CONTENTS

Tables

Preface

Producing this book has been a collective process in a number of ways. Over the past eighteen months we have benefitted from discussions with many individuals in both parts of Ireland and in Britain. In particular we would like to thank those present at the 1979 CSE conference for their critical response to our paper, which was an initial attempt to raise some of the questions with which this book deals. CSE Books has greatly encouraged us to complete the manuscript ahead of our original schedule and has involved us in every stage of the production process. We are indebted to Ian Knox for drawing the cover at such short notice. Several people made detailed comments on various drafts. John Downing provided very helpful suggestions on most of the chapters and James Wickham made extensive critical notes on the book as a whole. In the midst of many other pressing commitments, Les Levidow always found time to give the book his closest attention, supplying invaluable suggestions, criticisms and corrections throughout the re-drafting stage. Without such comradely assistance, producing this book would have been more of a headache and less of a pleasure.

Finally, although we have worked together closely, this is not a book written with three of us holding the pen. In that sense it is less than a fully collective product. Each chapter was written individually (see Contents), even though the themes, arguments and conclusions are the result of considerable collective debate.

Belfast, May 1980.

Note on the Authors:

Liam O'Dowd and *Mike Tomlinson* work in the Department of Social Studies, Queen's University, Belfast.
Bill Rolston works in the Sociology Department, Ulster Polytechnic, Belfast.

Graphics

Abbreviations

DUP   Democratic Unionist Party (led by Paisley)
ICTU   Irish Congress of Trade Unions
IRA   Irish Republican Army (*Provisional* IRA since 1969)
NILP   Northern Ireland Labour Party
NIO   Northern Ireland Office
SDLP   Social Democratic and Labour Party
RUC   Royal Ulster Constabulary
UDA   Ulster Defence Association
UDR   Ulster Defence Regiment
UVF   Ulster Volunteer Force
UWC   Ulster Workers' Council

1

Shaping and Reshaping the Orange State: An Introductory Analysis

Reform and Repression

Since 1972 the considerable ideological resources of the British state have been used to claim that the NI state was decisively reformed by a series of British 'interventions' which culminated in the demise of Stormont and the imposition of Direct Rule from Westminster. These interventions, it is suggested, not only prevented full-scale civil war but also implemented full civil rights for the Catholic minority while respecting the democratic wish of the Protestant majority to remain British. As for any remaining restrictions on civil rights or on progress to 'proper' social democracy in NI, the blame is put on those who dissent from the new arrangements, and on the deep and irreconcilable local antagonisms represented by an archaic amalgam of ethnic, religious and national identifications. The persistence of the most virulent of these antagonisms, embodied in the Provisional IRA, is portrayed as the sole reason for the continuation of 'the troubles', the mounting volume of repressive legislation and the curtailment of 'normal' citizens' rights. This legitimation process has been strengthened, both internally and internationally, by a series of ostentatious attempts to encourage a local compromise among elected representatives — each failure demonstrating the irreconcilability of the 'natives' and the extent of British commitment to pursuing a just settlement.

At one level this ideology is consciously used by British administrators and their supporters in the 'propaganda war'. Its success can be partly measured by the creeping paralysis which has rather surprisingly overcome the Left. Liberal and Left-wing analyses which have had little difficulty in recounting the repressive nature of 50 years of Unionist rule have been comparatively silent on the last eight years of Westminster rule.[1] The reasons are complex and have much to do with reactions to the persistence, nature and effects of the IRA campaign.

The militarisation of the struggle by the state and the IRA alike has helped to polarise positions on the 'NI problem'. On one side are those — including liberals, social democrats and many Marxists — who believe that, since 1972, the NI state has been either fundamentally reformed or that at least the conditions for social reform and class struggle have been improved. Thus NI is reformable even if reform is threatened by the continuation of 'the troubles' and the persistence of sectarian division. On the other side, more Republican-oriented analyses assert that the NI state is irreformable as a separate political unit. They also see British 'intervention' and the fall of Stormont as an important landmark marking not so much instalments of reform, as a substantial gain in the struggle for national liberation and the allied class struggle. Direct Rule and the repression of Catholics and Republicans which accompanies it are seen as confirmation of the continuity of the struggle against British imperialism.

Both sides are divided over emphases and tactics but still demonstrate a certain internal analytical and political coherence. The former displays an overriding concern to come to terms with the 'Protestant position', especially with the Protestant working class, denying the relevance of imperialism or the national question (see for example, British and Irish Communist Organisation publications; Boserup 1972; Probert 1978; Bew et al 1980). At least some of the implications of these analyses are given practical political content by what might be termed a 'politics of parity' which are practised by pressure groups and trade unions pressing for the application of the full 'benefits' of British social democracy to NI, and the fostering here of political parties along British lines. The anti-imperialist position, on the other hand, is much more concerned with repression rather than 'reform' and largely accepts and up-dates Connolly's position on the national question. Although internally divided with respect to IRA activities, anti-imperialism gives priority to British withdrawal and to the national question (see for example, Revolutionary Communist Group publications; Masters and Murphy 1978; Farrell 1976; Bell 1976).

This book does not attempt to arbitrate on this debate in some abstract or theoreticist fashion; instead it attempts to give some concrete substance to an argument which sometimes seems to deteriorate into the Left's version of 'Green' versus 'Orange'. In many respects the reformability/irreformability debate has become increasingly arid because neither side has advanced a sustained analysis of the role of the British state in NI *since* 1972. By and large both sides rest their cases on pre-1972 analyses of the Unionist state and take NI for granted as the major unit of analysis — implicitly accepting that the imposition of Direct Rule was an important watershed which constituted an 'intervention' by the British state in NI. Ironically this concurs with the dominant ideology of the British state which sees its 'intervention' as a response by an 'external' party to a bitter local squabble. When this squabble is transformed into the terminology of the Left it frequently becomes a futile battle of definitions over the 'status' of the NI struggle — is it an anti-imperialist war, a national liberation campaign, the dying kick of an obsolescent nationalism, or a conspiracy against the democratically constituted British/ Ulster nation? The result is often a type of *a priori* 'positionalism', in other words, a tendency to adopt postures on 'Ireland' which paralyse concrete analysis of the state and contemporary class forces.

In seeking to avoid another 'potted' analysis of the NI problem, complete with constitutional scenarios and chronologies of 'significant' events, we narrow our focus to NI as part of the UK state. Therefore we do not attempt to encompass all the forces, internal and external, which affect the state in NI; for example we do not discuss the relevance of developments in the Irish Republic, the EEC or the US. Instead we concentrate on the transition from Unionist to Direct Rule within the state, via a number of case studies of 'reform' or state intervention. Chapters Two and Three on regional policy and the trade unions are designed to illustrate the changing nature of the politics of capital and labour. Chapters Four and Five examine two areas — local government and housing — where the British state claims to have fundamentally reformed the abuses of the the Unionist government. Community politics (Chapter Six) encompasses at once a new area of state intervention and the emergence of a 'new politics' since the onset of 'the troubles', while Chapter Seven takes up perhaps the most contradictory area of 'reform' — the restructuring of the repressive apparatuses and its accompanying ideology.

The purpose of this introductory chapter is to provide an historical and theoretical context for the subsequent case studies.

It begins with an outline of the origins of the NI state in terms of the politics which led to the Partition of Ireland into 'Protestant' and 'Catholic' states in 1920/21. The second and third sections describe the way in which NI politics, between 1920 and 1968, were constructed around the link with Britain and around local sectarian and class divisions. The next section considers the main shortcomings in the conceptualisation and analysis of class and the state in NI, namely the uncritical measuring of NI politics in terms of British 'class' politics — preventing analyses from coming to terms with sectarian division. Finally an alternative approach is outlined, which accounts for sectarian and class division so as to inform the common argument running through the case studies.

Partition: Protestant and Catholic States

One of the factors which contributes to the current incomprehension of the NI crisis is the belief that the struggle is fundamentally insoluble as it is rooted in an archaic and unchanging historical antagonism between Protestant Unionists and Catholic Nationalists. Historical analysis shows, however, the changing nature of sectarian division and the emergence over time of many different 'solutions', of which Partition is the most recent. It is necessary therefore to specify the historical basis of Partition rather than accept NI (and the Irish Republic) as 'taken for granted' units of analysis.

Partition can be seen as a delayed constitutional resolution of far-reaching social revolution in 19th century Ireland. It was a belated and highly imperfect expression of the Protestant and Catholic class alliances which had been forged in the traumatic transformations of that century. Since the Reformation, Protestantism had become a distinguishing mark of the successive waves of colonisers who settled in Ireland as part of Britain's first colonial enterprise. In the North in particular, the Protestant-settler/Catholic-native dichotomy was complicated by the Anglican/Presbyterian divide among the 17th century planters, reflecting in part their respective English and Scottish origins. The 18th century marked the golden age of the colonial settlement through the consolidation of the Williamite settlement and the exclusion of Catholics from land-owning and politics. By the standards of the time Ireland was a highly developed economy in terms of agriculture and craft-based industry, facilitating the emergence of a type of colonial nationalism in the Protestant Irish parliament towards the end of the century. By then, however, the settlement was being undermined from within and without.

The beginning of the Industrial Revolution in Britain had major implications for Irish agriculture and industry, threatening the protectionist efforts of the Dublin parliament. In the North, the complex pattern of settlement produced a fissure between the more proletarian and Anglican tenantry and weavers in mid-Ulster and the largely Presbyterian United Irishmen concentrated in east Ulster. The latter, imbued with the ideals of the American and French revolutions as well as biblical fundamentalism, were the first promulgators of Irish Republican separatism. Led by middle class Presbyterians in Belfast and Dublin, they were supported by the independent weavers and tenant farmers in east Ulster (Gibbon 1975). By the late 1790s they had formed a tenuous alliance with the Catholic agrarian societies, which had long engaged in local struggles with the landed gentry, farmers and Protestant tenantry in the rest of Ireland.

The immediate result of the United Irish rebellion of 1798 was the Act of Union between Great Britain and Ireland in 1801 which abolished the Dublin parliament. Ironically in the light of later history, the Act was opposed by the newly formed Orange Order and favoured by the Catholic Church, which hoped for Catholic Emancipation under the new constitution. The rebellion in Ulster was savagely suppressed by British regiments and an Orange militia under the leadership of the Anglican gentry. As Gibbon (1975) points out, however, 19th century economic transformations undermined the social basis of Presbyterian Republicanism and precluded any long-term alliance with Irish Catholics. On a cultural level, the rise of Protestant evangelicalism helped to reduce if not obliterate political differences between Anglicans and Presbyterians. After 1850 Protestant revivalism was matched by a 'devotional revolution' among Catholics (Larkin 1972), sharpening the divide between popular Catholicism and Protestantism. Also, as language difference was reduced through the rapid decline of Irish, cultural differences became more polarised around religion. Even more significantly, however, Free Trade and the Industrial Revolution were beginning to transform the socio-economic structure and to shape the political alliances which became decisive in the Partition settlement. Far from undermining the salience of sectarian division in Irish politics, the Union settlement presided over its sharpening and reconstitution.

The overriding political force in 19th century Ireland however was the rise of popular Catholic Nationalism rooted in the first instance in the struggles over land. At a time when the commercialisation of agriculture and the undermining of craft-based industries was reducing the demand for labour *within* Ireland, there was an unprecedented population explosion. The Irish population (largely concentrated in rural areas) doubled between 1780 and 1840 reaching over 8 million or 45% of the total British Isles population. By 1851 however, catastrophic famine laid the foundation for a 'solution' to the population question through mass starvation, emigration and eviction of tenants. This outcome was shaped by the development of capitalist productive forces in Britain and elsewhere — at the same time facilitating the shift from tillage to livestock production in Ireland and ensuring a steady supply of Irish (and largely Catholic) labour power for British (and American) capitalist development.

Catholic class structure was far from homogeneous, however, and successive Catholic agitations over Emancipation, the Repeal of the Union, peasant proprietorship and eventually Home Rule were accompanied by sharp intra-Catholic struggles. The halving of the Irish population after the Famine conceals the decimation of agricultural labourers and cottiers who were forced to emigrate or to migrate to Dublin or Belfast where they became part of a small Irish urban proletariat. A still smaller number were absorbed into the lower ranks of the peasant proprietors created by the Land Acts. The political effects of the rural and urban proletariat (including the small peasants) were not negligible, however, as they were an important strand in the more radical section of Irish Nationalism and Republicanism — the so-called 'physical force tradition'. By the 20th century, the constitutional agitation for Home Rule was prosecuted by those who had emerged victorious from the class struggles on the Catholic side — a Catholic middle class of strong farmers, professionals and merchants supported by the newly installed peasant proprietors. Given political and ideological coherence by the expanding Catholic Church, these class fractions succeeded in forging an alliance with the English Liberals through the Home Rule Party against the crumbling Protestant Ascendancy. The political power of the latter was undermined by a succession of measures since the late 18th century including the abolition of the Dublin parliament, the gradual extension of the franchise, and the introduction of the secret ballot.

By the beginning of the 20th century, however, British political and economic interests in Ireland were much more complex than the political alliance between Irish Catholics and British Liberals seems to imply. This was due to the uneven development of capitalist accumulation in Ireland and the complexity of Irish integration into the UK social formation. While the Protestant landed gentry were in economic and political decline over much of the country, Ulster proved a significant exception. Here the Anglican gentry patronised the Orange Order, which was revitalised in the 1840s in response to Catholic agitation, thus linking the Orange alliance to British conservatism and the military establishment. Even more significantly, Belfast was becoming the only major centre of industrial capital in Ireland, creating the basis for an emerging Protestant bourgeoisie opposed to Home Rule — an alliance comprising the landed gentry, the Belfast commercial bourgeoisie and the new capitalists whose industries (shipbuilding, linen, and engineering) depended on British imperialism and Free Trade.

The new forms of accumulation translated the sectarian divisions of the tenantry into a new industrial setting by creating a Protestant and Catholic proletariat in Belfast. The new bourgeoisie which controlled Belfast was almost entirely Protestant, a product of the specific history of settlement in east Ulster. Unlike the rest of Ireland, there was no substantial Catholic commercial or professional bourgeoisie in Belfast. It followed or developed from the migration of Catholic labour to the city and came to appropriate a limited economic and political role in servicing its own 'community'. Under the new capitalist social relations, the Protestant proletariat tried to re-define the historic 'social contract' which had existed since the Plantation between elements of the Protestant tenantry and their landlords[2] by seeking to forge a specific and advantageous relationship with their new bourgeois masters. One consequence was a degree of preferential treatment for the Protestant working class over their Catholic counterparts in access to housing and skilled jobs. The Protestant bourgeoisie had a vested interest in such an alliance. On the one hand there was little basis for a local cross-sectarian bourgeois alliance which might have tempered their actions. On the other hand they were directly linked, at the upper levels at least, with the British imperial bourgeoisie and welcomed working class support in opposing popular Catholic agitation in Ireland as a whole, which threatened to weaken links with imperial Britain. This Protestant alliance pre-figured the Unionist anti-Home Rule movement on which the Stormont statelet was to be based.

The set of events leading to the Partition of Ireland in

1920/21 has been well chronicled elsewhere (e.g. Lyons 1973). It is seldom noted that in one sense Partition was a solution to a *British* rather than an Irish political problem. The different links of the British Liberals and Conservatives to political forces in Ireland threatened to cause major disruption among the British ruling class as Conservatives supported the Unionist defiance of the British parliament's Home Rule legislation. Furthermore the relative importance of Ireland, in population terms alone, had declined dramatically since the mid-19th century from 45% of British Isles population to around 10% by 1911. Yet successive agitations were making Irish politics more rather than less intrusive in British parliamentary affairs. Irish MPs, now over-represented in Parliament, were a major prop to the British Liberal Party in its struggle against the Conservatives and the nascent Labour Party. Irish withdrawal from Westminster helped to redraw political allegiances in Britain in the direction of the future 'two party system'. In Ireland, however, Partition looked to the past rather than the future. The Stormont statelet emerged as British imperialism itself went into decline and Belfast's major industries went into long-term recession; the Southern economy, notably agriculture, continued to stagnate, while depleting itself by remaining an exporter of capital, labour and livestock.

Nevertheless the terms of the Partition settlement continued to facilitate capital accumulation in the British Isles. They allowed the unimpeded extraction of capital and labour from Ireland as a whole — preserving the country as an important outlet for British manufactured goods and as a source of cheap food and military recruits. The links between Ulster and British capital were not disrupted by political divisions. Perhaps even more significantly, however, Partition ensured the victory of the most conservative elements in Irish politics both North and South. This victory, pre-figured by 19th century developments, confirmed and extended the sectarian moulds developed under the Act of Union.

The stabilisation of Ireland through Partition did not rest on a democratic consensus based on the ballot box. (The 1918 all-Ireland election which gave Sinn Fein a large majority of seats failed to provide the 'correct' result.) Instead it followed from the pragmatic recognition of sectarian and class divisions and their consolidation in the new political institutions. The precise form and territorial extent of the two new states owed much to extra-parliamentary action: the mass mobilisation of the Ulster Volunteers against Home Rule in 1912, the Easter Rising in 1916 and its aftermath, and more particularly two bloody civil wars in which the British government played a significant role — one in the North at the foundation of the Unionist state (1920/21) and the other in the South (1922/23). Ironically, in failing to create a 32 County state, Catholic Nationalist forces ensured a certain ideological consensus within the relatively homogeneous Southern state. In the North, however, the Protestant/Catholic division was institutionalised at all levels, perpetuating the question of state legitimacy as the central issue in Northern politics. In the process, the Labour movement was rendered largely irrelevant as a political force, thus precluding the emergence of a unified cross-sectarian coalition which might have seriously challenged the Protestant or Catholic class alliances.

The Marginality of 'Class' Politics

The beginning of the modern Labour movement in Ireland coincided with the Home Rule conflict between the 1880s and Partition. From the outset, its potential constituency was fragmented along the lines of skill, geography and sectarian division (see Chapter 3 on development of trade unions). Partition marked a major defeat for the Labour movement in both parts of the country, not in the sense that it immediately created new divisions where none existed before, but rather in that it had to accept political units drawn in such a way as to perpetuate its own marginality. The possibility of an effective cross-sectarian political alliance between the less industrialised Southern workers and Northern trade unionists was precluded, while sectarian divisions were accentuated within the Northern working class. The NI statelet certainly increased the weight of the Protestant working class within the state, not as a part of a cross-sectarian labour or trade union movement, but as a major component of an exclusivist Unionist class alliance.

   The marginality of Labourist politics in Ireland contributed to their growing centrality in Britain. As the Irish Question was dropped with alacrity from the British parliamentary agenda,[3] the Liberals were weakened by the removal of their Irish support in their competition with the emerging Labour party. The NI Unionist MPs became, in the main, irrelevant ciphers in the Conservative and Unionist Party. The considerable Irish component in the British working class was free to choose sides in the emerging Labour/Conservative struggle, free from the 'diversion' of the Irish constitutional question and the politics of territorial boundaries and repression associated with it. This tended to minimise the political expression of the sectarian and ethnic cleavages so prevalent among the Victorian working class in Britain. The politics of constitutionalism, 'territory' and sectarian repression now appeared to be a marginal and an exclusively Irish responsibility. The emerging Labour movement could portray its political struggle as a reasonably unambiguous confrontation with class oppression in the inter-war period. After the war, a liberal and social democratic (Labour/Tory) consensus emerged based on reconstruction and the increase in the absolute economic surplus (Harrison 1978:134ff). Substantial agreement over decolonisation contributed to the broader consensus, thereby largely insulating the question from British parliamentary politics.[4]

There was no such consensus underpinning parliamentary politics in NI, where there was *neither* a competitive party system based on liberal democracy *nor* an effective social democratic party. The nature of 'formal democracy' in NI is indicated by Table 1, which shows the remarkably high proportion of uncontested seats in the provincial parliament between 1929 (when PR was abolished) and 1969.[5] This lack of competitiveness is evident at all three levels of representation in NI — provincial, local authority and Westminster. 46% of total seats were uncontested in the Stormont parliament in this period, although the proportion for Belfast (21%) differs substantially from the rest of NI (57%). Outside Belfast there was continuous Unionist representation in 23 of the 32 seats over a forty-year period.

Table 1: Political Competitiveness
Northern Ireland General Elections 1929–1969

Area	No. of Seats	No. of Potential Contests	Uncontested No.	%
Belfast	16	160	34	21
Rest of NI	32*	324	184	57
Queens Univ	4*	36	22	61
Total	52	520	240	46

* Queen's University seats were abolished in 1969, but the same number of seats overall was retained by the creation of four new territorial seats in the 'Rest of NI' (in Antrim and Down). Elections to the university seats were by PR.
SOURCE: Elliott 1973

Remarkably, the Unionists never lost a seat outside Belfast in a constituency with a Protestant majority population. The Nationalists held three of these 32 seats continuously, while the remaining 6 seats returned mainly Nationalist candidates. In only *one* contest out of a possible 320 contests did a Unionist replace a Nationalist (Mid-Tyrone 1958) — when the Catholic vote was split — and the reverse never occurred. Thus, outside Belfast, politics involved sectarian voting focused totally on the Partition issue.

In the 16 Belfast seats, the same general picture applied with some complications. In a largely working-class industrial city, Unionists held 7 of the 16 seats continuously between 1929–1969 (these MPs included some Independent Unionists). The Nationalists held none continuously. The Catholic vote generally went to various types of anti-Partitionists, often with a Labour label. Only three Belfast seats were predominantly Labour-oriented, three were generally anti-Partitionist and two were marginal (see Elliott 1973).

At the local government level, uncontested seats were even more common. The Unionists gained 225 uncontested seats on Belfast Corporation between 1927 and 1967 compared with 36 for assorted Nationalists and only 12 for Labour candidates (Budge and O'Leary 1973:187). In Westminster general elections between 1922–1951, 40% of all seats were returned unopposed compared with 4% in the rest of the UK. This changed thereafter with the Sinn Fein practice of putting up abstentionist candidates in all constituencies. Only three of the 12 seats were marginal (and these had Catholic majorities). As in Stormont, Unionists have never lost a seat in a Westminster constituency with a majority Protestant population. The absence of party competitiveness on a liberal democratic model is striking. Indeed, the lack of ideological consensus is even more clearly shown by the fact that, during 50 years of uninterrupted rule in the NI parliament, the Unionist party supported only *one* bill introduced by an opposition member — the Wild Bird Act of 1931! (Harbinson 1973:119).

The absence of even a tenuous liberal consensus is matched by the weakness of a social democratic politics modelled on a British-type Labour party. The total number of Labour MPs elected to Stormont ranged from a minimum of two to a maximum of seven (in 1962) out of a total of 52. No Labour candidate was elected for a constituency outside Belfast, although one was returned unopposed in South Armagh in 1938 because of a

Nationalist boycott. Table 2 overstates Labour's electoral support beause of the high number of unopposed seats with heavy Unionist or Nationalist majorities. Even in Belfast there was no safe Labour seat. Only *one* Socialist MP has has been elected to Westminster (Gerry Fitt from 1966 to the present). Labour fared no better in local council elections — the NILP won on average, only 7% of the seats of Belfast Corporation up to 1967, compared with the Unionists' 78%. Labour never exceeded its 1920 performance in Belfast when it won one-fifth of the Corporation seats (Budge and O'Leary 1973:186-7). Not only was Labour support therefore small, it was localised and episodic and also highly vulnerable whenever the constitutional issue became paramount.

Table 2: Support for 'Labour' Candidates in
Stormont General Elections 1938–1969*

	NILP		Independent Labour†		Total Labour	
Election	Votes	% of Total	Votes	% of Total	Votes	% of Total
1938	18775	5.7	5480	1.7	24255	7.5
1945	66053	18.6	47360	13.3	113413	31.9
1949	26831	7.2	7970	2.1	34801	9.3
1953	31063	12.1	29711	11.6	60774	23.7
1958	37748	16.0	29819	12.7	67567	28.7
1962	76842	26.0	20239	6.8	97081	32.8
1966	66323	20.4	7697	2.4	74020	22.8
1969	45113	8.1	13155	2.4	58268	10.5

*   SOURCE: Elliott 1973
†   Independent Labour is a highly diverse grouping including Republican Labour, Irish Labour and Commonwealth Labour.

    Even if there was no major working class party of significance in the province it might be argued that Labour had considerable influence within the Unionist and Nationalist alliance. In Belfast, Nationalists' vulnerability to Labour influence was reflected in the Labour leanings of many Republican candidates and the tendency to vote for the NILP and Independent Labour. It was within Unionism, however, that Labour influence had greatest potential, given the large working class support for that party. In the event, that support was not reflected in the social class background of Unionist MPs. The Ulster Unionist Labour Association (UULA), created to mobilise the working class behind Unionism during the Home Rule crisis, illustrates the token way that official Unionism has recognised Labour representation. Although the UULA nominated a small number of Unionist MPs prior to 1925, it has failed to make a nomination since. As Harbinson (1973) notes, its earlier educational and 'social' function also disappeared, reducing its main role to the organisation of memorial services for Lord Carson. Harbinson (1973:213) estimates that only two of the nine Independent Unionist MPs elected to Stormont (all of whom had working class or lower middle class backgrounds) ever voted for even mildly socialist legislation. He does credit them, however, with an inadvertent contribution to the reform of the Unionist Party structure in 1946. Furthermore, on another level *official* trade unionism has had little impact on Unionist Party policies, as it was affiliated to the NILP (see Chapter 3).

Unionist representation was highly oligarchical. Ten of the 52 Stormont seats were more or less the preserve of individual Unionist families who were either from the big bourgeoisie or the landed gentry. Analysis of the occupational backgrounds of the officials of local Unionist associations and MPs indicates the depth of control in the hands of this class (see Harbinson 1973:81-2, 98ff, 107ff; McAllister 1977:70). Table 3 clearly indicates its overwhelming predominance among the elected representives of Unionism.

Table 3: Occupational Background of All Unionist Elected Representatives in the Westminster and NI parliaments (Percentages)

	Westminster 1921–74	NI Parliament 1921–69	NI Assembly 1974
Professionals, Managers, Executives and Large Landholders and Farmers	94	86	72
Clerical/Administrative Workers	—	3	14
Manual Workers (skilled and unskilled)	—	4	10
Others (Unclassifiable)	6	7	4
	100	100	100
Numbers	(65)	(161)	(50)

SOURCES: *Times Book of the House of Commons*, 1970, 1974, Harbinson 1973 and Nealon 1974

By 1973, of course, Official Unionism had splintered into several parties (Assembly figures allude to all Unionist parties) — a process later reversed as Unionists coalesced into two parties — the Official Unionists and the DUP. The initial fragmentation seems to have led to a limited democratisation, notably a rise in petty bourgeois and working class representation. There is thus a small but noticeable tendency for parliamentary Unionism to fall back on the lower echelons of the alliance in response to crisis, reminiscent of the attempts to involve the working class through the UULA in the days of the Home Rule struggle.

The main anti-Unionist party, the SDLP, contains few working class representatives either, despite its name.[6] Its leadership is of a different order to that of the Unionists, however, and indicates the different relationship of Catholics to the state and to capital. Eight of the 19 SDLP members in the 1973 Stormont Assembly were teachers, compared to only one teacher among the 18 members of Nationalist groupings at Stormont between 1945 and 1969. The latter contained five barristers, four farmers and four publicans, whereas the SDLP contained only two publicans and no farmers. These figures confirm the political importance of service within the Catholic community, while indicating the changing nature of such service resulting from greater contact between the state and Catholics, notably through the expansion of educational opportunity. The most striking difference between Protestant and Catholic representatives is the almost total absence of big business and landowning interests on the Catholic side and their considerable prominence on the Unionist side.

Of course voting patterns and the occupational background of MPs are an inadequate basis for assessing internal working class pressure for reform.[7] They simply demonstrate the extreme weakness of British-style social democratic politics in NI because of the inter-related issues of state legitimacy and sectarian division. Recent analyses of the NI state and its internal workings have all indicated the central significance of Orange clientelism which cemented the Unionist bourgeoisie to its mass support.

From the inception of the state, political power was concentrated in the hands of a small clique of civil servants and Ministers. The inter-war Unionist cabinet, a product of the boom years of local capitalism (pre-1914), read like an 'executive committee of Northern industry and commerce' with a few members of the landed gentry thrown in for good measure (see Buckland 1979; Farrell 1976; Bew et al 1979). This clique rested on the specific operation of Orange clientelism *and* British support. The Orange Order was the main institution which linked the Unionist bourgeoisie to its working class and petty bourgeois base; it was represented on the ruling Ulster Unionist Council and the vast majority of Unionist MPs and cabinet ministers were Orangemen.[8] A key element in the pre-Partition local authority system in the north-east of Ireland, its influence was extended into the new state apparatuses after 1920 (see Gibbon 1977). It concentrated in the inter-war years on the enshrinement of Protestant clerical influence within the state education system, (see Akenson 1973) and on the prevention of 'peaceful infiltration' by Catholics into public positions. In this it was highly successful: by 1943 only 37 of the 634 civil servants in administrative and technical grades were Catholics and there were no Catholics in the top 55 posts. The B-Specials were almost exclusively Protestant and, although the police contained some Catholics (17% in 1936), many were recruited from the 'loyal' Royal Irish Constabulary disbanded after 1921. Even then, however, the existence of a Catholic quota seems to have rested less on conciliation than on the RUC commander's stated aim of acquiring information on Catholic areas (Buckland 1979:20-22).

In the circumstances of capitalist crisis in the inter-war years, it was always more likely that the Protestant working class would seek to maximise their advantages within the Unionist class alliance rather than find common cause with their Catholic counterparts. The latter, largely excluded from the state apparatus, were highly dispersed; on the Catholic side, the Church continued to play in NI the role it held in Ireland as a whole throughout the 19th century — that of a quasi-state within a state. It continued to maintain a separate Church-controlled education system, and occasionally acted as arbitrator between different anti-Partitionist factions and as a negotiator with Stormont on behalf of the 'Catholic community'. Likewise, the Church was involved in health and welfare provision and generally 'organised' the social reproduction of the Catholic class alliance. Reproduction of the Protestant class alliance was thereby simplified as the state served to institutionalise the role of the Orange Order as a unifying and mediating force between the highly fragmented Protestant Churches in a way which counteracted the more centralised and monolithic Catholic Church. The exclusion of Catholics from the state apparatus, especially from the state education system, confirmed the notion of a 'Protestant state for a Protestant people' contributing to the ideological unity of the Unionist class alliance as well as to Protestant control of key occupations in the civil service and other state bodies.

Catholic/Protestant 'apartheid' in the arena of social reproduction was supported by a wide range of interests albeit for divergent reasons. The immediate inter-war period marked the high point of Catholic Church opposition to state intervention in health, welfare and education, north and south of the Border. The Catholic Church favoured a type of vocationalist or corporatist system to obviate class conflict. The system would be based on a principle of subsidiarity: it would be distributist rather than statist and would emphasise the role of the family, the local community, and voluntary organisations in social reproduction.[9] In this respect, Catholic ideology fused with Nationalist and Republican rejection of the state. This opposition was echoed by the ruling Protestant bourgeoisie for reasons which had more to do with conservative advocacy of laissez-faire; this local expression of British-style conservatism was also evident in the Stormont civil service, especially those sections in closest contact with the Treasury. However, this conservatism had to face populist Protestant pressure from the Orange Order and trade unions to force the state to combat the local effects of inter-war capitalist decline and the associated high unemployment rates (see Bew et al 1979). Such pressure often embraced demands for Catholic exclusion and repression — demands which greatly facilitated the management of class conflict on the Protestant side.

Thus while Partition left NI within the UK, an emerging social democratic state, 'class' politics on the British model were largely absent and the political reproduction of capitalist social relations took a very different form. Yet ironically, it was the emergence of social democratic politics in post-war Britain that was to open a gap between the Unionist Party and the Stormont state apparatus, leading to the fragmentation of the former and pressures to restructure the latter. The result was to undermine the previous political insulation of Stormont from Westminster *and* to force the restructuring of 'Catholic apartheid' vis-à-vis the local state.

De-Insulation and Crisis

Even in the inter-war period the British state (via the Treasury) had retained strict financial control of the Stormont administration. The latter had minimal control over revenue, with less than 20% of the total taxation. Of course this largely removed a potentially divisive 'class issue' from internal Unionist Party politics. However, Stormont technically controlled 80% of expenditure, though within limits laid down by the Treasury (Lawrence 1965:80, 190-1). Indeed the whole financial relationship with Britain served to minimise the element of Unionist discretion in apportioning the broad areas of state expenditure. The relationship included a rather loose commitment to parity of services which was transformed after the war into a more definite commitment to equalise standards throughout the UK in expanding areas of welfare state expenditure. Additionally, the war had already served to bring the Stormont administration more into line with British practices.

After the war there were major changes in the financing of the NI state. Between 1946 and 1963 overall revenue *doubled*, but expenditure (largely administered by Stormont) increased nearly *sevenfold* (Lawrence 1965:80). Moreover, greatly increased state intervention was concentrated, initially at least, in areas of acute political sensitivity i.e. in health, welfare, housing and education. Health and welfare expenditure increased from 1.6% of total expenditure in 1939 to over 19% in 1963. Education expenditure increased marginally in proportionate terms but greatly in absolute terms (Lawrence 1965:82). The overall effect of these interventions in the short run was to involve Stormont, to an unprecedented degree, in the reproduction of Catholic labour power — thereby undermining the role of the Church in this area. Catholics increasingly came into contact with the much expanded state apparatus. Even the Catholic working class in Belfast, in common with their Protestant counterparts, were benefitting from the new welfare state reforms. These reforms, however, were not so much the product of cross-sectarian working class politics as the result of importation via the British link — a link which served to divide them in most other respects.

The application of the welfare state measures to the North were not in the first instance a concession to local social democratic or Labourist politics but were presented instead as part of the benefits of the Union, the protection of which was the central plank of Unionist Party policy. At the end of the 1940s the PM (Brooke) was able to welcome the welfare state in the following terms:

> 'Perhaps the most important item for the people of this country is the agreed parity in social services and in other matters which exists between ourselves and our kinsmen across the water. It has meant prosperity. It has meant the removal of fear and want from many homes . . . The Island of Ireland has for centuries been part

of the United Kingdom and . . . I see no prospect whatsoever of Northern Ireland, which has been part of the whole, ever linking up with the portion of this island which now has separated itself from the British Crown. We owe our prosperity and our happiness to the fact that we are linked with the United Kingdom. That is the reason why industrially we are progressing, why our people are happy, why their health is better. Those are the reasons, and in maintaining this unyielding stand on the constitutional position the Government are inspired by the support of the Ulster people. Their well-being and their future and their happiness is in our hands, and we will hold it safe'. (HC Deb. V.33 c.37)

In spite of this paternalism, the political annexation of welfare state measures by the Unionist Party was somewhat contradictory. The Party voted against the measures at Westminster while implementing them at Stormont. To do otherwise would have been to risk loss of support to Labour in some Belfast constituencies and to expose the British link to unwelcome public scrutiny. There were also misgivings within Unionism that free state services would increase Catholic numbers, raising the old spectre of being 'out-bred' by Catholics and voted out of the UK.

Nevertheless the new measures were welcomed by the Protestant (and Catholic) working class and by a number of moderate Unionist civil servants and academics who were a little uneasy with conservative one-party rule at Stormont. For example, in an account of public administration in NI, a leading civil servant was able to designate the 20-year period after the war as the 'Positive Era' (Oliver 1978). NI's version of the British 'post-war settlement' was also informed by an economic analysis of the continuing crisis of the local economy and criticism of Stormont's laissez-faire attitudes, as well as its lack of effective economic planning powers. Indeed some wondered if, given the limits on the discretion and power of the Unionist state, it might be advantageous to remove the semblance of self-government altogether (Isles and Cuthbert 1955:166; Lawrence 1965). Additionally the Belfast working class were becoming restless at the continuing high unemployment rates as Britain approached full employment (see Chapter 2).

The introduction of the welfare state, and the subsequent involvement of Stormont in the restructuring of capital and in physical planning, did create tensions within the political status quo. The Stormont state apparatus (excluding the Unionist Party as such) increasingly came to act as the agent of the British state in implementing these reforms. For example the NI Housing

Trust, discussed in Chapter 5, had some pretensions to be free of direct Unionist Party control particularly at local authority level. It also demonstrated greater flexibility in building houses for workers for incoming industry while maintaining at least the appearance of technocratic impartiality in allocation. The 1947 Education Act increased state funding for Catholic education and opportunities for more Catholics to go to university. Regional physical planning tended to undermine the highly localised Unionist patronage system — replacing it with more centralised and bureaucratic decision-making. A case in point was O'Neill's 'presidential style' leadership (see Bew et al 1979). Faulkner, the spokesman for the populist right within Unionism in the mid-1960s, advocated reform of local government in line with modern planning requirements — a move distinctly unpopular with Orangemen at local authority level (see Chapter 4). Working class pressure for jobs led to the attraction of multi-national firms to NI, thereby leading to the uprooting and relocation of labour in the Belfast area. Finally the contradictions in the Unionist alliance were sharpened further with the onset of the Civil Rights movement led by Catholic university-trained activists who were the beneficiaries of the post-war reforms.

The post-war period, therefore, saw the erosion of an arrangement which eminently suited Unionist and British politicians alike. Until then, Unionists were able to obscure scrutiny of the actual workings of the link in the Stormont and Westminster parliaments while successfully maintaining that its preservation was the central question in local politics. British politicians were able to ensure the smooth bureaucratic functioning of devolution while avoiding the mire of Irish politics. Of overriding significance here was the delegation to the Unionists of responsibility for the coercion of the Catholic minority within the boundaries of the new statelet.

The collapse of 'law and order' between 1968 and 1972 was to challenge this arrangement, forcing British politicians to become reluctantly involved in a series of 'reformist exercises' to meet the complaints of the Catholic minority and above all to restore stability. This involvement by the British Parliament and Army was accompanied, however, by new strategies to distance NI politics from those of Britain. Bipartisanship emerged to forestall the possibility of dispute between Labour and the Tories over the actual management of the conflict. Furthermore, as our case studies show, the ideology of the 'neutral arbiter between warring factions' was stressed, as well as the institution of British

standards of administration. Moves were immediately made to
establish forms of local political compromise which might restore
stability, but as these failed, the appeal of military technocracy
grew as a means to the same end. This stressed 'containment' or
isolation of the contagion within NI — a strategy admirably
described in a recent suggestion by an ex-GOC that a 'hard
military casing' has to be maintained around NI to contain the
'explosive military mixture within, a mixture which will continue
to exist into the foreseeable future more or less as before'.
(Hackett 1979) A relatively successful refinement of this strategy
has been the attempt to confine 'the troubles' to certain 'abnormal'
areas of concentrated disaffection such as South Armagh and
West Belfast. As these areas are reduced in size and number, the
illusion of a gradual return to 'normality' can be maintained.

This is not to suggest that NI is being administered simply as
an unruly military province — on the contrary, the whole weight
of British civil administration is *combined* with military management. Indeed a militaristic technocracy is being increasingly
inscribed within legal and bureaucratic practices. This is
particularly evident from the case studies of community politics,
housing, and repression. It therefore becomes necessary to
examine the specific nature of the relationship between reform
and repression. Most liberal and social democratic states attain
some degree of legitimacy, in the short run at least, by
'partitioning' the apparatuses of repression — the army, police
and judiciary — from from other state institutions. Furthermore,
as Gough (1979:41) points out, the institutions of coercion tend
to be separated from the economically dominant classes — placing
the practice of coercion above sectional interests and equating it
with the 'public interest'. Once the existence of the repressive
apparatus is depoliticised in this way, 'legitimate' political struggle
can occur in other areas. A 'reformist' politics can then emerge to
forge an ideological consensus supportive of the state.

The Partition of Ireland helped to ensure that the 'compartmentalisation' of reform and repression was maintained in Britain
while effectively preventing it in NI. The police and B Specials
were directly under the control of the Unionist Party, more
specifically the Minister for Home affairs, prior to Westminster
intervention. While Protestant security forces for a 'Protestant'
state did help cement relationships among the class fractions
within Unionism, it scarcely depoliticised the repressive
apparatuses or contributed to the legitimacy of NI as a separate
political unit. The 'separation' of reform and repression was

accepted by *neither* the Protestant majority *nor* the Catholic minority. Between 1920 and 1968, Unionist 'law and order' remained inviolate from the modernisation of repressive apparatuses in Britain, contrasting markedly with the adoption of British welfare state measures. The reformist demands of the Civil Rights movement were immediately defined as a threat to the Unionist state not only by the local security forces but by the Protestant working class and petty bourgeoisie, despite protestations that the aim was 'British rights for British citizens'.[10] As the British state imposed reforms, it had to respond to the crisis (being a social democratic state) *as if* the 'compartmentalisation' of reform and repression was achievable in NI. In the last ten years British politicians have tried to encourage a local consensus politics which accept and justify this aim.

Problems of Analysis: Sectarianism OR Class?

It is not only the British state, however, which accepts the social democratic 'compartmentalisation' of reform and repression in NI. Many socialist and Marxist analyses do likewise in the sense that they counterpose sectarian and class division. The former is associated with repression, especially with the repression of Catholics under Stormont and Direct Rule. Class division on the other hand is more typically seen to concern reformist stuggles, e.g. the struggle for higher wages, better working conditions and welfare services. Given the centrality of the British state in NI, this characterisation of class struggle is more common, certainly within NI. Even those who emphasise repression and the anti-imperialist struggle would not deny the importance of class division in this sense or its relevance to everyday struggles. They fail to integrate these struggles into their analyses in a satisfactory way, however.

Those who concentrate on class division and class struggle abstracted from repression face a political *cul de sac* in the contemporary situation — 'class' politics in the recognisably British sense seems weaker than ever before, attracting only 3.6% of the votes in the last provincial election (Rose 1976:414) In the midst of a protracted struggle against the state, trade unions seem silent and ineffectual; worker kills worker in para-military struggle. The IRA campaign seems to sharpen working class dis-unity while remaining remote from workplace issues, while Protestant workers march to demand 'internment without trial' for their fellow Catholic workers (Bell 1976:92) or vote for

Paisley's sectarian populism.

In these circumstances the 'reformist' Left takes refuge in the idea that political 'modernisation' in the North is following the British path, despite the side-tracks of sectarianism and 'the troubles'.[11] This assumption is only too willingly shared by British politicians charged with managing the crisis and superficially there appears to be much evidence to support their argument. Over the long history of Anglo-Irish relations, many British political forms have been reproduced in Ireland, e.g. the civil service, trade unions, judiciary, elected parliaments, and even small-scale Labourist parties, both North and South. Since 1968 a whole range of British procedures and institutions have been introduced into NI. Of course these institutions are not seen as problematic *per se*; rather, the problem lies in the allegedly residual elements of Irish life, i.e. the proclivity to keep alive traditional antagonisms based on race and creed.

Our objections to this view are both theoretical and empirical. Theoretically it is based on a confusion between the actual history of capital accumulation in Britain and a model of the 'pure state of capitalist development'. Just because Britain *was* the first capitalist state does not mean therefore that it represents the apex of capitalist development today or that it manifests that process in its most advanced form. On the contrary the very fact that Britain *was* first has led to the construction of barriers to further accumulation, as the physical, industrial and social forms of the 19th century confront and resist the penetration of new forms of accumulation originating in the US and elsewhere. Therefore it is ahistorical and insular to see British class politics as the touchstone and epitome of the *progressive* development of social forces under modern capitalism. A wide variety of political systems from social democracy to fascism and populism have shown themselves to be compatible with the capitalist mode of production. British imperialism itself linked a wide variety of local political systems with liberal democracy at the 'centre' in order to further capital accumulation on a world scale.

The form of NI politics is, therefore, much less exceptional when considered in the wider international context. While it may be possible for the Left outside Ireland to ignore sectarian division either by seeing the crisis as a struggle of the undifferentiated 'Irish people' for national liberation or by seeing NI as a recalcitrant and backward province of the UK, it is much more difficult to evade its centrality living within NI. Here, analyses which stress cultural determinism and factors other than class are persuasive, eliciting a Left response based on a rather economistic and mechanistic understanding of the relationship between sectarianism and class. Cultural determinism is opposed by economic determinism. Sectarianism is put forward as a super-structural phenomenon, a set of ideas and practices which rest on some abstracted 'economic base'. Faced with the obvious historical and contemporary dis-unity of the Protestant and Catholic working class, stress is laid on the 'objective economic circumstances' which both share. Working class dis-unity is then attributed to a failure to recognise common interests, a type of false consciousness. Sectarianism, seen as a major part of this false consciousness, tends to be understood as a tactic (operated by the Unionist bourgeoisie or the British state) to divide and rule the working class; or else it is seen as a tactic used by elements in the working class — especially the Protestant working class — to bring pressure on the state to protect their privileges.

There are several variations on the economic-base/sectarian-superstructure argument. One suggests that objective changes in the economy are leading to increasing disconnection between the sectarian attitudes, ideas and practices in the superstructure and the 'base'. Thus the replacement of the local bourgeoisie by monopoly capitalists spells doom for the Orange system; multi-national executives and British administrators new to NI have not been conditioned to be sectarian and furthermore it is not in their 'objective' economic interest to be so when they arrive in NI (Boserup 1972; Probert 1978). Our case studies challenge such an analysis and suggest instead the up-dating of old sectarian divisions and the forging of new ones, side by side with monopoly capital and Direct Rule administration. There are those who emphasise a type of immiseration thesis suggesting that all workers in NI are being reduced to similar levels of deprivation by de-industrialisation, high unemployment and the peripherali-sation of the local economy (see Byrne 1979); however, they provide no convincing evidence to show that this is happening or that a common political consciousness is about to emerge in response. Chapter 2 suggests that there are still *degrees of misery* and these do correspond to sectarian divisions. Of course trade unions do seek to mobilise their members on a non-sectarian platform which stresses common economic circumstances. As Chapter 3 points out, however, trade union 'economism' is in fact a 'political' position. The fact that it is not recognised as such is a measure of the extreme weakness of economistic politics in undermining sectarian division. Indeed our analyses of regional policy, trade unions, housing and community politics suggest that this type of economism is highly compatible with sectarian division and may even serve to extend it.

The attitude of economistic analysis to the current NI 'troubles' is particularly instructive. Given the objective changes in the 'base', (which in one view was 'creating in the 1960s a *similar objective world* for Northern and Southern workers'), the re-emergence of sectarian conflict in the North is seen as an anachronistic aberration. It allowed

> 'the revival of the dying Northern capitalist class, as well as giving a new lease of life to the Southern capitalist class by distracting working class attention from the class struggle to a mythical national question'. (Sinn Fein 1977:148-9)

Thus the conflict is seen as preventing workers' unity rather than as expressing their abiding dis-unity. This view also suggests that the state stands somewhere 'above' sectarian conflict by virtue of servicing the objective interests of monopoly capital. Again our case studies fundamentally question such a characterisation by pointing to the ways in which sectarian division is being re-formed — not in the sense of undermining or rendering it irrelevant, but in the sense of its 're-creation' within the new state apparatuses, even within those which appear to constitute a British reform of Unionist abuses.

The British 'reforms' introduced after 1968 implicitly sought to detach sectarianism from class relations. To fundamentally reform sectarian division, however, would be to transform class division — an impossiblity for a capitalist state. The 'separate' issue of sectarianism had to be so defined as to create at least an illusion of 'reform'. Thus as Chapter 6 points out, the most blatant and de-stabilising manifestation of sectarianism had to be formally attacked. The Civil Rights movement's reformist demands had centred around the question of sectarian discrimination — an issue gratefully taken up by the state apparatus, re-defined in legalistic fashion and then conceded. An Ombudsman and a Fair Employment Agency were appointed, for example, to expose and combat sectarian *motivations*, attitudes and labour recruiting. The problem, of course, is to establish motivation in the first place and secondly to show that there were no extenuating circumstances. Instances of discrimination have proven exceedingly difficult to establish in NI. But where it might be possible to examine and occasionally influence the composition of some workforces, it would be a contradiction in terms for a capitalist state to suggest that landownership or the control of industry or banking should be balanced along sectarian lines. Even more specifically, in the case of NI, it would be impossible to insist that the local security forces should be balanced in the 'right' cross-sectarian proportions. Accordingly, this area was excluded from the remit of the Fair Employment Agency, although it was precisely the Protestant Unionist control of the security forces which underpinned the sectarian state from 1920 onwards. The weakness of analyses which counterpose sectarianism and class are mirrored therefore in the British state's separation of what can and can not be reformed.

An Alternative Analysis: Sectarian AND Class Division

The first step in combatting the deficiencies of the foregoing analyses is to confirm the importance of social divisions other than class in all historical capitalist societies. Sectarianism is not a superstructural phenomenon floating free of an abstracted economic base which in turn is divided into classes. In NI sectarian division is a *material* reality which has been constituted and re-constituted throughout the history of capital accumulation and class struggle in Ireland as a whole. It is not merely an overlay on class divisions to be seen as something which is either more or less important than class. As a material reality it has a history embedded in colonisation, industrial revolution and the emergence of new class forms under capitalism. Class in NI, as elsewhere, is not simply a matter of an 'economic relation' — it cross-cuts politics, ideology and culture. Class relations and the material reality which they express cannot be experienced in a pure or abstract form. The brief discussion of the historical background to Partition and the analysis of NI political relations since 1921 confirms the ubiquity of sectarian division. Class relations in NI were only experienced as *sectarian class* relations. Sectarian division is itself a particular historical division of class, or more precisely of class fractions, cemented together in Protestant and Catholic class alliances. In other words sectarian division is a class phenomenon and *vice versa*.

The peculiar ideological power of sectarianism resides, in part, in the durability of a popular, everyday rhetoric which recalls, for example, the siege of Derry in 1689 and the siege of the Bogside in 1968 as landmarks in an unchanging struggle between Catholics and Protestants. Thus history recurs rather than develops, and the sectarian struggle must be 'settled' prior to the solution of any other political question. Of course this popular view of history also helps legitimate capital accumulation in NI and capitalist state structures which rest on this accumulation. The apparently unchanging rhetoric of sectarianism fixated on 'historical events' even allows successive Secretaries of State to assert that history must be *forgotten* in order that the business of reform and modernisation can be advanced.

Popular sectarianism is more than a 'view of history', however. It is, as Burton (1978:37) points out, a form of ideological social relations of pervasive importance in everyday life. It is a practical and necessary social skill to be able to 'tell the difference' between Protestants and Catholics. Thus the 'immutable' historical division becomes a contemporary and mundane reality.

> 'Telling [the difference] is based on the social significance attached to name, face and dress, area of residence, school attended, linguistic and possibly phonetic use, colour and symbolism. It is not based on undisputed fact but as an ideological representation is a mixture of 'myth' and 'reality'. Aspects of the process are certainly contentious among members of the community itself...'

Thus in NI, voters, workers, trade unionists, council tenants and community groups generally operate with a tacit or explicit sectarian prefix, despite frequent protestations to the contrary. This is no accident or atavistic survival immmune to modern political forms, for sectarianism in the ideological sense does not merely obscure class differences, it also *reveals* the materiality of sectarian division at all levels in NI. This division amounts to near apartheid in many areas of social life, which does indicate a *continuity* with history if not its recurrence. Segregated housing, schools, churches, recreational facilities and workplaces testify to the importance of the division which is at its *sharpest* in urban working class areas. Many empiricist accounts of NI stress the lack of contact between Catholics and Protestants but confuse physical segregation with the absence of inter-sectarian relationships. For example, Boal *et al* (1976:83) observe:

> 'Two ethnic national groups in Northern Ireland can be visualised as composing two distinct societies with little or no interaction between them, both essentially "normal" societies, except that the presence of the other group functions as an external enemy'.

In failing to go beyond what is directly observable, this statement refuses to recognise that the relative lack of contact is itself an expression of an underlying social relationship. Catholics and

Protestants do relate to each other in many ways but the crucial relationship is via the state. Since 1920 this state has remained the UK state either in the shape of devolved Unionist government or Direct Rule. Geographical segregation is an expression of the sectarian class relations through which this state operates, and on which its very existence depends.

The conflict over territorial boundaries is not a question of some instinctual 'territorial imperative' or an abstract argument about the territorial completion or incompletion of the national liberation struggle (as some nationalists and their critics maintain). It is not the struggle over the territorial extent of the state *per se* which denies the state its legitimacy. Schools, churches, shops, factories and farms which constitute the physical terrain are a *stake* in the sectarian and class struggle within NI. The Border is the over-arching manifestation of hundreds of internal sectarian boundaries which designate Protestant and Catholic space. A recurring theme in our case studies is the extent to which both Unionist and Direct Rule governments have used these divisions to maintain a form of political stability in NI. It is here, at this concrete level, that the inter-penetration of reform and repression, sectarianism and class are most evident. Churches, schools, housing estates, firms, parades, flags, riots, and intimidation are physical manifestations which serve to delineate and reproduce territorial divisions on sectarian and class lines. It is in recognising, shaping and perpetuating these divisions that the state in NI assumes its peculiar form.

Footnotes:
1. There are exceptions to this general statement; for example Boyle *et al* (1975) have evaluated the operation of the legal system and Darby and Williamson (1978) have examined state responses to 'the troubles'. In general, however, this type of analysis accepts, rather uncritically, the administrative categories laid down by the British state, i.e. the compartmentalisation of the NI problem into its discrete technocratic components, security, education, social services, etc., thereby failing to grasp the overall thrust of reformist policy. Marxist and other socialist accounts have not examined the recent anatomy of the British state in NI in a holistic way. They have been primarily concerned with the pre-1972 Stormont state and with socialist positions on the Irish problem (e.g. Farrell 1976; Bew *et al* 1979; McCann 1974; Morgan and Purdie 1980).
2. Miller (1978) sees contractarian ideology as central to the understanding of Protestant politics, rooted in the religious and political

traditions of the Ulster and Scottish Presbyterians. In Ulster the landlords had the political and military support for the Protestant tenantry to preserve the plantation and the Williamite settlement. In turn landlords were expected to protect the tenantry from the encroachment of the Catholic natives. Miller suggests that the 'conditional loyalty' of 'Loyalists' to the British state is based on a modern version of this historic social contract.

3. Lyons (1973:700) suggests that the Westminster Parliament spent on average only two hours per annum discussing NI between Partition and the outbreak of the current crisis. Of course a convention also developed that Westminster would not discuss the affairs for which Stormont had responsibility.

4. Colonial struggles did threaten to highlight the links between overseas 'repression' and the post-war 'reformist' state. Labour/Tory agreement on dismantling the Empire did help to insulate 'repression' from 'reform' in a political sense. If the 'unsolved' Home Rule Question had been a major item on the agenda of the Attlee government it might have weakened the subsequent British 'post-war settlement'.

5. Political scientists often attribute lack of political competitiveness to the mechanics of the 'straight vote system', where minorities are under-represented. However, neither pre-1929 or post-1969 electoral experience suggests that PR fundamentally alters the Unionist/anti-Unionist voting patterns in NI as a whole, or the political salience of the basic divide, even if some choice within the two blocs has become possible.

6. The SDLP was originally a coalition between Civil Rights activists, including Belfast MPs on the one hand and some Stormont Nationalist MPs on the other. Since 1975 Labourist representatives such as Paddy Devlin and Gerry Fitt have left the Party, weakening its political support in Belfast.

7. The Outdoor Relief riots of 1932 and the protest against redundancies and unemployment in the early 1960s are frequently cited examples of extra-parliamentary working class action. Whatever their short-term political effects they made little political impact on the central Unionist/anti-Unionist divide.

8. The Orange Order is formally entitled to 122 of the 760 seats on the Ulster Unionist Council and 18 out of 300 on its Standing Committee. Furthermore many of the constituency delegates are Orangemen. Only three members of all Unionist cabinets between 1921 and 1969 were not Orangemen when first elected. Three other Ministers — Orangemen when elected — left the Order later. One resigned when his daughter married a Roman Catholic, another was expelled for attending a Catholic ceremony as part of his public duties and a third resigned on becoming Minister for Community Relations. Of the 95 Stormont MPs who never achieved Cabinet rank, 87 were Orangemen. Three of the remainder were O'Neillite MPs elected

for the first time in 1969 (and who have since left politics). Every Unionist Senator but one in the NI Senate, between 1921 and 1968, was an Orangeman. Only two of the Westminster MPs (both women) were not members of the Order in the same period (see Harbinson 1973:90-91).

9. Here the Catholic Church was advocating in Ireland a politics and social philosophy which had emerged from the Catholic social movement on the Continent (see Whyte 1971 on Catholic policy in the Irish Republic). As applied in Ireland it contained a mixture of anti-communism, anti-materialism, and opposition to foreign (particularly British) influences. It advocated a version of the corporate state resting on small property holders and the 'traditional values' of Irish rural life — self help, neighbourliness, etc.

10. This early Civil Rights slogan has now been ironically adopted by recent Orange marches which have demanded tougher 'security measures' from the British government to protect the rights of Protestant citizens.

11. In a peculiar sense some anti-imperialist positions also accept this view by default, by appearing to reduce the question of class struggle to 'Troops Out'.

Who's doing well out of the troubles?

While thousands of people are being thrown out of work by violence, living in fear of violence — some people are living high.

The men of violence are feathering their own nests by extortion, robbery and murder.

It could be different — we can restore, through the rule of law, more freedom and hope for the future.

Where all our efforts and resources go into the search for new investments and more jobs. Where we are able to enjoy the better things in life.

IT'S OUR CHOICE — BUT . . .

7 years is enough

Northern Ireland Office (NIO) poster campaign, November 1976

2

Regional Policy

Regional policy may be seen as the state's most explicit response to the uneven spatial development of capital in post-war western Europe. The growth of multi-national enterprise and the increasing specialisation and fragmentation of the labour process has facilitated the mobility of industrial production across regional and national boundaries — superimposing new spatial and physical patterns on those laid down in the 19th century. Simultaneously the growth of social democratic politics placed an onus on states to ensure full employment. These political demands came to have a regional emphasis as high unemployment rates persisted in the old centres of 19th century industry, where redundant physical and productive plant posed barriers to the new forms of capital accumulation. NI, and in particular Belfast, was one such area, although it lacked a social democratic politics along British or Continental lines.

To a large degree the viability of a separate NI state in 1920/21 rested on the concentration of Protestant (and Unionist) industrial capital in the Belfast area, which in turn was integrated into the Glasgow-Liverpool complex, at a time when British imperialism was a major world force. Concentration of capital meant concentration of labour, stratified in terms of skill, workplace and sectarian division. Two broad phases may be distinguished. The first saw the mechanisation of linen and the creation of a linen complex between 1840 and 1880. A large proportion of the migrants to Belfast in this period were Catholic peasants driven off the land by famine and by the shift from tillage to livestock production. In the second phase, 1880–1911, the other side of Belfast's industrial complex took shape as shipbuilding and engineering provided large-scale employment for skilled Protestant males.

In 1945 NI's economy still rested on its 19th century

foundation. It was highly specialised around linen, shipbuilding, engineering, and agriculture. Two-thirds of the total population and almost 80% of the insured workforce were concentrated within a 30-mile radius of Belfast. The major industries were highly export-oriented and susceptible to the cyclical crises of international capital. Unemployment, remaining consistently high in the inter-war period, reached a peak of 29.5% of all insured workers in 1938. The shipyards had reached an all-time low in 1933/34 and over 56% of all linen workers were unemployed by July 1938, compared with six per cent in 1927 (Buckland 1979:52-53). At the height of the unemployment crisis war broke out — providing a reprieve for the major industries. Output and employment in linen, shipbuilding/engineering and agriculture expanded as part of the war effort and NI reached its lowest ever unemployment rate (3.8%) in 1944. No sooner had the war finished, however, when the precarious nature of capital accumulation and employment became apparent once again, confronting the Unionist state with a dilemma present in one form or another since its foundation. On the one hand it was forced to facilitate the restructuring of the traditional industrial sector while maintaining employment, especially among its working class supporters. On the other hand it had to ensure that the incoming industries did not upset the balance of sectarian power on which the very existence of the state depended. The creation of the state had made the politics of sectarian majorities and territory crucial in NI as a whole *and* within its constituent parts. Competition for jobs, public expenditure and various forms of patronage had become invested with the whole panoply of questions surrounding sectarian class relations (and the sectarian head-count) which were critical to the nature and existence of the state as a separate unit.

Employment and the Restructuring of Capital

NI quickly reverted to high unemployment rates in the post-war period, although they never attained 1930s levels (when an average of 20-28% of the insured population had been out of work). Rates persisted at between three and five times the UK average. After the war-time low an immediate post-war peak of 10.2% was reached in 1952 with subsequent rates of over seven percent in 1958, '63, '67 and '71. It was not until the current crisis of international capital, however, that unemployment was to surpass its 1952 level. After 1975 the rate began to rise to over seven percent, reaching well over ten percent two years later, and over 15% by August 1980 (See Isles and Cuthbert 1957; Murie 1970; Dept. of Manpower Services [DMS] Gazette 1978–9). Furthermore, relatively high migration rates depressed the unemployment rates — masking the extent to which NI was a locale for an industrial reserve army. The overall migration and unemployment figures obscured major internal variations among different areas and sections of the population. Barritt and Carter (1962:120-24) estimated that between 55% and 58% of emigrants between 1937 and 1961 were Catholics even though they formed only one-third of the total population. Likewise several towns in the south and west often had unemployment rates more than double the NI average.

The post-war restructuring of the central sectors of the economy led to job losses and to pressure on the regional government to assist incoming multi-national enterprises to provide alternatives. Tables 1 and 2 demonstrate the changing employment patterns in broad outline.

Table 1: Percentage of Employees in Main Industrial Classifications, 1952–1979

	1952	1959	1965	1971	1979
Agriculture Fishing/Mining & Other Extractive Industries	5.6	5.4	4.0	3.0	2.1
Manufacturing	44.9	39.7	37.3	36.3	27.3
Construction	8.4	8.8	9.7	8.4	7.3
Services	41.1	46.1	49.0	52.3	63.3
Total	100.0	100.0	100.0	100.0	100.0
N =	466,000	437,479	465,205	473,241	513,650

SOURCES: Isles and Cuthbert (1957) and *DMS Gazette*, 1-3, 1978/79.

Table 2: Self-Employed: Percentages in Main Industrial Classifications, 1959–79

	1959	1971	1979
Agriculture/mining etc.	76.1	62.2	63.6
Manufacturing	2.4	2.8	2.8
Construction	2.6	9.8	10.6
Services	18.9	25.2	23.0
	100.0	100.0	100.0
N =	105,716	81,443	75,750

SOURCE: *DMS Gazette*, 3, 1979

Three broad phases can be distinguished with respect to manufacturing employment using these statistics.[1] Between 1952 and 1959 there was a marked decline mainly due to the contraction of linen employment. In the next period, 1959–71, manufacturing employment was almost stabilized, mainly because of a dramatic increase in external investment in NI promoted by an active regional policy. The third period was marked by a fall-off in outside investment and renewed decline in manufacturing employment. Throughout the whole post-war period there was a spectacular reduction in agricultural employment as it became more capital-intensive. Simultaneously there was a dramatic growth in services which accelerated after 1971. Although self-employment continued to fall after 1971, its rate of decline slackened considerably. Agriculture accounted for most of the decrease as self-employment actually increased in the other categories between 1959 and 1979.

Despite the overall increase in the working population, these gross figures conceal important shifts. Total male employment actually fell by 19,000 (5%) between 1959 and 1979, while female employment rose by over 65,000 (almost 40%). Over 32% of the latter was part-time, however. Mainly as a result of the growth in services, part-time employment accounted for nearly 18% of total jobs in 1978 compared to only 8% in 1971; 78% of all part-time jobs were held by women (*DMS Gazette* 1979). Table 3 gives a more precise account of the decline of traditional sectors and of the extent to which new industries provided alternative employment. Between 1959 and 1971 the decline in shipbuilding and textiles was largely offset by growth in the food/drink/tobacco, engineering and rubber industries. Thereafter all the major manufacturing sectors (except the 'other' category) contracted, notably textiles, clothing and engineering. The slower decline in shipbuilding masks a massive state investment of £35m in 1972 (*NI Economic Report* 1973) which failed to provide any of the projected 4,000 extra jobs that year. The rate of increase in service employment accelerated dramatically after 1971 although much of it was part-time work. This increase was mainly due to the growth of professional and scientific services (especially education and health) and of public administration and defence as the British state became directly involved in administering the area.

Throughout its history NI has remained a highly specialised fragment of the UK economy — closely tied to the changing fortunes of British capitalism. Insofar as the Stormont government

*Table 3: Changes in Employment
(Incl. Self-Employment), 1959-78*

	Absolute and Percentage Employment Changes, 1959-78		Average Annual Employment Change	
	Numbers	*%*	*1959-71*	*1971-78*
Agriculture/ Mining etc.	−44,700	−42.5	−3,042	−588
Manufacturing (Total)	−33,950	−19.2	−168	−3,952
Food/Drink/ Tobacco	+1,488	+7.0	+403	−468
Shipbuilding	−13,630	−60.5	−1,004	−72
Engineering	+4,524	+28.5	+828	−780
Vehicles	−4,957	−34.5	−272	−177
Textiles	−25,235	−44.9	−1,164	−1,262
Clothing/ Footwear	−7,798	−30.7	+31	−1,025
Other Manufacturing*	+6,689	+690.3	+514	+1
Construction	+5,127	+12.4	+512	−192
Services (Total)	+108,860	+49.1	+3,584	+7,784
Professional/ Scientific services	+62,615	+144.6	+2,565	+3,658
Public administration/defence	+23,479	+83.8	+594	+1,970
TOTAL	+35,911	+6.6	+884	+4,340

* Mainly rubber industries
SOURCE: *DMS Gazette*, 3, 1979

had any overall economic policy, it was one of maintaining and strengthening integration with the UK. This put distinct limits on diversification. Unlike the South, where the protectionism of the 1930s encouraged a diverse (if weak) industrial base, such questions did not arise in NI. The explicit aim of reducing dependence on British markets was common to all Southern political parties even if it met with little success until EEC membership in the 1970s. The North, on the other hand, had no internal debates on the merits of protectionism *versus* free trade and remained heavily export-oriented. NI, as a separate unit, is much more export-oriented than neighbouring economies. For example, taking the value of exports as a percentage of Gross

National Product in 1967, NI exports accounted for 70% (55% to Britain, 15% to other countries). Comparative figures for other countries were, Irish Republic (25%), UK (14%), Germany (16%), Netherlands (34%) (*NI Economic Report* 1968).

NI's political autonomy under the devolution settlement was not founded on financial or economic autonomy — a reality which placed major constraints on local regional policy. Despite Unionist ministers' oft-stated aim of diversifying the economy, this was not allowed to disturb the degree of integration with the UK. Nugent (1946:167) interpreted the policy of diversification cautiously: 'we have built around our well-established industries new undertakings of the type which act as supports to our older industries'. Although there have been major internal transformations within the textile sector (synthetic fibres replacing linen) and within shipbuilding/engineering, Table 4 demonstrates the continued specialisation of Northern manufacturing industry in four major industrial sectors:

Table 4: Percentages of Total Manufacturing Employment in the Four Major Industrial Sectors, 1952–78

	1952	1959	1971	1978
Food/Drink/ Tobacco	11.4	11.9	15.2	15.9
Textiles/Clothing	51.2	46.6	38.7	34.3
Shipbuilding/ Marine Engineering	11.6	13.0	5.5	6.3
Engineering (incl. vehicles)	14.3	17.2	21.6	21.0
Total	88.5	88.7	81.0	77.5
N =	185,330	153,892	138,985	108,751

SOURCES: Isles and Cuthbert (1957:63) and *DMS Gazette*, 3, 1979

The economy actually became more specialised between 1952 and 1959. Thereafter the main factor in diversification was the transformation of the textile industry and the resultant contraction of employment. While the economies of North and South have been growing more alike in broad structural terms since 1960, the inherited effects of prior state policy and historic economic structure have ensured a more diverse manufacturing base in the South (Black 1977:47-51).

In any case, given the ideology of the Stormont government

and its lack of economic powers, the political framework of formal regional policy was largely determined by the British state. A relatively passive regional policy existed in Britain between 1951 and 1958 in conditions of near-full employment. Investment grants were small and the industrial development certificates (IDCs), which were intended to divert industry to the disadvantaged regions, were frequently ignored. A period of transition followed, leading to a much more active policy under the Labour government between 1964 and 1970. This corresponded to the most active period of policy in NI under the O'Neill administration. After 1970 regional planning agencies were expanded as local versions of the National Enterprise Board, but the IDC policy was relaxed in response to what was now termed the 'inner city' problem, which appeared to be common to all regions. There was a move away from 'blanket regional subsidies' and more emphasis placed on restructuring sectors of industry (see Moore *et al* 1978; CSE State Group 1979:42-43).

Regional policy in NI has operated within the broad UK framework with significant modifications in response to local conditions. In the inter-war period Stormont was forced to operate the *Loan Guarantee Act* to aid local industry. From the inception of the state, the British government facilitated cheap loans through banks and insurance companies which were used by Stormont to aid shipbuilding in particular, under the watchful eye of the local state's bank — the Midland (Buckland 1979:116-18; Bew *et al* 1979:91-92). By the end of the inter-war period manufacturing was divided into two main sectors — shipbuilding/engineering dominated by the increasingly state-financed shipyards and three major Belfast engineering works,[2] and a highly competitive and fragmented linen complex. As the long-term decline of local capitalist enterprise as an employer of labour resumed after the war, the Unionists sought to maintain Protestant working class employment by encouraging incoming industry through the *Industrial Development Acts* while simultaneously aiding local capital through the *Re-equipment of Industry Act*. An important intra-Unionist tension was exposed here. Local capitalists in the linen complex, with a reputation for low wages and unreliable employment, strongly resented state help to incoming industry which was increasing competition for labour especially in Belfast (Steed 1974:401). As early as 1946 Walter Smiles (1946:162), employer of over 3,000 workers in Belfast Ropeworks[3] and chairman of Belfast Chamber of Commerce, sounded a warning:

> 'I detect a tendency in modern industrial development to sacrifice the old for the benefit of the new. Greater ballyhoo is given to a couple of dozen girls making a new television set in a backyard than to a well-established industry which has supported thousands of men and their dependants for a hundred years or more. Ulster industrial tradition is about 200 years of age with a record of craftsmanship which still survives even the modern technique of mass production. The stern Huguenot and Scotch Presbyterian character developed industries under difficulties. These industries are deeply rooted in the soil of Ulster. Though we do not breed as many Grand National winners as Eire, we turn out useful ships, machinery and linen.'

Local capitalists, strongly represented in the Unionist cabinet, fought a rearguard action throughout the 1950s in the face of pressure from the NILP and academic economists for more systematic state intervention to combat employment and the new competition for labour from externally-owned industry. However, the Unionist Party's long-term preoccupation with maintaining the status quo and with reproducing sectarian class relations seems to have gripped local capitalists. Local investment and 'entrepreneurship' was at a low ebb. Only 10% of the new state-assisted plants resulted from local initiative; where local investment did occur, it came mostly from long-established tobacco, textile engineering and mechanical engineering concerns rather than from new firms (Steed and Thomas 1971:350). The government's Local Development Enterprise Unit (LEDU) complained consistently in the 1970s of the dearth of new innovations or technical ideas (Busteed 1976:180).

By the beginning of the 1960s large-scale redundancies in the shipyards, combined with the continuing decline in linen employment, highlighted the failings of local capital and the lethargy of the Unionist Party in developing a coherent programme of intervention. Some Protestant defections to the NILP in Belfast and rumblings of discontent from Unionist backbenchers led to the replacement of Brookeborough, PM for 20 years, by O'Neill in 1963. Other factors were also conspiring, however, to usher in a series of Stormont initiatives in formal regional policy. NI civil servants were now operating what Green (1979:17) terms an 'expenditure-based system' free from the notional idea of a balanced NI budget. They were free to make a case to the Treasury for particular developments. Finally regional policy was being revived in Britain anyway.

Restructuring the Physical Environment

Regional policy meant more than merely subsidizing traditional and incoming industry, however. It also involved the state in renewing the physical environment to accommodate the restructuring of production. Here state intervention expressed the contradictions of a capitalist development itself which, in Harvey's (1978:124) words, must

> 'negotiate a knife-edge path between preserving the exchange values of past capital investments in the built environment and destroying the value of these investments in order to open up fresh room for accumulation. Under capitalism there is a perpetual struggle in which capital builds a physical landscape appropriate to its own condition at a particular moment in time, only to have to destroy it, usually in the course of a crisis, at a subsequent point in time.'

Given the existing powers of the NI state and the concern of Unionism to maintain control of local sectarian territories, physical planning was potentially of much greater interest to the Party than more generalized economic planning. Proposals to restructure the physical environment emerged towards the end of the war. Stormont had come under a greater degree of central British control as part of the general war effort. Between 1945 and 1951 five Stormont Command Papers appeared as the local response to reconstruction. These asserted the necessity for state intervention to build roads, plan industrial location, increase house building and reshape physical infrastructure and communications.[4]

In the event the Unionist Party was considerably less keen than the local civil servants to embark on such a far-reaching state programme of physical planning. The Reports were shelved. Unionist politics at Stormont and in the local authorities did not revolve around such apparently 'rational' and grandiose conceptions. Instead the strategy was to respond in a piecemeal and ad hoc manner to demands and pressures emanating from the different levels of the Protestant class alliance. Ritual assertions of sectarian and partitionist rhetoric in reply to the anti-partition campaign of the time helped maintain Protestant unity but only constituted a part of the total response. There was the practical political problem of facilitating local capital accumulation as well as the problem of maintaining Protestant employment. The setting up of the NI Housing Trust and the adoption of educational and social services reforms did not represent any Unionist enthusiasm for the British welfare state but rather a pragmatic recognition of the constraints of devolution and the potential consequences for unrest among their working class support if the reforms were not implemented.

The explicit planning strategies of the O'Neill administration in the 1960s concentrated on the physical infrastructure of the Belfast Region in particular, in order to accommodate and influence the changing industrial base. The new policy was replete with the 'growth centre' and 'New Town' rhetoric of 'objective' planning while its implementation sought to marry the new rhetoric with the practice of reproducing Unionist hegemony. Infrastructural development was concentrated on the 'Protestant' towns of Antrim/Ballymena and Lurgan/Portadown (renamed Craigavon) which were designated as New Towns. New Town Commissions were set up in 1965 to supplant the relevant local authorities and to produce integrated plans for housing, industry and retail centres. The central planning document was the Matthew Plan which had been commissioned by Stormont civil servants in 1960 (for background, see Oliver 1978:81). Matthew defined a Belfast Urban Area and a Greater Belfast Region (see Map 1) placing a stopline around Belfast to prevent further industrial and housing growth on the urban periphery. Labour was to be directed to the New Towns and the other growth centres in the Greater Belfast Area.

Belfast Corporation, more interested in motorway development than in housing, eventually commissioned consultants to plan the long awaited redevelopment of inner Belfast between 1965-69. These joined the transport consultants whose plans eventually helped to displace almost 4,000 families from the inner city (Wiener 1975). Both sets of plans resulted in the spread of urban blight and the hastening of out-migration. The new high-rise flats in Protestant and Catholic West Belfast were a monument to the low priority attached to working class housing need compared to the alacrity with which the state facilitated incoming capital.

Roads and communications were a priority. Between 1964–69 expenditure per capita on roads was 50% higher in NI than in the UK was a whole. The M1 and M2 motorways linked the New Towns to Belfast — neatly outlining the economic region designated by the planners and favoured by the Unionists. The *Benson Report* (1963) recommended the rationalisation of the railway network further isolating the rest of NI from the developing Belfast Region. Advance factories were mainly

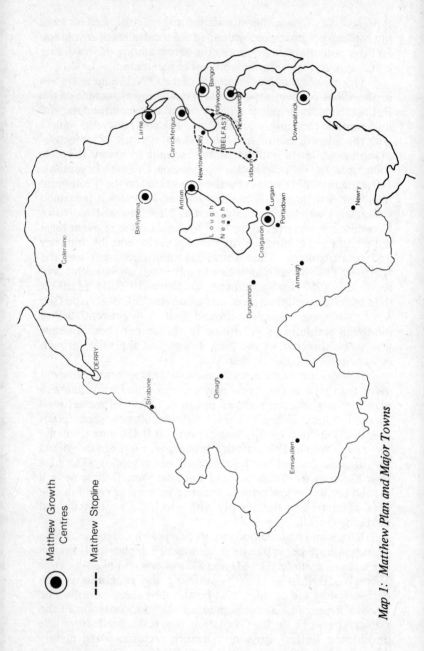

● Matthew Growth Centres

┊ Matthew Stopline

Map 1: Matthew Plan and Major Towns

concentrated in this region until at least 1966 (Walsh 1979:12; Micklewright 1970), leading to the consolidation of what the *Quigley Report* (1976) was later to term the 'dual economy'.

For many in the emerging Civil Rights movement, the new planning policy was seen as simply a further example of sectarian discrimination — a new 'plantation of Ulster'. The main thrust of the criticism did not go much beyond allegations of discriminatory motives which favoured 'Protestant' towns and areas in the east over the predominantly Catholic west and south. One of the civil servants centrally concerned with the new plans sought to justify them on 'objective' planning criteria by explaining that the east had always had 'far more locally generated drive, private and commercial as well as municipal' (Oliver 1978:182). The new commissions and public bodies were still monopolised by the Unionist bourgeoisie, however; and despite O'Neill's policy of 'hands across the Border and the sectarian divide', the technocratic veneer of planning wore a little thin at times. The siting of Craigavon and particularly the New University of Ulster in the 'Protestant' market town of Coleraine rather than in Derry owed much to the local politics of sectarian majority. Perhaps the *Lockwood Report*'s (1965) most convincing technocratic argument for locating the university in Coleraine was that it would be near Aldergrove Airport and would therefore allow 'easier access to British academia'. In general, however, the more important point was not sectarian motives as such but that the 'requirements of capital' were easily reconciled with existing sectarian geography and domination.

Initially there was little internal Unionist opposition to the *Matthew Report*. On the one hand it appeared to meet Protestant working class demands for jobs, while on the other it appeared to consolidate the Protestant majority in NI as a whole by concentrating development in the Belfast Region, which contained 75% of all Protestants compared with only 48% of all Catholics (see Table 5).

Table 5: Sectarian Composition by Region, 1971

	Protestants	Catholics	Total
Belfast	250,940 (27.9)	115,259 (24.1)	411,091 (27.0)
Environs of Belfast	418,688 (46.6)	115,844 (24.2)	579,119 (38.1)
Rest of NI	229,582 (25.5)	246,816 (51.7)	529,430 (34.9)
	892,210 (100)	447,919 (100)	1,519,640 (100)

SOURCE: NI Census, Religion Tables (1971)

Furthermore major industrial growth was to be concentrated in the environs of Belfast, where Catholics accounted for a highly dispersed 20% of the population, thus avoiding Catholic West Belfast and the west of the province.

While these considerations may not have occurred to Matthew they did concern the Unionist local authority system, which itself was threatened by Matthew's suggestion to centralise planning powers and rationalise the archaic complex of local government units. These policed the local sectarian boundaries through housing allocation, employment and control over land use (see ch. 4). They faced their first challenge not from the Civil Rights movement but from the planners. At the height of the internal crisis in Unionism between 1965 and 1973, it was significant that the only resolution on the Party's annual conference agenda opposing the leadership was concerned with the procedures and effects of planning directives (Harbinson 1973:58). In the event the complete centralisation of planning powers did not occur until 1973 under the Ministry of Development (later the Dept of the Environment). By 1975 the regional growth centre policy had been greatly attenuated, with almost as many growth centres as there were new District Councils.

The Location of Manufacturing Employment

It is easy to exaggerate the extent to which formal physical planning shaped the type and location of incoming industry. As Parson (1979:58) points out, Ireland — both North and South — may be seen as a type of 'reserve area' for British and international monopoly capital. It acts as a locale for an industrial reserve army, a receptor for capital selectively exported from the core, a market for goods produced in the core, and a source of political conservatism.

NI offered a particular combination of these characteristics in the post-war period. Long before the Matthew Plan, new textile and engineering industries had located in Castlereagh, Lisburn and Newtownabbey on the outskirts of Belfast. GEC and Courtaulds had set up major plants in Larne and Carrickfergus, respectively, in the 1950s. The designation of Antrim New Town followed rather than preceded the location there of its major industry (British Enkalon) in 1963. In fact the Matthew Plan may be read as an attempt to control these developments by dispersing industry more widely within the

Doing business in Northern Ireland

"I decided to roll the dice..."

Some well-known manufacturers in Northern Ireland

Some thirty American firms have factories in Northern Ireland today, with total capital investment of about $700-million.

"A better attitude toward work than in many parts of the world..."

AVX Corporation
H. J. Heinz
Coleraine ● Monsanto

Limavady
Ballymoney

Londonderry
Hoechst

Ames Textile
Brunswick

Irish Sea

Du Pont
United Technologies
VF Corporation
Courtaulds
Plastic Capacitors

Ballymena
American Brands
Michelin

Larne

G.E.C.
Courtaulds

I.C.I.
Courtaulds

Carrickfergus

Antrim
Akzo

Michelin
Fruehauf
Camco
ITT

Bangor

National Distillers
Textron

Oneida

Belfast ● Ford

Newtownards
VF Corporation

Omagh
Nestlé

Grundig
Tenneco
TRW Mission
American Brands
British Petroleum

Norton
Unilever
Euroweld
PX Nuclear
Hughes Tool

S. H. Camp

Craigavon

Dromore
Warnaco

Ballynahinch
Plessey

General Foods
Goodyear
St. Joe Paper
Demag

Enniskillen
Ball Corporation

Armagh

Downpatrick

Irish Republic

Newry
International Rectifier

● Warrenpoint
Synthetic Industries

NORTHERN IRELAND: THE OPPORTUNITIES ARE THERE. THE PROFITS ARE THERE.

Mr Louis Ritchie, Industrial Development
Organisation for Northern Ireland,
Ulster Office, 11 Berkeley Street, London W1X 6BU
Telex: 21839

Please send me more information on Northern Ireland

from *Fortune* magazine (USA), 1977
colour supplement paid for by Northern Ireland government

Belfast Region — thus opening the way for urban renewal in inner Belfast. The impact of industrial restructuring is indicated by Table 6:

Table 6: Percentage of Manufacturing Employment by Region

	Belfast	Environs of Belfast	Rest of NI	Total
1959	55	28	17	100
1966	52	28	20	100
1971	43	34	23	100
1978	38	36	26	100

Regions are based on amalgamation of Employment Exchange Areas (currently named Employment Service Office Areas). See Map 2.
SOURCES: Micklewright (1970) and *DMS* unpublished statistics.

The major feature of the redistribution of manufacturing employment is the declining industrial base in Belfast. In fact the Table grossly understates the decline within the city, as the Belfast Employment Exchange Area includes the new post-war industrial suburbs of Castlereagh and Newtownabbey. The de-industrialisation of inner and West Belfast has further reduced the job prospects of working class Catholics, who have been overwhelmingly concentrated in the west of the city since 1969. The percentage of total manufacturing employment in the Environs of Belfast and in the Rest of NI increased significantly after 1966 — possibly suggesting that the local state's 'dispersal' policy was beginning to take effect. It is difficult to disentangle the determining influences here, however, as the locational requirements of incoming firms may have encouraged dispersal in any case, as they did in the Irish Republic. By the mid-1960s there were indications of labour shortage in the Environs of Belfast, where new investment had been concentrated in the post-war period. For example the major Courtauld's factory, at Carrickfergus since 1950, was experiencing competition for labour by 1965 from other new factories such as ICI, Michelin, Standard Telephone and Cables and Carreras, all within a nine-mile radius (Garnsey 1965:57).

Table 7 gives a more precise breakdown of manufacturing employment between 1959 and 1978. The Table reiterates the dramatic decline of manufacturing in Belfast throughout the whole period and the widespread effects of the high rate of

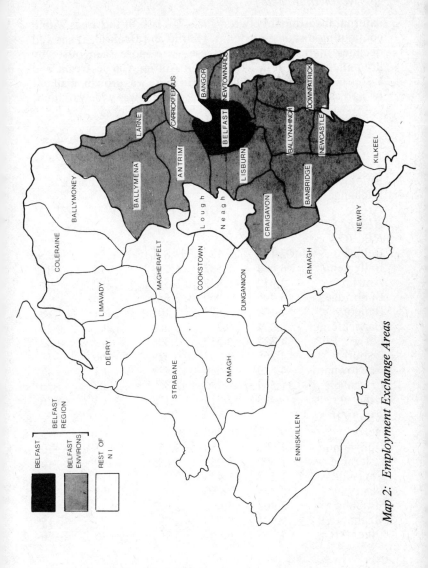

Map 2: *Employment Exchange Areas*

external investment between 1959–71. Two of the areas within commuting distance of Belfast (Larne and Banbridge) showed declines in this period but these were more than offset by dramatic growth in nearby areas in Antrim, Carrickfergus and Lisburn. Outside the Belfast Region there was growth in all but two areas — Dungannon and Newry. There was wide variation,

Table 7: Regional Manufacturing Employment, 1959-78

Employment Exchange Areas	Numbers Employed			% Change	
	1959	*1971*	*1978*	*1959-71*	*1971-78*
BELFAST REGION					
Belfast	102,130	75,128	53,871	−26	−28
Ballymena	6,694	7,582	6,778	+13	−11
Antrim	3,652	6,933	5,548	+90	−20
Banbridge	3,700	2,960	2,684	−20	−9
Bangor	1,100	2,879	3,101	+161	+8
Carrickfergus	2,054	6,213	5,588	+202	−10
Larne	4,337	3,510	2,396	−19	−32
Lisburn	4,266	7,162	6,329	+68	−12
Newtownards	4,529	4,588	3,827	+1	−17
Craigavon	11,554	14,780	12,369	+28	−16
Other Areas	2,418	2,513	3,178	+4	+26
REST OF NI					
Derry	9,921	10,358	9,797	+4	−5
Dungannon	4,002	3,280	2,953	−18	−10
Coleraine	1,800	3,943	3,685	+119	−6
Enniskillen	1,267	3,473	3,373	+174	−3
Newry	3,348	3,260	3,211	−3	−1
Strabane	2,201	3,082	2,622	+40	−15
Magherafelt	1,601	2,700	2,294	+73	−15
Other Areas	4,763	6,907	5,105	+45	−26

SOURCES: Micklewright 1970; *DMS* unpublished statistics

however, between the spectacular growth of Coleraine and Enniskillen and the near stagnation of Derry, the largest town in the western region. The generally precarious nature of capital investment in NI is clearly demonstrated by the decline of employment after 1971 in every area except Bangor and some small towns south of Belfast. Not only did external investment decline but many of the new factories set up in the 1960s contracted. Here the much-vaunted 'New Town' and 'growth centre' policies seem to have had little effect. Since 1971 Craigavon and Antrim have shown rates of decline as high (if not higher) than other centres. The experience of other towns seems to depend more on the specific locational decisions of particular firms rather than on their status as 'growth centres'.

Next we take a closer look at the transformation of the economy in two key sectors to illustrate the politics of industrial restructuring in more concrete terms.

The Politics of Restructuring: Shipbuilding/Engineering

From the late 19th century onwards this sector provided employment for the central core of the skilled Protestant working class. Not only was the industry concentrated geographically in inner Belfast, it was also dominated by four large firms — Harland and Wolff, Mackies, Sirocco and Shorts. Shipbuilding and engineering workers were highly unionised and formed a critical support plank in the Unionist class alliance on which the state was built. Even when these workers occasionally deserted official Unionism to vote for the NILP or for independents, their support for Partition was not in doubt. Labour and capital depended on free trade under the aegis of the British state. The fortunes of Shorts and H & W, in particular, became closely linked with British state financing and with defence contracts after 1920/21.

The political centrality of the organised engineering workers affected both the nature and extent of restructuring. Massive grants and loans to the shipyards and to Shorts aircraft factory ensured the survival of these firms, albeit with greatly reduced workforces.[5] The survival of the shipyards in particular was of major symbolic significance to Unionism. Eventually both Shorts and the shipyards came under direct state control. Nevertheless Stormont's interventions seemed to be largely of the ad hoc variety until the mid-1960s. Money was provided to keep the major firms afloat while new engineering complexes were encouraged on the outskirts of Belfast. New firms such as Hughes Tool Co., ICL (later closed) in Castlereagh, Standard Telephone and Cables and Camco in Newtownabbey as well as Simms Steel and Grundig in Lisburn were set up with state help and provided alternative employment for workers made redundant in the traditional firms. Between 1959 and 1980 the proportion of the engineering labour force employed in the four traditional firms declined from approximately 75% to 50%. The remaining 50% of employees worked in over 150 firms, ranging in size from 1,000 to 20 employees (*Belfast Telegraph* 31/3/80). The increasingly diverse complex of firms was matched by a considerable diversification of output, both within the traditional plants and among the newcomers.

There was little involvement of Catholic workers in the industry. The small engineering plants in West Belfast went into decline. No major engineering plant was located there with state help until the abortive Strathearn Audio scheme in 1974 at the time of the 'power-sharing' executive. The new 'engineering suburbs' were built by the NI Housing Trust (see Ch. 5), housing mainly skilled Protestant workers. Some Catholics did move from the inner city and formed sections of the new estates, but it appears that these were not employed in the new engineering works to any great extent. In 1971 the Catholic proportions of Lisburn, Castlereagh and Newtownabbey District Council areas were 15%, 9% and 15%, respectively — figures probably reduced further as people crowded back into West Belfast in response to the political crisis.

Although the rapid decline of shipbuilding has been broadly offset by diversification and the relocation of skilled Protestant workers, the industry remains highly vulnerable to international recession and to the vagaries of government decisions. Contracts for oil tankers, oil drilling equipment and aircraft components are highly competitive internationally. Other UK shipbuilding and engineering regions compete for government contracts. Developments in micro-electronics threaten traditional skills and NI has so far failed to attract significant numbers of firms using the new technology. Perhaps the most visible trend is the growth of the car components industry, widely dispersed throughout the province, epitomising the fragmented nature of multi-national production (Perrons 1978). Recent American investment has centred around the 'showpiece' De Lorean

newspaper ad from the Northern Ireland Development Agency (NIDA), 1979

sports car company in West Belfast which promised 2,000 jobs at
a cost to the state of £53m. Employment continues to decline,
however — sharpening the competition for jobs and so placing
acute pressure on the militancy and effectiveness of trade unions.

The Politics of Industrial Restructuring: Textiles/Clothing

Textiles (notably linen) and clothing manufacture have been
central to the history of capital accumulation in NI. Textiles/
clothing still remains the most widely dispersed industry. Isles
and Cuthbert (1957:114), in phraseology which neatly encapsu-
lates their 'enclave' view of NI, noted that linen was the 'principal
medium through which industry has reached out to the small
centres of population in the interior'. However throughout its
history it has been closely linked to extreme fluctuations in world
trade. Thus three wars — the American Civil War and the two
World Wars — created boom conditions in the local industry
which were succeeded by recession, entailing a decline in local
flax growing, bankruptcies and decreasing employment (Dohrs
1950).

Nevertheless in 1948 Dohrs estimated that one quarter of
the world's capital equipment of linen spinning and weaving was
located in Belfast and that NI produced over a quarter of the
world's production of linen (the other major producer being the
USSR with 48%). 50,000 were directly employed in spinning and
weaving — 61,000 in the linen industry as a whole, of whom a half
was in Belfast. In 1952 textiles/clothing taken together was by far
the largest industrial sector with 43% of total manufacturing
employment and 79% of female manufacturing employment.
Textiles employed 1½ times as many women as men, clothing 7
times as many women as men (Isles and Cuthbert 1957:63).
Compared with shipbuilding/engineering, therefore, it was
heavily female, much more geographically dispersed and more
balanced in sectarian composition. Sectarian balance was largely
numerical, however, as location affected the composition of the
workforce in any particular mill. Furthermore the various levels
and trades within the industry were stratified on sectarian
grounds — often within the same firm. At one end of the scale
were the overwhelmingly Protestant and Unionist owners and
managers; at the other end were the largely female and
disproportionately Catholic labourers who worked under the
most arduous and unhealthy conditions in the spinning mills.

The linen complex proved highly resistant to rationalisation in the post-war period. At the beginning of the 1950s it contained over 400 plants engaged in seven different processes with relatively little vertical integration. The industry was controlled by fiercely competitive family firms which looked with disfavour on amalgamation. While they welcomed state aid they strongly resented state interference. Government attempts to encourage linen research, planning and marketing failed to stem the decline of the industry in the face of competition from man-made fibres (even within NI), Asian textile imports, and political developments which facilitated the supply and finishing of textiles in Latin America and China (Steed 1974:406). Although over 90% of production was exported, Steed observes that the complex knew remarkably little about its markets. Highly traditionalistic, it failed to develop a managerial elite to do market research and to manage its labour force at a time when competition for labour was acute, especially in Belfast. The major force for change, however, was the local impact of new British synthetic fibre corporations; these grew rapidly through acquisitions in the 1960s and showed 'virtually no interest in adding linen firms to their multiple fibre, multiple plan, multiple city operations' (Steed 1974:408). By 1970 only 200 plants remained, by now much less linen-orientated and more integrated, although less cohesive in terms of intra-industry links. This number was reduced by a further 25% by 1979, but by then the character of the industry had been completely transformed.

Corporations such as Tootal, ICI and Carrington Viyella control a range of textile and clothing firms. Courtaulds alone controls 22 plants throughout NI (*CIS Anti-Report* No. 10). The new corporations have imposed a new pattern of industrial location on the old which on balance seems to have widened the gap between Protestant and Catholic workers — still leaving both susceptible to the uncertainty endemic to the international conditions of the industry. The most clear-cut locational changes have occurred within Belfast, notably in the inner city and West Belfast. Here the juxtaposition of Protestant and Catholic workers (often within the same mill) has been largely obliterated by far-reaching de-industrialisation. New investment has been concentrated in growth centres such as Carrickfergus, Antrim, Ballymena and Craigavon. Coleraine, a town with little textile tradition, has become a major centre for overseas textile investment through the arrival of Montsanto (USA), Hœchst Fibre (West Germany) and Sperrin Textiles (Netherlands). The shift in

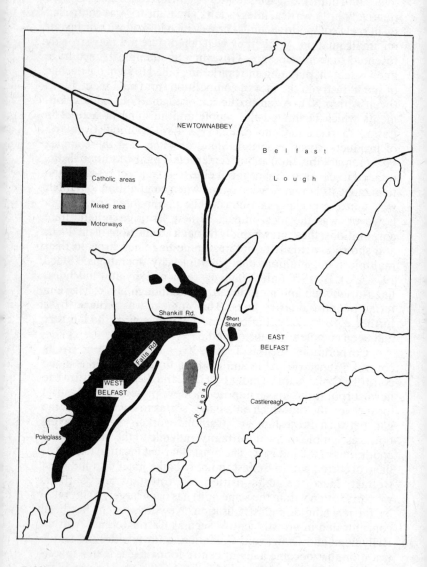

Belfast Urban Area (excluding Lisburn)

location has favoured Protestant rather than Catholic areas and male rather than female employment.

Between 1960 and 1973 the traditional textile sector lost 27,000 jobs of which 20,000 were female jobs. Most of the new jobs were for men (Black 1978:50). For NI textiles the years 1966–73 marked the high point of investment, building on the earlier post-war investment in that sector. Output increased by 109% in this period as growing capital-intensity reduced the workforce in the sector. By 1976 one-fifth of all UK employment in man-made fibre was concentrated in NI (Quigley 1976:53). Most of the industries attracted to NI in this period were in the textile/clothing sector. Between 1959 and 1972 four industrial categories — textiles, engineering/shipbuilding, construction and food, drink and tobacco — made up 75% of NI's industrial production. Of these four, textiles showed the most rapid increase with a growth in output of 7.5% per annum compared with 6.5% p.a. in construction and 2.6% in food, drink and tobacco and 0.8% in engineering (Gibson 1975:203). The international crisis in textiles led to large-scale lay-offs and closures in the new multi-national sector between 1973 and 1979. Courtaulds and ICI alone shed 1,200 jobs (Cooper and Lybrand 1980:34). The recession hit the clothing industry heavily after 1971 — again affecting females and Catholics disproportionately. Clothing employment decreased by 30% between 1971 and 1978 (NIEC:1979). Thus as multi-national corporations adjust their 'global' strategies in response to the oil crisis and to the changing patterns of trade between the EEC, the US and the Third World, the major 'growth' sector in the NI economy is undermined.

Reproducing Sectarian Division: The Marginality of Catholics

Twenty years of regional policy have done little to improve the job security of Protestant or Catholic labour. Even the skilled working class (mainly Protestant) has worked in industries such as shipbuilding and aircraft production which are notoriously sensitive to the capitalist cycle. The new synthetic fibres industry has proved to be similar in this respect. The precarious nature of capitalist development in NI has not reduced, however, the salience of sectarian division in the working class. This becomes clear when the position of Catholics is examined closely.

The transformation of the occupational structure since the beginning of the twentieth century has demonstrated trends evident in other industrial societies. Agricultural employment and skilled (craft-based) manual work have declined while non-manual occupations of both the professional and unskilled variety have increased. Bew *et al* (1979:166-168) and Aunger (1978) show how these trends have worked out differently for Catholics and Protestants. Basing their calculations on the censuses of 1911 and 1971 they show that there has been an expansion at the top and bottom of the Catholic social scale. The proportion of Catholics in professional and managerial occupations increased from 5% to 12%, compared to an increase among Protestants from 8% to 15%. On the other hand the proportion of unskilled Catholic manual workers has also increased from 20% to 25%, while this group has actually declined among Protestants from 18% to 15%. The proportion of skilled manual jobs has decreased for both Catholics (from 24% to 17%) and Protestants (from 34% to 19%). In the case of Protestants, however, skilled manual workers, when displaced, do not appear to have moved downwards into the semi/unskilled manual occupations. (The latter accounted for 40% of Protestant occupations in both 1911 and 1971.) Instead the proportion of Protestant non-manual workers has increased dramatically from 26% to 41%. In the case of Catholics, however, semi/unskilled manual occupations increased from 48% to 52%, semi-skilled non-manual occupations actually decreased as a proportion of Catholic occupations, while professional/managerial occupations increased markedly.

With the exception of the professional and managerial category, therefore, the occupational distribution has worsened for Catholics and improved somewhat for Protestants over the intercensal period. (This excludes agricultural occupations.) The apparent anomaly of an expanding Catholic professional class reveals, on closer inspection, its reliance on servicing its own community. Teachers and clergy account for 34% of this occupational group among Catholics, compared with 19% among Protestants. Furthermore 56% of this group work in 'social reproduction' occupations, education, health and welfare services — compared to 29% of the Protestant professional group. On the other hand the Catholic middle class is dramatically under-represented in industrial and financial occupations. Catholics account for only 7% of company secretaries, 12% of managers, 11% of engineers, chemists and biologists, 13% of commercial travellers and insurance agents and 17% of accountants. On the other hand, 73% of publicans are Catholics, 50% of waiters, 49% of hairdressers, 48% of domestic housekeepers and 43% of nurses (all figures based on 1971 Census figures after Aunger

1978 and FEA 1978). The structure of middle class occupations reveals the extent to which the Catholic middle class are marginal to the control of capital accumulation in NI. It does not appear that the penetration of monopoly capital has reduced the local political importance of the Protestant bourgeoisie. There is certainly little evidence that it has created a Catholic industrial bourgeoisie with whom it might compromise.

Examination of sectarian divisions among 'employees in employment' in 1971 also suggests that there are deep and systematic differences between the Protestant and Catholic working classes even at the end of a period marked by active regional policy and considerable external investment in NI. Table 8 shows differences in the main productive categories:

Table 8: Selected Industrial Classification by Religion, 1971

	% Catholic	% Protestant	% Not Stated	N
Food/Drink/Tobacco	21.4	60.9	7.7	(25,797)
Engineering (inc. Vehicles)	16.3	75.9	7.8	(37,287)
Shipbuilding	4.8	89.5	5.7	(9,654)
Textiles	23.6	69.1	7.3	(41,701)
Clothing/Footwear	40.1	50.7	9.2	(25,289)

SOURCE: NI Census, Religion Tables (1971)

The overall proportion of the economically active population enumerated as Catholic was 28.2% in 1971. In general Catholics were under-represented in manufacturing, forming only one-fifth of the male workforce there, compared to approximately one in three in agriculture/mining and one in four in the service sector. The high representation in clothing and footwear is accounted for by female employment. Only 12% of the labour force in the tobacco industry was Catholic — reflecting the location of the Rothman and Gallaher firms which control the industry. Catholics accounted for 37% of the employment in construction, but despite this overall over-representation they accounted for only 18% of the managers, builders and contractors within the industry compared to 51% of the plasterers and bricklayers and 55% of the labourers (FEA 1978:14; NI Census, Religion Tables 1971).

Clearly, then, Catholics (especially males) are under-

represented at the point of manufacturing production. Furthermore they do not form large concentrations of manual workers in
any major industrial sector to compare with the status of
Protestants in engineering/vehicles and shipbuilding. This greater
geographical dispersion was already indicated in Table 5. The
sectors with greatest Catholic representation — agriculture and
construction — are those which show greatest internal differen-
tiation and geographical dispersal.

   The restructuring of manufacturing employment in terms of
geographical location and production has accommodated rather
than challenged sectarian divisions. In a limited sense the form of
restructuring in the early 1960s was a direct response to Protestant
labourist demands. By 1965 the O'Neill administration could
claim to have effectively ended the revival of the NILP by
providing new jobs for redundant Protestant workers in the
Environs of Belfast. By 1970 unemployment rates in the major
sub-areas of the Belfast Region ranged from 2.2% to 5.5%. Even
in the period 1959-71 rates had been relatively low in these areas
compared with the Rest of NI. Table 9 demonstrates the effect of
the international recession since 1970 on the three 'economic
regions' within NI.

Table 9: Regional Unemployment, 1970–79

	1970 %		1979 %	
Belfast	32	(43)*	31	(38)*
Environs of Belfast	19	(34)	24	(36)
Rest of NI	49	(23)	45	(26)
	—	—	—	—
	100	(100)	100	(100)
Total unemployed	32,714		62,763	

*Figures in brackets denote regional share of manufacturing
employment in 1971 and 1978 respectively.
SOURCES: Murie (1970) and *DMS NI Unemployment Figures — Press
Notices*

   Despite some diversion of new jobs to the Rest of NI after
1966, unemployment was still extremely high in 1970 — notably
in Derry (11.3%), Strabane (16.9%), Enniskillen (12.9%) and
Newry (13.9%). High unemployment rates do not appear to
have translated into political pressure capable of diverting new
manufacturing jobs to these areas. This is not surprising when it

ıs recognised that Catholics were disproportionately represented among the unemployed — comprising 45% of the workforce outside the Belfast Region and 61% of the unemployed.

In some areas there were enormous Protestant-Catholic differentials in unemployment. In 1971, at the end of the period of high external investment and before the onset of the current recession, 23% of Catholic males were unemployed in Derry compared with 8% of Protestant males. Comparable figures for Strabane were 23% and 11%, respectively; Newry and Mourne, 20% and 11%; and Dungannon, 22% and 8% (FEA 1979, based on District Council data in the 1971 census). Even more significantly, Catholic unemployment rates exceeded Protestant rates in *each* of the 26 District Council areas in NI; in Belfast, for example, 19% of Catholic males were unemployed compared to 8.5% of Protestants. Even in those areas where new investment was concentrated and which were overwhelmingly Protestant, Catholic male rates still vastly exceeded Protestant rates (see Table 10).

Table 10: Percentage Male Unemployment Rates in Selected Industrial Growth Centres, 1971

District Council	Catholic	Protestant
Castlereagh (East Belfast)	15.3	4.6
Lisburn	8.3	4.3
Newtownabbey	11.3	4.7
Antrim	9.0	3.5
Ballymena	10.1	6.2
Carrickfergus	11.8	6.3
Larne	9.6	4.7
Craigavon	14.3	5.1

SOURCE: Fair Employment Agency (FEA), 1979

Clearly regional policy has done little to reduce the marginality of the Catholic working class. Under Direct Rule and the impact of international recession, manufacturing employment has contracted in all but one of the Employment Exchange Areas. Although the crisis in the textile and clothing industries has affected both Catholic and Protestant labour, there is no evidence to suggest that the margin of Catholic disadvantage has been reduced. Areas of traditionally high unemployment such as Derry, Strabane, Newry and Dungannon have now even higher male unemployment rates of 19%, 31%, 23% and 22% respectively (male unemployment, *DMS Press Notices*). The greatest absolute increase in unemployment has been in the Belfast 'Travel to Work' area[6], however, where the number of unemployed males has increased by *two and a half times* and female numbers have almost *quadrupled* in the five year period 1974–79 (*Quigley Report* 1976; *DMS Press Notices*).

While Belfast in general has much unemployment, certain areas within the city are much worse. Much of inner and West Belfast has become an industrial wasteland. In 1978 there was an estimated 31% unemployment among economically active household heads of the Catholic-only wards of the city. The rate reached over 50% in the Falls and over 40% in Whiterock, New Lodge, and Grosvenor. The rate in Protestant West Belfast was also much higher than the NI average at 17.4%, reaching over 30% in one ward. Viewed alternatively, the purely Catholic wards to the west and north-west of the city contained only 21% of Belfast households in 1978 but 43% of the city's unemployment by 1979. Protestant West Belfast contained almost 11% of total households and over 11% of total unemployment (NIHE *Belfast Household Survey* 1978; *DMS NI Labour Market Guide* 1979). The major landmarks in West Belfast are now army bases. Indeed the army recently appropriated one of the few remaining industrial sites for use as a base — removing two small factories in the process.

The collapse of employment in West Belfast and the immobility of the labour force there has prompted both Labour and Tory governments to give large subsidies to new firms on the fringe of the area. Significantly these are mainly American — e.g. De Lorean, General Motors (seat-belts), and the American Monitor Co (electronics). They are part of an upturn in overseas investment in NI since 1978 but to date most of the new jobs remain in the 'promised' or 'promoted' category. Furthermore the Tories' public expenditure cuts threaten to reduce the financial incentives to prospective investors.

The private/public sector distinction has become increasingly meaningless in NI as the state has become more heavily involved in the support of existing industry through the NI Finance Corporation (later the NI Development Agency) and the Local Enterprise Development Unit (LEDU). NI reliance on high-cost energy (e.g. electricity generation based on oil) has forced the state to provide large fuel subsidies to keep many firms in business.[7] Massive assistance has been given to firms such as Courtaulds in Derry and Carreras for modernisation, in order to 'safeguard' existing jobs. In practice this has meant large-scale redundancies as these firms become more capital-intensive. The Unionist Party's more ad hoc approach to external investment in the 1960s has now been replaced by the highly centralised 'selling of NI' as a package to would-be investors. In Roy Mason's (18/10/78) words:

> 'We have created a package of financial inducements which is one of the best in Western Europe. My policy is if you have a good product go out and sell it. NI is a good product so that is exactly what I and my ministers have done.' (NI Office Information Service)

'Selling NI' does little to oppose sectarianism. Far from providing opportunities for cross-sectarian mobilisation on the 'crisis of the economy', unemployment and state intervention merely highlight the nature of sectarian class division by encouraging competition, both between workers for scarce jobs and between areas for 'scarce' factories. In other words the capitalist state must manage rather than resolve existing divisions.

The state's major response to economic restructuring has not been subsidies to manufacturing industry, however, but the expansion of employment in social reproduction — i.e., in services (now over 63% of total employment in NI) and in direct government employment. Public sector employment alone grew from 35% of total employment in 1974 to over 40% in 1979 (*DMS Gazette*, 3, 1979). This expansion does not appear to have minimized sectarian division and Catholic marginality, however. The 1971 census suggests that the proportion of Catholics in services amounted to approximately 25% at that time. Those services outside the public sector showed contrasting pictures. As the occupational data suggest, Protestants were over-represented in Insurance, Banking and Business Services — there out-numbering Catholics by almost *five to one*. On the other hand, distributive and miscellaneous services had Catholic proportions close to (or above) the average — reflecting the sectarian division. Services in the public sector (e.g. professional and scientific services) show the effects of state support for the segregated educational system and for the large numbers of Catholic doctors, nurses and lawyers servicing their own community.

In key areas within the public sector, however, there was a heavy concentration of Protestants. Catholics accounted for only 13% of senior civil servants and were out-numbered *five to one* in the power industries. The latter have proved critical politically in the successful UWC strike of 1974 and the abortive Paisley strike in 1977. In each case Protestant workers brought significant pressure to bear on the British state.[8] The other key public sector area is 'public administration and defence' which has increased rapidly in line with the 'troubles' and now accounts for over 10% of total employment. In 1971 only 18% of employees in this sector were Catholic compared with 73% Protestant. Since then the numbers of police have been increased dramatically (less than 10% of them Catholic). In addition, the full-time and part-time UDR has been doubled, providing a significant source of alternative income and jobs for Protestants in times of high unemployment.

The Politics of a 'Normal' Regional Policy

Formal regional policy has been British state policy from its very inception. The social democratic compromise on which it was based, when applied to NI, obscures and even denies the centrality of sectarian class division. Isles and Cuthbert (1957), still the main administrative *cum* academic handbook on the NI economy, does not mention it; neither do the plethora of planning reports in the 1960s and '70s.[9]

Even when the so-called 'security situation' is taken into account, it is seen as an aberration — an extraneous limiting factor of economic development. The *Quigley Report* (1976), the most comprehensive recent account of the economy, observes rather apologetically, 'we feel bound to take note of the impediment to economic progress which the security situation creates'. 'Taking note', however, simply means evaluating the dis-incentive to external investment posed by the IRA campaign. In spite of this Quigley (1976:4) sees a ray of hope in the general gloom:

> 'Nevertheless, we take comfort from the fact that economic and industrial issues are much less a matter of political controversy and dissension in NI than in most other parts of the western world.'

Here the report fails to recognise that the very same situation which produced the 'security problem' *also* produced the lack of 'political controversy' presumably associated with Left-Right splits elsewhere. Even so, perhaps Quigley is more realistic than those on the Left who live for the day that social democracy and 'British standards' of political debate become a reality in NI.

On occasions when the question of sectarian division is addressed, some rather traditional assumptions come to the surface. A case in point is Thomas Wilson, later to become NI's chief economic planner in the 1960s. In an edited book, *Ulster under Home Rule* (1955), he allows himself to speculate on the 'intensity' of Catholic grievances and their tendency to over-statement. He does not attempt a quantitative or technocratic analysis of these grievances but attributes them instead to a type of 'spiritual discontent' resulting from partition. He argues that there is no *a priori* reason why Catholics should have one-third of the university chairs or of administrative posts in line with their share of the population:

> 'ability and inclination, together with the competition of people from outside Ulster altogether, may dictate differently. As for business life, Presbyterians and Jews are probably endowed with more business acumen that Irish Catholics.'

He goes on to assert that in any case Catholic grievances are not always very 'real'.

> 'They have less to complain about than the U.S. negroes, and their lot is a very pleasant one as compared with the nationalists in, say the Ukraine ... For generations they were the underdogs, the despised "croppies", the adherents of a persecuted religion, who were kept out of public affairs by their Protestant conquerors. They were made to feel inferior, and to make matters worse they often *were* inferior, if *only* in those personal qualities that make for success in competitive economic life'. (*author's emphases*) Wilson (1955:208-209)

Here the whole history of capital accumulation in Ireland and the changing nature of sectarian class relations is reduced to a problem of individual psychology permeated by racist assumptions. In the process the historical experience of the Protestant working class is ignored or implicitly identified with that of the Protestant capitalist class. Wilson's attitude is not merely eccentric; it was shared by the all-class Unionist ideology of the 1960s and '70s which sought to combat the disruption caused by the restructuring of the economy on the one hand and by Catholic agitation on the other. Central myths of Protestant self-reliance, enterprise, thrift and loyalty were contrasted to the improvidence, fecklessness and disloyalty of Catholics who were prone to rely on state welfare rather than work. Factors such as the relatively higher fertility of Catholics played a dual role; on the one hand it helped explain their economic disadvantages while on the other it epitomised their potential danger to the Protestant majority if they were not controlled. In the specific circumstances of NI this ideology was useful to the Protestant working class and the petty-bourgeoisie in forcing Stormont and the Unionist Party to reconcile economic restructuring with the preservation of their marginal advantages. For the Unionist middle classes it offered a means of maintaining the integrity of the state and the class alliance in a situation of flux and transformation. In the event, of course, the Unionist bourgeoisie failed and in the end were content to transfer to Westminster the political onus of reproducing sectarian class relations.

One of the consequences of economic restructuring in the 1960s was the growing gap between the Unionist Party and the Stormont statelet. The Party's close identification with the existing economic order led to major internal tensions as this order began to collapse, making the Party a defective vehicle for regional policy on the British model. Traditional sources of investment within NI dried up; of manufacturing employment generated between 1945 and 1973, only 13.6% is said to have emanated from domestic sources.[10] Between 40-50% of manufacturing employment is now in externally-owned firms — roughly the same proportion as the Irish Republic. Unlike the Republic, however, the great weight of new investment was of British origin (allowing for the difficulty in labelling multi-nationals). By 1963 only four per cent of the North's manufacturing employment was in non-British firms — a figure which rose to 17% by 1971. By 1979 only 13% of the manufacturing workforce were employed by American companies (*Ulster Commentary* May '79). In the Irish Republic US firms accounted for 42% of jobs promoted between 1960 and 1976; only 21% came from Britain, 14% from West Germany and 23% from other sources (Walsh 1979:10-11).

Political upheaval did not lead directly from changes in an abstracted 'economic base', however. Throughout the post-war period the Stormont state apparatus was being transformed, not as a result of changes internal to NI, but as an agent of welfare state reforms and of British regional policy. Hitherto NI-British relations had been obscured behind a wall of bureaucratic secrecy and Westminster conventions. Now the 'internal'/'external' division began to break down as Stormont civil servants — in Green's (1979) words, 'de facto integrationists to a man' — pushed ahead with implementing social reforms and regional policies funded by the British state. The Unionist Party struggled unsuccessfully to annex the 'benefits' in order to preserve the political status quo in the face of intra-Unionist tension and Catholic agitation. This scenario has led many to celebrate the 'cleansing of the Augean stables' brought about the British intervention and the onset of 'modernisation'. Massed forces of monopoly capital — the British state, presumably including the British army — are undermining the Orange system of sectarian division and anachronistic politics (see Boserup 1972). The major obstacle now is seen to be the IRA campaign and the 'green fog' of Irish nationalism. On one level history is being rewritten to show that, while Partition was a good idea, devolution under the Unionist Party was not (see Buckland 1979). Others, more concerned with contemporary political projects, work to reproduce in NI the politics of the 'respectable' British parties. Thus the aim is the transformation of 'official Unionism' into a British-type Conservative Party, the resurrection of British-type Liberalism through the Alliance Party, or — most unlikely of all — the building of a Labourist Party to unite the working classes.

This chapter has argued that the so-called modernising forces, far from undermining sectarian division, instead construct it anew in a contemporary form. Just as Courtaulds do little to undermine apartheid in South Africa (see CIS No. 10), so also they do little to reduce sectarianism in Dungannon. Here, as in many other instances, multi-national capital does not merely replace 'traditional capital' but acquires existing firms and transforms their Protestant owners into middle management. For example, within seven years of their arrival in Dungannon, Courtaulds had presided over a 27% decline in the labour force of the firms they acquired. The total outcome would scarcely suggest an upsurge of cross-sectarian class politics in a town where the sectarian head-count is finely balanced and where the historical constancy of the population must be understood in the context of local estimates which suggest that over 40% of all Catholic children in the area emigrate before they reach 25 years of age (Hall 1979:8-10).

Even more important, however, is the British state, which increasingly provides a platform for the coalescing of the old and new industrial bourgeoisie in managing the local economy. Here, the more durable traditional capitalists can join local middle management, and directors of multi-national enterprise new to NI, in restructuring a regional fragment of the British economy.[11] The SDLP (1980) may complain rather plaintively that the Unionist middle classes still monopolise state agencies and commissions, thereby contradicting the principle of power-sharing, but Atkins (the Secretary of State) can respond in terms which echo Thomas Wilson 25 years earlier: that appointments are made on the 'basis of ability and willingness to serve'. British reform may have weaned sections of the local bourgeoisie from the excesses of sectarian rhetoric, but at a fundamental level the British state still has to differentiate between the Protestant and Catholic middle class because it is a capitalist state. While the Catholic professional middle class have grown to service their own community under the British welfare state, they have remained marginal to industrial production and the upper reaches of the state apparatuses.

Likewise the Catholic working class have remained marginal to industrial production. The foregoing analysis of 'regional policy' has shown that there are clear and unequivocal reasons why Catholic protest is not based at the workplace and why the central political and military struggle appears so remote from production-based issues. Restructuring has maintained — if not extended — the marginality of Catholics; the largest concentrations of urban Catholic males are not on the shop-floor but on the dole queue and in Long Kesh. This is not to argue that Catholics live entirely 'outside' the economy. On the contrary, they are well represented in the migrant labour force, in agriculture, construction and in industries with high labour turnover — as well as in the industrial reserve army. Even more obviously, Catholic areas such as Newry and Derry are reserve areas *par excellence*, attractive to 'fly-by-night' firms which set up with massive state aid and quickly abscond to reap another round of benefits in some other 'development area'.[12]

The Protestant working class, on the other hand, are now directly dependent on the British state to maintain employment in the key manufacturing sectors. The dependence runs in both directions, however, since their consent (or at least their tolerance) has been proven necessary for the British state to manage the NI conflict. Both the Protestant working class and petty-bourgeoisie strenuously opposed the restructuring of Stormont as a betrayal. The political project of the Direct Rulers and the integrationists is to show them that they have a role to play in combatting terrorism and repressing dissent from the new arrangements — a dissent which is now 'criminal' and 'unjustified', since all 'legitimate' reforms have been granted since the early 1970s. Regardless of abstract commitments to 'partnership' and 'power-sharing', the practical effect of British state policy has been to widen the gulf between the Catholic and Protestant working class. Even issues which encourage cross-sectarian mobilisation, such as the public expenditure cuts, can become divisive as competition for ever scarcer resources becomes sharper.

Despite protestations of reform and neutrality, with periodic manifestations of 'good intentions', sectarian division is being incorporated and institutionalised in new forms within the heart of an expanded British state apparatus in NI. The process is being re-legitimised as part of the democratic will of the majority to remain British. Simultaneously the *responsibility* for maintaining sectarian division is laid exclusively at the door of the IRA, who seek to thwart the will of that majority by conducting a campaign of violence from urban Catholic ghettoes and rural enclaves.

On the contary, an examination of 'regional policy' demonstrates the extent to which sectarian class relations are embedded within the fabric of the NI social formation. The British state has now assumed absolute economic and political centrality; it controls production and social reproduction without having to confront an oppositional politics which link workplace and community issues. It is not enough for us to explain the resultant 'political impasse' as part of a grand administrative strategy to divide and conquer. It arises, more fundamentally, from the specificity of capital accumulation in NI and from the British state's role in maintaining the conditions appropriate for new forms of accumulation.

NOTES

1. Strictly comparable employment statistics are available only from 1959.
2. Mackies (textile engineering), Shorts (aircraft and aircraft components), Sirocco (general engineering).
3. The Ropeworks provide a classic example of industrial restructuring. Originally a major source of female employment close to the shipyards, it has now moved to the outskirts of Belfast and reduced its workforce by approximately 90% from its 1946 level.
4. Cmd 224, *Housing in NI*, 1944; Cmd 225, *Location of Industry*, Interim Report, 1944; Cmd 227, *Planning Proposals for the Belfast Area*, Interim Report, 1945; Cmd 241, *Road Communications in NI*, Interim Report, 1946; Cmd 302, *Planning Proposals for the Belfast Area*, Second Report, 1951.
5. In the 1960s the British government assisted Stormont in providing grants and loans of £11½m. to H & W and £16m. to Shorts (Lyons 1971:746). Under Direct Rule, between January 1975 and December 1979, the British government provided £103m. in grants and loans to H & W (cited in *Belfast Telegraph* 7/2/80).

6.   Belfast 'Travel to Work' area is an amalgamation of Belfast, Lisburn, Bangor, Newtownards, Carrickfergus and Larne Employment Exchange Areas.

7.   Economic analyses have always stressed the cost of fuel to industry (particularly the importation of coal) as the major 'natural disadvantage' of NI as a location for industry. 'Remoteness' and 'separation from the mainland' combined with 'lack of indigenous energy resources' have become part of the conventional wisdom which explains the continued weakness of the regional economy. Accordingly the British government has now ensured that the cost of electricity to NI industry is comparable with that in the rest of the UK. Electricity production in NI is 90% based on oil compared to only 16% in Britain. The oil crisis has raised major difficulties for the massive new Kilroot power station now under construction. This station was planned on the basis of wildly inaccurate forecasts of future energy demand and now must be re-planned to switch the emphasis from oil to coal-based generation (Tomlinson 1980).

8.   The power workers were a key element in the UWC strike which forced the Labour government to concede on 'power-sharing'. The Tories also appeared to recognise the crucial significance of power workers in British politics as a whole. A Conservative Party committee, chaired by Lord Carrington, produced a secret report which observed: 'Strong unions and advanced technology operated by their members, particularly in the fuel and power industries, mean that no government these days can "win" in the way that Mr Baldwin's cabinet triumphed during the General Strike of 1926, by maintaining essential supplies and services' (*The Times* 18/4/78, cited in Parkin 1979:87).

9.   Cmd 479, *Economic Development in NI* (Wilson Report), 1965; *NI Development Programme 1970-75* (Matthew, Wilson and Parkinson), 1970; *NI Regional Physical Development Strategy*, 1975–1995.

10. *Labour Research* (1977:36-7) estimated that of 75,000 jobs provided by the 36 largest manufacturing companies in NI only 9,600 are controlled from within NI.

11. Facile predictions which suggest that the penetration of monopoly capital serves to undermine sectarian division within the North, and the Border between North and South, do not stand up to close scrutiny. Two long-serving trade unionists take a more realistic view, suggesting that businessmen are unlikely to engage in a highly visible initiative to promote cross-border cooperation. They go on to suggest: 'they [businessmen] are very sensitive to the limits created by community tensions; when they encounter them, they will attempt to accommodate them, not override them, and it would be wrong to expect them to do otherwise' (McCarthy and Blease 1978:369).

12. The *Belfast Bulletin* Summer 1979 details the high turnover of firms in the Newry area. In Derry the closure of the government-aided BSR (Birmingham Sound Reproducers) made 2,000 workers redundant in 1967. Since 1961 the former owner, now living in Switzerland, has maintained a farm of 3,000 acres in North Donegal. This farm, one of the largest in Ireland was put for sale this year (*Belfast Telegraph* 18/1/80). Even areas with traditionally low unemployment rates are not immune to sudden closure decisions. In 1978 the Ballantyne Sportswear Co. in Coleraine used the pretext of a minor trade dispute to dismiss 260 workers and move to Scotland, to a new factory grant-aided by the Scottish Development Authority. Prior to this the company had experienced only one (three-day) strike in 20 years of operation (*Irish Times* 13/11/78).

do you really believe in
"A BETTER LIFE FOR ALL"
in Northern Ireland?

Can you answer these questions truthfully:—

Do you believe in:—

	YES	NO
1. The right to live free from violence, sectarianism, intimidation and discrimination;		
2. The right to security of employment and well paid work;		
3. The right to associate freely and to advocate political change by peaceful means;		
4. The right to good housing accommodation;		
5. The right to equality of educational opportunity;		
6. The right to adequate social services to protect the well-being and living standards of the aged, the young, the sick, the unemployed and the socially deprived.		

Belfast *Telegraph*, 18 November 1976

3

The Limits of Trade Unionism

The relationship between labour and capital, although in essence one of constant mutual antagonism, has changed as capitalism has developed. This has resulted in a changed role for trade unions. From being isolated, reviled and suppressed historically, they have become a relatively legitimate and integral part of the operations of contemporary capitalism.

Critics of this process argue that such institutionalisation threatens to transform the relation between labour and capital into one of peaceful co-existence (see Hyman 1973). They attack official trade unionism for being reformist, economistic and self-restricting, and their politics lead them to explore the means of challenging capital outside the arena of trade union politics, and to exploit the contradictions within this politics to ensure that trade unions become a greater threat to capital.

Yet, many who are prepared to criticise the theory and practice of trade unions in a 'normal' society falter when they address the same questions in NI. Seeing NI as totally abnormal, they are grateful to find *any* reformist space, no matter how resricted or economistic, on the grounds that indigenous social democratic politics need encouragement. Anxious to find havens of normality in an abnormal society, to discover evidence of 'proper class politics' where sectarian relations pervade the whole society, they leap at the opportunity that trade unionism in NI offers. Here at least is a veritable island of social democracy in a sectarian sea.

The image of the trade unions as a haven of normality is one that the official trade union movement in NI has long had of itself. But that self-image has been sharpened as a result of a decade of political crisis and has become standard currency in the trade union movement's presentation of itself.

'The trade union movement remains as the one valid voice of working people. It is also one of the voices of sanity in the community.' (ICTU 1977:58)

This self-image emerged early in the present 'troubles'. In previous sectarian violence, the trouble on the streets had often begun in the shipyards, or had at least spread there. The history of the shipyards reveals numerous riots, expulsions of Catholics and socialists, and deaths. Yet, on August 15, 1969, the day after 11 people had died in gunfire and 800 Catholic homes had been burnt down in Belfast, there was no violence at all in the shipyards. Fifty shop stewards hastily called a mass meeting to which they presented a resolution that simultaneously appealed to level-headedness, economic self-interest and reaction.

'This meeting of shipyard workers calls on the people of NI for the immediate restoration of peace throughout the community. We recognise that the continuation of the present civil disorder can only end in economic disaster. We appeal to all responsible people to join with us in giving a lead to break the cycle of mutual recrimination... Furthermore, we demand that the government and the forces of law and order take stronger measures to maintain the peace'. (See McInerney 1970:12)

Sandy Scott, a shipwright, shop steward and NILP official, addressed the mass meeting, arguing that violence would lead to the cancellation of orders, redundancies and possible closure. A Methodist minister invoked a prayer and the resolution was presented to the meeting. It was passed unanimously.

The shop stewards saw the result as the triumph of 'reason' over 'emotion and sectarianism'. The government judged it likewise. Scott received an MBE, and government publications from that time have been as eager as the movement itself to sing the praises of trade unionism.

'Sectarianism is contrary to trade union policy... Both the membership and the leadership of the trade union movement in NI reflect the balance in the community... Members with all types of religious affiliation, as well as atheists and communists, have played a full part in the development of trade unionism... with hardly an exception, sectarianism stops at the factory gates'. (NI Information Service 1979)

However, if congratulation, by self or others, is to be more than a mere grasping at straws, there must be evidence of a reality behind the image. Such evidence would at very least need to reveal a history of the pursuit of class politics on the part of trade unions in NI, as well as a vibrant trade union movement at present. The growth of Belfast as Ireland's first industrial city meant not only that there was a proletariat in the north-east, but that it was agitating on similar issues to its confrères in similar cities in Britain. Consequently, there is a long history of trade unionism in NI. In fact, the Woodworkers' Club of Belfast is the oldest recorded such club in the British Isles, dating from 1788. Belfast Trades' Council, now approaching its centenary year, has a reputable record in pursuing issues of import to the working class in Belfast, Protestant and Catholic. Furthermore, contemporary membership figures suggest a strong NI trade union movement. Approximately 57% of workers are unionised (a rate slightly higher than in Britain but lower than in the Republic) and about 90% of those are in unions affiliated to the Irish Congress of Trade Unions (ICTU) through its NI Committee (NIC). The NIC has become legitimised not only in the eyes of its members, but also in the eyes of the state.

> 'There has also been a growth in influence at government level. We are taken seriously now and our cooperation is sought, after decades during which we were ignored'. (Carlin 1979)

In short, there appears to be a united and influential trade union movement paradoxically representing a divided working class. Given that appearance, criticisms of reformist trade unions, however correct, can be dismissed as threatening the very survival of a rare and precious forum of social democratic politics. The priority is to protect the haven of normality, despite the reformism and self-restriction.

There is, however, one major fault in this approach — namely, that trade unionism and sectarianism are seen as opposites. Trade union organisation alone is said, not least by trade union officials, to counteract sectarianism. Sectarianism, if it exists, is seen to exist outside trade unionism, or, if inside, only as a regrettable aberration. However, the scrupulous search for examples of trade union organisation (Bleakley 1955; Carr 1974) is in itself futile. Integrated as it was into the early Industrial Revolution in the British Isles, Belfast not surprisingly exhibited many features similar to those which emerged in other industrial cities, including active trade unions and trades councils. In fact, failure to find examples of such working class organisation in 19th century Belfast would be exceptional. It is necessary therefore to go beyond the chronicling of trade union organisation. When that step is taken, it becomes obvious that sectarianism and trade unionism are not opposites, except in the realms of abstract analysis. Trade unions in a sectarian society cannot remain insulated from the society of which they are a part. Where sectarian relations prevail, trade unions, like other elements in the society, reconstitute and reproduce those relations. Trade unions, as they developed in NI were simultaneously about class politics *and* sectarian politics.

The Development of Sectarian Trade Unionism

As elsewhere, trade unions in the north of Ireland emerged in three separate phases. There was, firstly, the emergence of craft unions, later the growth of unions for skilled manufacturing workers, and finally, the unionisation of the unskilled. The emergence of the phases of trade unionism is not remarkable. Much more noteworthy is that sectarian division was a part of the *normal* operations of trade unionism in Ireland from the beginning. That is not to say that trade unionists in the 19th century were unceasingly sectarian in their attitudes and utterances; it is to emphasise that divisions in the working class were necessarily reconstituted in the movement that sought to organise that class. Consequently, developments which had one connotation in a non-sectarian setting took on a different meaning in a sectarian setting. Thus the sectionalism and exclusivity evident in the development of trade unions elsewhere became in the North of Ireland precisely sectarian sectionalism and sectarian exclusivity.

Catholics had been 'allowed' to join the guilds in Ireland from 1793, thirty-six years before Catholic Emancipation (Ryan 1919:71). But such a liberal gesture was in fact meaningless in a situation where the mass of Catholics were peasants. In fact the guilds and early craft unions were Protestant organisations, reflecting the class structure of Ireland at the time. As the peasantry began to move to the towns — a process accentuated by the famines of the mid-19th century — the craft unions closed ranks to protect their jobs and position. An understandable reaction in its own terms, this was a move that came to have sectarian consequences also. Thus, when in 1808 the Cabinet Club in Belfast agreed to admit 'no strangers' until the current period of unemployment had passed (Bleakley 1955:23), the strangers were in effect not just non-cabinet makers, but also were more likely to be non-Protestants. In fact, the two most volatile issues among the craft unions in the 19th century — apprentice ratios and the closed shop — were in part sectarian.

Craft unionists who were also Protestants found themselves threatened by an influx of non-craft unionists who were also Catholics.

There thus emerged a working class divided into two fractions: on the one hand Protestant and more skilled, on the other Catholic and less skilled. Early trade union organisation reflected this division of unionised skilled Protestant workers from non-unionised unskilled Catholic workers. Nor was the division broken down as a result of the spread of the 'new model' unions, or 'amalgamateds', from the 1860s. In Ireland these organisations were merely extensions of the British 'new model' unions. This gave rise to problems later. It also caused division in mid-19th century Belfast. The amalgamated unions organised skilled manufacturing workers; in Belfast these workers — shipwrights, boilermakers, engineers, etc. — were Protestant. Consequently the amalgamated unions became, at least initially, Protestant unions. Such objective division had subjective consequences. As Beatrice Webb commented after a visit to Belfast, the skilled workers were 'contemptuous and indifferent to the Catholic labourers and women who were earning miserable wages in the shipyards and linen factories of Belfast' (cited in Bleakley 1955:33). Whether such contempt derived from the exclusivity of the skilled, from sectarian attitudes and/or from sexist attitudes hardly matters to those at the receiving end of it.

When the unskilled attempted to organise, however, in the third phase of trade unionism they faced even more severe opposition. The beginnings of the organisation of the unskilled occurred early in Belfast. For example, the National Union of Dock Labourers, formed as a result of the 1889 Dock Strike in London, already had a branch in Belfast by 1890. But it was some years before the struggle of the unskilled reached its zenith, culminating in the strikes in Belfast in 1907 and 1911, and the great lock-out in Dublin in 1913. In Belfast the opposition to that struggle was fiercest on the part of the employers and the state. In this context it is important to note that the attempt at organisation by the unskilled was seen by the authorities as no more than an attempt by Catholics to organise, because in fact that it is what it predominantly was. Thus, although the main disturbances of the strike of 1907 took place around the docks, the army was billeted on the Catholic Falls Road, and it was there that they opened fire, killing two young workers, both Catholic (see Irish Transport and General Workers Union 1959:16).

It was not only from such sources that opposition came.

Workers themselves, divided on the intertwined bases of religious affiliation and skill, were not easily united on the question of organising the predominantly Catholic unskilled. James Larkin had some success in 1907, not least because he was an official of an English union and therefore less open to attack by Loyalists on the grounds of national allegiance. James Connolly, who came to Belfast in 1911 as an official of Larkin's newly-formed Irish Transport and General Workers' Union (ITGWU), had much less success, not least because he represented an Irish union and thus his national loyalty was open to question. He was well aware of the difficulties of organising in Belfast. For example, his first successful steps in supporting and organising mine workers in Larne were thwarted overnight by the actions of local clergymen who had only to whisper to the men that Connolly represented a Southern union to have them abandon not only Connolly but the strike as well (Connolly 1975:30-33).

Those who sought to advance the cause of trade unionism in the North of Ireland were faced with the double bind of a divided clientele and an institutionally divided movement. The problem was that to attempt to unite the working class itself was to go beyond a 'straight trade union' task into the realm of politics. Not only did the chances of success in such an endeavour appear slim, but taking political stances outside purely trade union issues would certainly drive away one or other section of the divided clientele. Consequently, as trade unionism grew, it did so along the lines of least resistance. The chances of institutionally uniting the movement were better, but such unity had to be totally apolitical. The trade union movement could only exist on the basis of the least common denominator between divided workers. It is for this reason that a number of characteristics came to the fore in trade unionism in the North. The movement, in as far as it existed at all, could most successfully do so on the basis of centralised rather than mass organisation; Connolly's syndicalist dream of 'one big union' found little support in the North. Furthermore, the central organisation had to concern itself primarily with avoiding 'politics'. In other words, economism represented the limits of the movement to organise and agitate; wages and conditions were not necessarily seen as political issues.

The beginnings of centralisation occurred in the last decades of the 19th century. Belfast Trades Council, the first in Ireland, was formed in 1881, and in 1889 trade unionists from all over Ireland participated in the attempt to set up a Federation. The Federation later incurred the wrath of its Northern affiliates by organising a Sunday sports meeting. The sabbatarian Northerners withdrew hastily and the Federation collapsed. Five years later, however, they united institutionally with other trade unionists in Ireland under the banner of the Irish Trade Union Congress (ITUC).

Given the sectarian division of labour in the North, unity was possible, for the most part, only at an institutional level. The institution thus became disproportionately important in Northern trade unionism. Furthermore, economism became equally important because the only way the institution could survive was by avoiding those political issues upon which its clientele was divided and by concentrating exclusively on economic issues. Lastly, the all-Ireland nature of institutionalism proved constantly fragile. In retrospect, it appears amazing that the ITUC, an all-Ireland body, should have been formed at the height of the Home Rule crisis. The survival of such a body was only possible, however, as a result of wooing Northern trade unionists. As time went on that process of wooing itself became institutionalised, even if the marriage was never consummated.

Trade Unionism and Unionism: Mutual Acceptance

Bleakley (1955:83) notes that Northern trade unionists were 'ever anxious to avoid the charge of introducing "politics" into trade unionism'; they were consequently 'quick to hesitate' when it came to open discussion of such matters as the national question. He adds:

> 'How successful the policy of avoiding politics was is revealed in the total lack of reference to politics in 19th century trade union documents'.

But, despite its avoidance of politics, economism *is* a political position, not just by default, but also because it requires a definition of the correct target against which trade union demands can be directed. In the North the target was Britain. Many trade unionists saw themselves, as a result of the Union, as an integral part of the British trade union movement, struggling against British capitalists for better wages and conditions. This outward-looking stance is frequently equated by McCarthy (1973) and others with internationalism, and is contrasted with the parochial demands of Southern trade unionists caught up in solely nationalist fervour.[1]

But such a conclusion misses the point that neither position was merely cerebral, but represented the recognition by similarly reformist leaderships in the two parts of Ireland that their future fortunes lay with different bourgeoisies. In the South the trade unions played a part, albeit sometimes reluctantly, in the struggle for national independence between 1916 and 1922. In the North there existed what Hechter (1975:234-263) has termed 'servitor imperialism', that is, the recognition by sections of the working class that their best interests were bound up with the imperial interest. Clashes such as that between Connolly and William Walker in 1911 were therefore not merely between 'green socialism' and 'orange socialism' (the conclusion being that what Ireland sorely lacks is a contingent of 'red socialists'), but between two fractions of a divided Irish working class with differing interests. It is too facile to argue that Northern trade unionists were economistic while Southern ones were not; both held economistic outlooks but with different political targets. As Purdie (1980:10) succinctly concludes:

> 'Connolly saw the Union between Ireland and Britain as a barrier to progress, for the Labour Movement as much as for the nationalist movement. Walker on the other hand saw progress being won for the Irish working class through its association with the British working class . . .'

The partition of Ireland thus called for a reappraisal on the part of trade unionists North and South. On the one hand, the more nationalist Southern trade unionists found their aspiration for national independence only partly fulfilled. On the other hand, the Northerners found themselves in a state of partial Home Rule which they had previously opposed. Consequently, neither set of trade unionists was completely enamoured of the constitutional arrangements, but that did not prevent their respective representatives, through the Irish Labour Party (ILP) in the South and the NILP taking on the role of official opposition in Leinster House and Stormont respectively in the early 1920s.

Despite the partitioning of Ireland the institutional unity of trade unionism remained intact. The ITUC did not split, although the NILP severed its direct links with the ITUC in 1924, to be followed in 1930 by the ILP. All the same, although Northerners like Sam Kyle continued to play a leading role in the all-Ireland body, there is no denying that Northern influence waned. In 1929 only 17% of delegates to Congress were from NI, compared with 32% in 1901. (The figure today is approximately 25%; *Belfast Bulletin* 1979:3).

In the 19th century the relationship between Irish-based and British-based trade unions had never been a particularly happy one. After partition the situation worsened, as is evident from the long-standing feud between the ATGWU and the ITGWU in the 1930s. Although this conflict was unusually bitter, it was not unique. The tension was often managed through certain working arrangements based on territoriality. Thus, when the Electrical Trades Union (ETU) applied in 1932 for affiliation to the ITUC, Congress agreed, provided the ETU confine its activities to the North. In 1943 the break between the two sets of trade unions finally came. The British TUC invited trade unionists to a two-week conference, the first week being for those from allied countries only, and the second for both 'allied' and 'neutral' trade unionists. Given that the Republic was neutral while NI was not, the ITUC Executive, being Southern-dominated, attempted to side-step the dilemma by declining the invitation. Belfast Trades Council, on the other hand, agreed to attend and the whole matter came up for debate at the 1944 Congress. A new ITUC executive was elected and for the first time the British-based unions were in a majority. The new executive reversed the previous decision and sent delegates to the London conference. As a result, in 1945 the ITGWU and ten other Irish-based unions left the ITUC and formed the Congress of Irish Unions (CIU).

By 1949 both the ITUC and the CIU began to show signs that they were concerned to restore some institutional unity to Irish trade unionism. But progress towards this goal was slow. In 1953 the executive of the ITUC passed a resolution declaring that it was anxious for unity; the CIU replied that it was also anxious, but 'on the basis of the Irish trade union movement being wholly Irish-based and controlled' (cited in Bleakley 1953:167). How this latter demand could be assimilated with the retention of Northern allegiance to an all-Ireland congress was the dilemma. Yet, the dilemma was solved. In January 1955 the Provisional United Trade Union Organisation (PUTUO) was formed, with equal representation from the ITUC and the CIU; its brief was to 'produce a constitution ... for the establishment of a single, national trade union centre for the whole of Ireland' (PUTUO 1957B:4). By 1959 a joint constitution was agreed and the two congresses merged to form the Irish Congress of Trade Unions (ICTU).

This seemingly impossible feat was accomplished as a result of recognising partition to the point of wooing Northern trade unionists to the Southern-dominated Congress by giving them autonomy. This is in fact how the ITUC had been operating for some years. In 1939, before the split, William O'Brien of the ITGWU had astutely concluded that: 'If the great body of trade unionists in NI are to be associated with us, it would be necessary to allow the fullest measure of autonomy in that area' (cited in McCarthy 1977:149). Consequently, in 1942 the ITUC established a sub-committee for Northern affairs — there was no such body for Southern affairs — and in 1944 that sub-committee became the Northern Ireland Committee (NIC). At first the NIC showed 'considerable timidity' in exploring its autonomy (McCarthy 1977:316). But by the 1950s, although still formally a subsidiary body of the ITUC, the NIC was operating as a totally autonomous body as regards NI affairs. In 1957 its first full-time officer was appointed. So, by the time the PUTUO was charged with making 'special provision for NI' (PUTUO 1957b:44), the NIC was well established. It was logical that the PUTUO should do nothing to dismantle its growing autonomy. In fact, the NIC proved the perfect mechanism to allow the Northerners to belong to an all-Ireland Congress, while allowing the old CIU supporters, confined for the most part to the South, to pursue their more nationalist aspirations.

From that time the ICTU has operated as two trade union movements, each working relatively independently of the other in each of the two states brought about by partition. At annual conferences Southern delegates only vote on Southern issues, and Northern delegates only on Northern issues. The ICTU's quarterly *Trade Union Information* has separate articles on the North and the South, the vast majority on the latter. And definitive works on trade unionism treat North and South as separate organisations, which they are, often without doing justice to the North. McCarthy (1973:17), for example, warns the reader at the outset:

'We shall be concerned essentially with the Republic. However, NI will appear in our discussions from time to time'.

The NIC was firmly established as a legitimate element in the ICTU from the beginning. However, it was some time before it was legitimised in the eyes of the NI government. The Unionist Party, being conservative, was wary of trade unionism. Even though the General Strike of 1926 had not spread to NI the *Trade Disputes and Trade Unions Act (NI)*, closely modelled on British anti-General Strike legislation, was introduced in 1927. Added to this initial conservatism was an antagonism towards the ICTU as an all-Ireland body. Consequently, the NIC was not officially recognised by Stormont. In the absence of formal recognition there was an uneven relationship between the NIC and different government departments. The Tourist Authority, for example, had invited the NIC to nominate representatives; the Ministries of Health, Commerce and Education had negotiated with the NIC. So, there was recognition after a fashion. But the different departments could pick and choose whom to consult and when. In effect this meant they were willing to deal with individual unions, but more wary of dealing with the NIC. The Ministry with whom arguably the NIC most needed a working relationship — Labour — consistently refused to have any dealings with the NIC. Its Minister, Ivan Neill, said in 1950:

> 'We are glad to consult with . . . individual trade unions . . . but we do not particularly favour consultation with an alternative self-constituted body whose head office is in a foreign country' (cited in McCarthy 1977:334).

At the same time there were cogent reasons to include the trade unions in the decision-making process. Stormont had begun to take an active interest in planning in a desperate attempt to stem the decline of the economy. Such planning was impossible without close consultation with the unions. Furthermore, a convergence was afoot in the 1950s. The NIC was also concerned with the decline and began to argue in terms of increasing state intervention to boost investment.[2] It was economically irrational to believe that government and trade unions, with increasingly similar concerns and proposed solutions, should be kept apart for long.

However, there were still the two problems of the Trade Disputes legislation and the all-Ireland affiliations of the NIC to be overcome. By the late 1950s the NILP, having reached a strength it had not had since 1925, was arguing strongly for the repeal of the Trade Disputes legislation. They pointed out that the repeal of the similar legislation in Britain had been one of the first acts of the Labour Party on taking up office in 1949, and argued for repeal in NI on the grounds of parity.

> ' . . . the fact of the matter is that we are British trade unionists. It is all right to be British citizens; it is all right to be British employers, but apparently it is not all right to be British trade unionists. The great majority of our people are British trade unionists'. (W.R. Boyd, NILP, HC Deb. V.43 c.663)

But interestingly the government response to the NILP's demand worked to the detriment of the NILP, while bolstering the position of the NIC. The legislation was repealed, except for sections four and eight. The latter required unions in NI with headquarters outside the UK — in practice, Southern-based unions — to register in NI.

Section four stated that unions could not automatically wage a political levy on their members. If a member wished to support a political party through his/her union, then s/he must opt *in*; in Britain a levy was collected unless the member opted *out*. As a result of such legislation from 1927 the NILP had received very few finances by way of political levies — only £2,500 in 1956, for example (see HC Deb. V.43 c.738). So, it was certain that the parity of legislation between NI and Britain which the NILP demanded would have provided much more finance and helped strengthen the Party's position. By refusing to repeal this section the government drove a wedge between the NILP and the trade unions. It is plausible to argue that this was done deliberately. As the Attorney General told the NILP:

> 'If honourable members opposite had an 80% majority they could speak on behalf of the trade unions, but so far as I know they can speak only on behalf of 20%' (HC Deb. V.43 c.810).

At a time when the NILP's strength was growing, the way in which the legislation was changed contributed, if not towards stemming the NILP rise, at least towards making it more difficult. At the same time, it marked the first tentative moves towards the recognition of the NIC. O'Neill expressed himself in terms which, despite the paternalism, offered some hope for those who wished the NIC to become legitimate in the eyes of the state.

> 'We do not take the view that good industrial relations are necessarily the product of legislation. Circumstances may dictate emergency legislation — but in the normal way we believe that good industrial relations are more firmly based upon a spirit of good will and mutual confidence between employer and worker'. (HC Deb. V.43 c.978)

In 1958 the *Trade Disputes and Trade Unions Act* (*NI*) 1927 was amended, and six years later the NIC was formally recognised by Stormont. By that time the NILP's star had waned.

The Cost of Legitimacy: the NIC and Repression

The institutionalisation and co-option of the trade union movement in NI had a disproportionate significance because of the sectarian division of the working class. In NI a trade union movement hardly exists outside this institutional level. The co-option of the NIC in 1964 is therefore a significant watershed. From that point the NIC stood as a bridge between an increasingly centralised and reformist state and a divided working class. And since Direct Rule the importance of such a bridge to the British state in NI has become even more obvious. On the one hand the NIC's economism represents the limits of a divided working class' ability to make demands upon the capitalist state. On the other hand, the NIC has become an element in the state's management of a divided working class. For economism, as has been said, *is* a political position, requiring the NIC to come to terms with the NI state.

The mutual acceptance of the NIC and the NI state was therefore of benefit to both parties. The NIC became the 'rational' voice of labour, thus acquiring a niche in the reformist state. The NI state for its part had a close relationship with a 'respectable' body that could deliver the goods. In this sense the state has done better out of the arrangement. What the trade union leaders have gained is 'direct access at all times to ministers in NI' (NI Information Service 1979). What the state has gained is a body that will deliver 'respectable' labour politics and act as the first line in policing 'non-respectable' labour politics.

The co-option of the NIC required it to come to terms with the repression and sectarianism of the state. For forty-two years the trade unions in NI had little scope to mount active opposition to sectarianism and repression because of their relative marginality to the normal democratic channels. With the NI state and the NIC accepting each other's legitimacy in 1964, the way was opened for some trade unionists to confront the question of sectarian discrimination and to agitate for civil rights within the confines of the NI state. But what appears as new-found militancy is merely the trade union movement finding its feet — attempting to be for the most part what a 'normal' trade union movement should be in a 'normal' society. Criticism short of rebellion became possible. Thus, in 1964 Belfast's Transport House was the venue for a conference on civil liberties organised by Belfast Trades Council. In 1966 the NIC published a pro-civil rights document, *Citizens' Rights in NI*.[3] And in 1967 there were four trade union representatives on the thirteen-person executive of the newly-formed NI Civil Rights Association (NICRA; see NICRA, 1979:8). But interestingly, most of the trade unionists active on the issue of civil rights were also members of the Communist Party. They succeeded in moving the NIC towards a pro-civil rights position. But the NIC never gave its full support to NICRA itself. Consequently, when civil rights developed into guerrilla war, the Communist Party was isolated from the trade union movement on this issue, as well as from the increasingly Republican mass movement which developed.

From that point the NIC has done little to confront issues on which labour movements in other societies might be expected to agitate. In short, its acceptance by the state was acquired at a cost — the acceptance of, or at least turning a blind eye towards, the 'carnival of reaction' (Connolly 1975:53). This is not to impugn the sincerity of individual trade unionists, nor is it to ignore the very real dilemma of officials who attempt to be part of the reformist apparatuses of the state while at the same time opposing its repressive apparatuses. It is to emphasise, however, that by playing a role in the reformist state in NI, the NIC has had to play a role also in the repressive state.

The paradox is most apparent in those reformist bodies concerned with 'reforming' repression. The case *par excellence* is the representation of the NIC on the Police Authority. This quango was formed in 1970 as part of the British attempt to reform, and in the process make more efficient, a discredited Royal Ulster Constabulary (RUC). In theory, the Authority has the right to hire and fire the police, officers and lower ranks. In practice it has a less prestigious role, as Chief Constable Kenneth Newman reminded it when he pointed out that it could hire but not fire him (see Holland 1979:17). In 1978 the two trade union representatives on the Police Authority were Jack Hassard and Bob Allen. Hassard has a well-earned reputation for taking up issues of repression, but he made little progress in his repeated attempts to have the police investigate certain specific instances of police brutality. As a result he withdrew from the Police Authority in 1979 and the NIC subsequently withdrew Allen as well.

Shortly after Hassard's resignation the whole question of police activities became a major issue with the publication of the Bennett Report, especially the claim of Police Surgeon Dr Irwin that he had examined numerous injured suspects whose injuries could have been caused only by police brutality. Yet, despite a row at the 1979 ICTU Annual Conference, where many delegates accused the NIC of inaction as regards repression, Terry Carlin, NI officer of the ICTU, took Hassard's place on the Authority.

Questioned on his action, Carlin proved evasive. Speaking, presumably on behalf of the whole NIC, he stated:

> 'We had to decide whether the ICTU was better off or on the Authority and we decided on balance that it was better to have our members serving on it. We'll be explaining our position fully at next year's NI Conference' (Carlin 1979)

— by which time, perhaps, a lot of the anger will have subsided and Carlin's action will be reluctantly accepted as a *fait accompli* by those in the trade union movement more actively opposed to repression than he.[4]

But, one does not have to look only at those bodies concerned with 'reforming' repression to see the impotence of the trade union movement in the face of repression. With Direct Rule, NI's notorious *Special Powers Act* was replaced with the *Emergency Provisions Act* and later the *Prevention of Terrorism Act*. Internment gave way to indefinite periods of remand for 'suspected terrorists', heavy-handed interrogation at Castlereagh and other holding centres, jury-less courts, criminalisation and H-Blocks. By any liberal, let alone socialist standards these contentious issues would seem to require attention. It would not seem too difficult to regard certain activities of the British state in NI as repressive and oppose them.

But 'repression' is not a neutral concept. In NI it is defined as a Republican issue. True, respected groups such as Amnesty International, the NI Bar Council and the prison doctors have publicly condemned repression, but for the most part to talk of repression at all is to be seen as a taking a pro-Republican stance. Propaganda is seen as an integral part of the war, and no one should be allowed to promote propaganda on behalf of Republicans by gracing their sufferings with the title of 'repression'. This is the attitude of the establishment in NI, and it is also the attitude dominant in the NIC. In some unions, in fact, to be even suspected of being a Republican is a surer ticket to ostracism than suspicion of communist affiliations.

In response to charges of inactivity on the question of human rights — charges which originated with the influential Longshoreman's Union in the US and which were raised at the International Transport Confederation meeting in Vienna in 1978 — the NIC issued its *Memorandum on the Protection of Human Rights in NI* (NIC 1978). In it the contentious issues which some in NI would call repression are merely alluded to. Emergency legislation, for example, is opposed on the grounds that it 'often diminishes the rule of law'. Excessive remand is criticised because

> 'after an absence of several months the worker concerned meets considerable difficulties in regaining his former employment, either because suspicion still attaches to that person in the mind of the employer or because the job has been filled'. (NIC 1978:5)

That is as far as the NIC can go to uphold human rights within the structures in NI.

The impotence of the trade union movement derives precisely from its role within the state structures. Even at its best, when it condemns repression, it does so from the minor position of a timid voice of conscience clamouring for the attention of politicians and administrators who are more partial to the louder advice of military advisers. But, even then, its actions belie its words. The NIC is content to protest, as the *Memorandum* notes, merely through letters to the Chief Constable of the RUC and meetings with the Secretary of State.

In short, the NIC's position vis-a-vis the repressive state is to attempt to 'cool out' the worst excesses of the state. This requires it to police those of its members who wish to go further than that. Thus, although the ICTU Annual Congress has passed motions calling for the repeal of repressive legislation, the furthest the NIC can go is to urge the state to be cautious:

> 'emergency legislation should only be enacted for a specified period of time and should require renewal by Parliament and should not be renewed beyond the duration of the crisis' (NIC 1978:5).

That willing self-castration of the NIC is perhaps the most remarkable facet of its legitimacy. Even when a trade unionist, Brian Maguire of AUEW/TASS, died by hanging while in police custody, it was not the official trade union movement which led the protests, but a small group of trade unionists calling themselves TUCAR, Trade Union Campaign Against Repression. But TUCAR suffers the isolation of all those who take up the issue of repression within the trade unions. It was dismissed as a Republican front organisation, even when it took up the death of a comrade.

Parenthetically, it should be added that even TUCAR was confined by the structural nature of repression; willing to act, it was unsure whom to act against. When Maguire died in Castlereagh, it picketed Transport House, thus angering trade union officials who could not see how they could be held responsible for Maguire's death. Likewise, when a member of TUCAR was held under the *Prevention of Terrorism Act* in England, the group picketed the Belfast office of Sealink, the company which owned the boat on which the arrested man was travelling. TUCAR's well-meaning actions were defused by the lack of specificity of its targets. Such aimlessness derived from the structural position in which TUCAR found itself. Furthermore, based as it was on the support of Catholic workers primarily in West Belfast, where unemployment and precarious employment abound, it became increasingly difficult for TUCAR to mobilise support after the closure of the two factories where its base was strong, Antrim Crystal and Strathearn Audio.

Self-Restriction: the Trade Unions and Sectarianism

The issue of repression raised by Catholic workers can be dismissed by the NIC on the grounds that to tackle it would be to alienate Protestant workers. Thus, the refusal to take up the issue is judged by the NIC not as a failure, but as one aspect of its most precious asset, its non-sectarianism. Yet, sectarianism is at the very base of NI society. Given that, it is difficult to understand how the trade union movement could be integrated into the structures of the NI state and yet be actively opposed to one essential element in these structures. Non-sectarianism need mean no more than that the trade union movment, like the present reformist state itself, is opposed merely to the most blatant manifestations of sectarianism.

Trade union officials for the most part do not make blatantly sectarian statements. There are differences among unions and between those statements meant for public consumption and those uttered behind closed doors. The trade union officials' public image is mainly one of non-sectarianism in speech, but there is little reason for self-congratulation in that alone. The trade union movement's claim not merely to be non-sectarian, but also to be one of the few bodies in NI to be so, would seem to require more evidence than the mere absence of sectarian speech.

Take the following *faux pas* of the NIC, for example. At the beginning of 1978 the redevelopment of the Short Strand area of Belfast was planned. An inquiry was arranged, and objections were invited from any interested parties. Two unions, AUEW/TASS and the Sheetmetalworkers, at the nearby engineering works of Sirocco, entered an objection on the grounds that the redevelopment of the area would prevent the planned expansion of the engineering works and would lead to a loss of jobs that could result from the expansion. To all appearances the incident was a straightforward one, with a clash of interests between unions and residents on the issue of jobs versus houses in a limited space. But nothing in NI is so straightforward. Sirocco has traditionally offered skilled employment to Protestant workers. Short Strand is the only Catholic working class ghetto in predominantly Protestant East Belfast. The issue was one of Protestant jobs versus Catholic houses. Moreover, there was evidence that there was not just a simple conflict of interests here, but that at least part of the reason for objection was related to sectarian division. AUEW/TASS voiced their

> 'grave concern at the building of a new housing estate at the East End Factory, bearing in mind that workers have previously been recipients of abuse'. (Letter of St Matthew's Tenants' Association to Terry Carlin 1/8/78)

The NIC was involved in this impasse from the beginning because the most vocal objector, Andy Barr, Communist Party member and member of the Sheetmetalworkers Union, was also a member of the NIC. The issue was raised at the NIC annual conference in Derry in March 1978, and as a result Terry Carlin was instructed by conference to negotiate in the matter. The residents met with Carlin a number of times but became convinced that he was not neutral. Not only did he agree with the unions' objections, but he seemed to act increasingly as a spokesperson for management. For example, at a subsequent meeting it was Carlin who outlined Sirocco's position:

> 'Because of the company's involvement in the confidential nego- tiations, it was not in a position to take part in further meetings [with the residents] at this stage' (minutes of meeting 18/9/78).

So the residents, through St Matthew's Tenants' Association, approached the Belfast and District Trades Union Council for support. A heated meeting resulted at the Council in September 1978. Eventually, an arrangement was worked out between the trade unions, the government and the management of Sirocco, whereby the company did expand its operations, with the help of generous government finance, but not in its Short Strand plant. The management also agreed to draw more of its workforce from the area surrounding the plant; it has not done so as yet.

Towards the end of the dispute the NIC sought to justify its role publicly.

> 'The Committee and its officers have sought throughout the discussions to act as conciliators in a difficult situation in which there are conflicting demands for the needs of industry on the one hand and on the other, the legitimate demand of a small community for new housing of an adequate standard'. (NIC Press release 5/10/78)

Thus, the NIC acted as if sectarianism was not a factor in the situation. To be non-sectarian in this sense is easy; it merely requires that one ignore the very real undertones that exist when issues of jobs and houses are raised in NI. The NIC could ignore these undertones only when they remained precisely that, when the sectarianism in the situation was muted. It recognised the sectarianism only when it came to the surface. In fact, the suspicion is that, had it not come to the surface, the NIC would have been content to continue to act as if sectarianism was not a factor. But it is a strange 'objectivity' that acts as if reality was different from what it is and gears its whole strategy towards hoping that reality will change to suit the partial view. More, it is an 'objectivity' which in the circumstances becomes partisan. It is, as in the case of Sirocco and Short Strand, sectarianism by default.

The NIC is content to leave muted sectarianism undisturbed. It is only when reality presents itself in unavoidably sectarian colours that it has been moved to pursue an active non-sectarianism. In this area its greatest claim to fame is the Better Life for All Campaign (BLFAC). This campaign originated in Newry in 1976 in the aftermath of particularly vicious assassinations in South Armagh. Trade unionists in Newry started a petition of protest, 'The People's Declaration', which was soon taken up by the NIC. Andy Barr of the NIC summed up the hopes of the BLFAC organisers when he stated:

> 'The choice for NI people is therefore to resign themselves to the paramilitaries to fill the vacuum, or to do as trade unionists have done — support a constructive set of proposals which hold out the prospects of peace and prosperity for the people' (ICTU 1977: 493).

There are a number of difficulties in such a campaign. Firstly, as Bill Webster of Derry Trades Council, a supporter of the BLFAC, stated:

> 'It is extremely difficult to win support for a campaign to get a

better life for all in a state which has always encouraged one section of its workforce to get a better life for themselves at the expense of the other section' (cited in National Labour Movement 1976:7).

That criticism in itself does not necessarily spell failure; it does, however, point to the magnitude of the task facing any campaign pursuing working class unity in NI. A much more crucial difficulty is the problem of strategy. The NIC's view is that violence will be ended through the united activity of trade unionists. But such unity in action is precisely the problem. This strategy is therefore idealist. A divided working class is a symptom of an underlying problem. And it is that problem which must be the target of strategy. Any strategy that aims at the symptoms only is bound to be less than successful.

The initial euphoria about the campaign waned quickly. By March 1977, Webster was complaining that 'in the minds of many trade union activists the BLFAC has ceased to exist' (cited in *Belfast Bulletin*; 1979:9). However, it had not so much died as disappeared into the smothering bureaucracy (see Morrissey and Morrissey 1979) from which it emerges only in the reports of the NIC to ICTU annual conferences and in press statements.

The euphoria regarding the BLFAC was never justified by subsequent events. Yet it is to this one campaign that the NIC points as proof of its active non-sectarianism. This is because on other occasions its record is even poorer. When sectarianism has expressed itself not only blatantly, but immediately in the trade union movement's own arena, the workplace, the total impotence of the NIC has become apparent.

In the UWC Strike of 1974 the NIC, sure that the strike would fizzle out, was content to call upon people to continue working. As support for the strike grew and intimidation increased, essential services ground to a halt. Finally the NIC organised a back-to-work march led by Len Murray. The march was too little too late. Only 200 people turned up to be stoned by jeering strikers (see Fisk 1975). In its impotence in the face of loyalism, it mirrored the reaction of the state itself to the strike.

However, three years later both the state and the NIC responded differently on the basis of their previous experience. In the Paisley/Baird lock-out of 1977 Mason was able to defuse the situation by dint of feverish meetings with the Protestant power-workers, whose support for the UWC had been a crucial factor in the UWC's success. As for the NIC, it worked hand-in-

THE ULSTER WORKERS' COUNCIL

give notice that:

If Brian Faulkner and his colleagues vote in the Assembly on Tuesday, 14th, to support Sunningdale, then

There will be a General Stoppage

Workers' dependents are advised, in such an event, to apply for Supplementary Benefit immediately.

Advice Centres will be available in all areas.

After 6 p.m. (Tuesday, 14th) all essential services will be maintained, and only action by Mr. John Hume will rob the housewife, the farmer, and essential services industries of power.

Watch this Space for Future Information

Belfast *Newsletter*, May 1974

glove with Mason and made no independent contribution towards opposing the lock-out, not even an abortive back-to-work march. The only advice it could give workers in a leaflet was:

> 'If you or your colleagues have been intimidated report the matter to the Police. Very urgent. Phone 999' (cited in Labour and Trade Union Co-ordinating Group 1977:14).

The NIC would surely be happy to accept the metaphor that it is a hapless jockey astride two horses pulling in opposite directions. Thus, when TUCAR tried to march under its own banner in the 1978 May Day parade, it was forbidden on the grounds that the UWC had not been allowed to march in previous years. Similarly during the April 1980 unofficial strike of NUPE members over British Army presence and surveillance in the Royal Victoria Hospital, the organisers were dismissed by NUPE officials and the NIC as being motivated by sectarianism — a charge not levelled, however, at the two branches of NUPE which have demanded the expulsion of the shop stewards who led the unofficial action.

In apparent neutrality the NIC condemns anyone who attempts to mix politics and trade unionism. So, the NIC sees itself as controlling the Republican horse by ignoring repression, thus claiming that it has done nothing to drive away the Loyalist horse. With its conscience thus clear, it is free to curtail the Loyalist horse when it threatens to bolt. The impotence and retreat of the NIC in the face of Loyalist disruption at the point of production, however, smashes that metaphor. The partisanship of Loyalist workers is less incongruent with the underlying structures of the Northern state than the partisanship of Republican workers. The latter is in a very real sense tangential and easily dismissed by the NIC, as in the case of TUCAR. But the former partisanship is much more central and not so easily dismissed. Roy Mason, in a reply to Troops Out advocates within the Labour Party, summed up this non-neutrality well. It is well worth quoting from his letter at length as it portrays not merely the state's view, but the official trade unions' view in as far as they are integrated into the state.

> 'The policy you suggest takes very little account of the many "unionists" who are also members of the British trade unions and support goals for which the Labour Party stands. Such "unionists" value membership of the UK because it enables them to live in a modern secular industrial society where the rights of workers and individuals are well developed. Your policy would involve a

government saying to such people, that life in a very different society was to be imposed on them. As you will know, there are major moral and cultural differences between Irish society and British society. These may be illustrated by reference to prevailing views on education, censorship, contraception, divorce, abortion, homosexuality and so on. How would the Labour Party justify its support for unity to those whose allegiance to Britain is based on a shared appreciation of that society which is in large part the creation of the Labour movement?' (Cited in Hemel Hempstead Constituency Labour Party 1979)[5]

Given the centrality of Protestant workers to the economy, the issues relevant to many of them, often couched in the blanket term 'security', are less tinged with opprobrium than those issues of relevance to many Catholic workers. Moreover, the militancy of Loyalist workers is less easily combatted, even if the will is there; they are more likely to have a point of production than Catholic workers, and at that point are more likely to be skilled workers. It is thus disingenuous of the NIC to argue that it is non-sectarian because it is equally against Loyalism and Republicanism. Integrated as it is into the state, it cannot be.

Selling the Workforce

The pay-off for the trade union movement which results from its integration into the state structure of NI is not a vibrant non-sectarianism. It is that the movement is legitimised. As such, it claims to be able to influence decisions in NI. The question is: just what kind of influence is it able to exert?

The answer lies in the nature of the NI economy and the state's attempt to combat its decline by trying to attract foreign investment. In that endeavour it plays one important trump card: the docility of labour. The Department of Commerce delights in playing this card in its glossy literature. It points out that productivity is higher in NI than in the rest of the UK; with a base line of 100 for 1963, productivity had risen to 158 in the UK overall by 1975, but had risen higher in NI, to 177 (Department of Commerce 1976:21). Moreover, the number of days lost through strikes in NI is low; an average of 253 days lost each year per 1,000 employees between 1960 and 1973, compared with an average of 602 for the Republic and 288 for the UK over the same period. (Figures from Economic Research Section, NI Department of Commerce.)

Foreign capitalists are quick to see the importance of the relative docility of labour, and usually mention that factor as an important one influencing their decision to invest in NI. Sam Fox, Chairman of Synthetic Industries Inc., the first US firm to begin production in NI since the 'troubles' began, stated that he was attracted by

> 'the healthy attitude of the worker towards his [sic] job and his company; this attitude is characterised by a willingness and a desire to work' (cited in *Ulster Commentary* 364, January 1977:6).

The trade union movement, similarly faced with the decline of the economy, is equally eager to attract foreign capital because it provides employment. And, like the state, the movement also plays the trump card of the docility of labour. The problem is that when selling the workforce becomes the priority, it can conflict with what should be the most important function of a trade union movement, the protection of the jobs and wages of its members.[6] It may be argued that to entice foreign investment is one way of guaranteeing more jobs and better wages in the long run. Yet, in the short run, a commitment to presenting an image of docility can paralyse the unions, leaving them less able to agitate on issues such as low pay and redundancies, and more willing to police those whose activities might damage the image.

Certainly it would appear that trade union officials bend over backwards in dealing with the management of foreign concerns. And management is grateful, as this testimonial from Camco of Houston, Texas and Co. Antrim shows:

> 'We have lost almost no working time through industrial disputes over several years. When we require to modernise or replace equipment we discuss our needs and objectives with the trade unions and to date we have had their full cooperation' (cited in *Workers' Research Unit Bulletin* 1978:32)

The problem is that modernisation can often include redundancies or closure. Thus, Dupont's £29m re-capitalisation programme (£24m of which is to come from the NIO), announced in 1977, will ultimately mean the loss of 200 jobs. In such situations the trade unions are often reduced to the role of mere consultant on redundancies and closures.

Policing those who might damage the image of docility is not a full-time concern of union officials. The fact that the working class is divided means that the bureaucracy is challenged only infrequently. The trade union movement, such as it is, thus resembles a body with a head and limbs which somehow miraculously survives without a torso. There is, for example, no independent shop stewards' movement. And the challenge from those workers who attempt to organise to the left of the NIC is as yet slight. Consequently, what is most threatening to the NIC's position is the possibility of workers organising in such a way as to challenge the bureaucracy and its economism. When unofficial action and 'politics' coincide, trade union officials act with firmness and alacrity. The April 1980 NUPE action, already mentioned, caused consternation in NIC ranks not only because it was unofficial, but also because it took up the issue of repression. John Coulthard pulled no punches when he stated in an interview during the strike: 'If you don't clobber unofficial action, it keeps coming back again and again' (Radio Ulster 10/4/80). Economism and official control are thus necessary concomitants in NI trade unionism. The need to 'cool out' less docile trade unionists also partially explains the fragile relationship which exists between the NIC and some trades councils. There are sixteen trades councils, many of which were formed or reconstituted as a result of the BLFAC. They have in common a relative independence from the NIC. This can lead to positions which contravene the NIC's pursuit of self-restriction and non-controversiality. Belfast Trades Council, for example, has been highly critical of government 'security' policy.

> 'Are all the reports of ill-treatment at Detention Centres, Harass-ment of Prisoners, etc., emanating from the opposing factions within the community with startling unanimity, to be swept under the carpet?' (Belfast and District Trades Council 1978:2).

It could be concluded that the policing of its own 'extremists' is a fair price to pay to ensure that the trade union movement can deliver the goods to its members. But it is arguable that in fact it delivers little. 78% of NIC-affiliated trade unionists are in British-based unions. (14% are in NI-based unions and the remaining 8% in Southern-based ones; see Trade Union membership surveys conducted by NIC 1977 and 1978.) Consequently, many decisions and negotiations which affect trade unionists in NI do not occur within NI. Even when it comes to action over the cuts, an area where the NIC has scope to operate locally, it seems prepared to lead only from behind. The thrust for 'anti-cuts' activity comes from the public sector through such unions as NI Public Service Alliance. The willingness of members of this union to go beyond the leadership has led the General Secretary on at least one occasion[7] to bemoan the presence of political agitators in the union. The opposition of the NIC itself to the cuts would appear to be more rhetorical than real. Its recent document (NIC 1979) seems initially militant, but the main threat to government is that the NIC will be less willing to participate in future dealings with government than it has been in the past.

> 'Let us give warning to Government in no uncertain terms. If its "contribution" to the jobs action programme is to create further redundancies both in the public and private sectors . . . then Government cannot ask the trade union movement . . . to give a constructive response to these destructive policies' (NIC 1979:10).

So, the state has benefitted more from the legitimacy of the NIC than have rank and file trade unionists. The NIC links the reformist state and the divided working class, 'uniting' the latter by avoiding 'politics' and policing those less eager to avoid politics. As a consequence it may well 'influence' government as Terry Carlin argues, but not in any aggressive way. In fact, it smothers aggression in order to maintain its position. It cannot abandon the selling of the workforce, because it considers that an essential element in stemming economic decline. So, it substitutes advice for criticism, lobbying for activism. Its influence is that of a manager, not an opponent.

Conclusion

The notion that there are non-sectarian havens of normality in NI is an ideological one. Yet it is a powerful notion which, in the case of trade unionism, has led to the attempt to create such a haven at the institutional level in the form of the NIC. But real politics in NI is simultaneously about class and sectarianism. Consequently, the space actually available for trade union politics is severely restricted. This is evident from the history. It is evident from the present relationship of the NIC to its members on the one hand and to the state on the other. And it would remain so even if more 'proper class politics' were imported — a strategy urged by the Campaign for Labour Representation in NI 1980). As Connolly (1975:40-41) concluded about trade unionism:

> 'The historical backgrounds of the movement in England and Ireland are so essentially different that . . . the phrases and watch-words which might serve to express the soul of the movement in one country may possibly stifle its soul and suffocate its expression in the other . . . the doctrine that, because the workers of Belfast live under the same industrial conditions as do those of Great Britain, they are therefore subject to the same passions and to be influenced by the same methods of propaganda is a doctrine

almost screamingly funny in its absurdity'.

NOTES

1. One such example is McCarthy's (1973:48) assessment of Jack McGougan of the Tailor and Garment Workers' Union; he 'represented the careful, constructive, socialist trade union tradition which had done a great deal to restore unity, and which later was to succeed in gaining recognition of the ICTU from the government of NI'.

2. The PUTUO convened a one-day conference on the economy on 23 November, 1956 at which a *Memorandum on the Present Economic Situation of NI* (see PUTUO 1975a:42-50) was discussed. The Memorandum, which urged increased state intervention to boost investment, was strongly influenced by two economists at Queens's University, Carter and Black, at a time when two other economists at the same university, Isles and Cuthbert (1957), were advising the government in similar terms.

3. According to the Workers' Association (1974:12), Terence O'Neill's response to this document was that the NIC was 'moving out of its sphere in industrial matters into essentially political issues'.

4. When Jack Hassard again raised the question of trade union representation on the Police Authority at the NI conference of the ICTU, David Wylie, on behalf of the NIC, reminded conference that Hassard's resignation was a personal decision. He added that 'there was an extensive and co-ordinated campaign to discredit the RUC and he appealed to delegates to let their heads rule their hearts in this matter and support the NIC in the difficult problem it and its representatives had' (cited in *Belfast Telegraph* 17/4/80).

5. This quotation is all the more amazing given that Mason, while Secretary of State in NI, did nothing to legalise abortion, capitulated to fundamentalist Protestant opposition to homosexual reform, and presided over a partial reform of divorce legislation.

6. Dohrs (1950:196-7) points out that in 1950 only 20% of the labour force in the linen industry was unionised and concludes that the main obstacle to unionisation was 'religious sectarianism'. In the rare instances when strikes occurred they might be broken by scab workers of the other religious persuasion. Dohrs suggests that Protestant workers had to overcome their 'religious affinity' with the management before becoming involved in agitation. Accordingly he argues that textile unions in NI pursued much more limited aims than their British counterparts. 'Their principal objective has been the increase in wage rates rather than the broad plans for the amelioration of working conditions, shorter hours and other activities associated with trade unions elsewhere'.

7. Jim McCusker, General Secretary of the NI Public Service Alliance, and a member of the NIC: 'Obviously every one of us has our own political opinions, but we must not abuse our positions within the union to further our own political beliefs' (cited in *Belfast Bulletin* 1979).

4

Relegating Local Government

The Framework of Reform

In 1973 NI's local government system was transformed. This was the first major reorganisation of the administrative framework of local government since 1898.[1] Local government was stripped of all its major functions — education, housing, planning and social services — and left to empty the bins, sweep the streets, tend the parks and bury the dead. Reorganisation was pushed through by the British state, which had been engaged in far-reaching local government reform since the 1960s. The reorganisation of London's local government system in the mid-1960s was accompanied by the establishment of a regional tier of planning boards and councils. During the latter part of the decade various Commissions reported on the efficiency, staffing and management of local government outside of London, the outcome of which was the reform of local government throughout the UK between 1973 and 1975 (see Cockburn 1977).

These developments are the most apparent facets of an attempt to resolve the ongoing political and economic crisis of the state as it has emerged in the decades following the European war. Much of the empirical work on the role of the state in Britain has centred on an analysis of state expenditure on the basis that the state now spends over half of Britain's Gross National Product (Barratt Brown 1972, O'Connor 1973, Gough 1975), but it is seldom recognized that one-third of public expenditure is channelled through local government. As Bennington (1976) observes, the budget of the Greater London Council is exceeded by fewer than thirty nation states in the world. In Britain, the relative importance of local government in the consumption of public revenue has increased in the recent past. Local government spending since 1969 has expanded faster than growth in Gross Domestic Product and faster than the rate of inflation, and the proportion of central government grants in local budgets jumped from the 1969 figure of 36% to 41% in 1975 (Hepworth 1978: 38).

The current level of government expenditure especially reflects the involvement of the state in aspects of social reproduction and in the provision of productive infrastructure. With respect to local government, as Saunders (1980) shows, these functions correspond firstly to local authority provision of housing, education and social services, and secondly to the provision of physical infrastructure (such as roads, drainage and car parks) and planning services to aid capital accumulation. As one of the textbooks on local government finance puts it,

> 'local authorities have become significantly more involved in the redevelopment of communities, partly because of the continuing housing problem, but more particularly because of the recognition in the country generally that if Britain is to retain its position as a leading industrial power then the country's social infrastructure must be radically changed and modernised' (Hepworth 1978: 23).

Housing eats up 21% of total local authority expenditure, and environmental services, roads and transport a further 22%.

Capital debt incurred by local government stood at £18,800m in the spring of 1974 and approximately 60% of this sum is financed commercially. The vast bulk of the debt (70%) arises from borrowings to finance housing projects. But the significance of local government attempts to manage the urban crisis go beyond this relation to finance capital. Cockburn argues that 'the city is as necessary to capitalist reproduction as the factory is to capitalist production', and explains that this is the fundamental reason why

> 'the financial crisis of the state at the local level has been experienced most acutely by the local authorities of the big cities, where the rate base was static or declining yet the nature of the physical environment and the conditions of the population demanded above average public spending'. (Cockburn 1977: 64)

The above observations are clearly relevant to NI prior to reorganisation. Local government has performed similar reproductive functions and has had to come to terms with a financial and environmental crisis notably concerning the organisation of the city of Belfast. Similar international corporate management techniques have been applied to local government problems in NI, as in Britain.[2] Even on the crude basis of expenditure patterns, however, it is clear that local government in NI is not a simple microcosm of British trends. For example, expenditure by local authorities on roads was exceptionally high in the 1960s, increasing *eleven-fold* between 1955 and 1965. Housing expenditure, on the other hand, in spite of a 300% increase in the capital programme between 1961 and 1967, accounted for just ten per cent of local authorities' combined revenue and capital expenditure in 1961 and 14% in 1967.[3] Both factors testify to the historical specificity of local government in NI indicating a political commitment to the development of physical infrastructure and a lack of a corresponding commitment to social reproduction.

Superficially, it might appear that the main reason for centralising all the major state services in NI was the failure or inability of the local government system to provide the appropriate conditions for capital accumulation, especially those concerned with labour reproduction. This does not, however, address the specific political relations of which local government is a part and moreover encourages a view of the present system which understates its ideological and political significance. It suggests that reorganisation belonged to the 'logic' of capitalist development rather than to the political contradictions which accompany that development.

The form which reorganisation took can only be understood through historical analysis of local government as a major institution through which the Unionist Party moulded the sectarian substructure to socio-economic relations. The political shape of local government in the North was largely characterised by a one party, Protestant-Unionist control from well before the partition of Ireland until the early 1970s. The system served to exclude the Catholic-Nationalist opposition and was a remarkably impenetrable forum of Unionist power and patronage which, before the British welfare reforms of the 1940s, governed most aspects of state services with the notable exception of the police. In the post-war period it continued as a site for reinforcing the hegemony of the Protestant bourgeoisie, for the further crystallisation of sectarian territories and for the rationing of employment and housing. The political forces which produced the solidity of the local government system need to be appreciated from the outset. From such a starting point a number of factors can be seen to have unsettled this form of domination and to have contributed to the 'solution' of local government's crisis following the direct intervention of British ministers in the late 1960s.

One Dimensional Local Government

The invincibility of the Unionist local government system was carefully constructed and maintained from 1920 onwards. At the creation of the Northern state, the local government system was part of the battleground of the division of Ireland. As a complement to the repressive actions of the A, B and C Specials, the political and administrative apparatus of local government was immediately altered to defend and consolidate not only the new state's territory but also the subsequent supremacy of its Unionist political rulers. The details of the changes are worth repeating because they reveal something of the unwillingness of Britain to meddle with the formal political autonomy of the North after the passing of the *Government of Ireland Act* in 1920. In addition, they illustrate the manner in which Nationalist opposition in general, and Protestant working class protest in particular, would be dealt with under the new regime.

Just before the supervision of local government was transferred to the new Ministry for Home Affairs in December 1921, the Northern parliament passed the *Local Government (Emergency Provisions) Act* which enabled the Ministry to dissolve elected councils refusing either to function or to administer any Act relating to local government. Potentially, nearly one-third of all local authorities in the North might rebel against the Belfast government since some twenty-five councils, mainly adjacent to the disputed border, were controlled by Nationalist majorities following the 1920 elections, which had been held under proportional representation (PR). A rebellion of this sort would strengthen the South's claim particularly over Fermanagh and Tyrone Counties. In the event, twelve councils and several Poor Law Boards of Guardians were replaced by Ministry-chosen Commissioners and, as Farrell (1976: 83) notes,

> 'the Commissioners appointed were not chosen to placate local opinion. The Commissioner for Armagh and Keady Urban Council was Colonel Waring, later to become a county commandant of the B Specials'.

But the long-term strategy lay in minimising Nationalist representation once the border issue had been settled and elected local councils restored. Thus PR was abolished and elections delayed until the notorious gerrymander of ward boundaries could be devised. There was some resistance to the abolition of PR shown by Protestants from within the North as well as some disapproval demonstrated by Britain. Thompson Donald, an Ulster Unionist Labour Association MP representing East Belfast in the new parliament, argued that the measure was being rushed through the House with the implicit aim of stifling Catholic representation, but without consideration of its effect on the Protestant working class vote. As he put it,

> 'the Local Government (NI) Bill is to meet certain demands. It certainly does not meet with my approval, and I take very strong exception to the Bill which will be known in the future as the 'Coercion Act'. . . I am simply voicing the opinion of the working classes when I bring the matter forward' (HC Deb. V.2 c. 917).

The Prime Minister's (Craig) response to this was simple and blunt. Every Ulster MP at Westminster had opposed the introduction of PR in the 1920 Act

> 'convinced so far as the South and West were concerned that PR would secure no benefits for Loyalists there, and so far as we are concerned in the North, we would be prejudiced by having PR as part of our electoral system whether for the Parliament here or for local government' (*ibid* c. 920).

Of course PR had been imposed by the British in 1920 (only two Irish MPs at Westminster had supported it) firstly to minimise the Sinn Fein vote in the South, and secondly, to ensure some minority representation in the North. Rather than confront the Unionist government's abolition, Britain, in a gesture of disapproval, merely delayed for a couple of months the granting of Royal Assent. This was the only occasion on which the formal power of ratifying Northern legislation was publicly exercised against the Unionist government. In future, political relations between the two governments would be largely buried in the secrecy of civil service administration.

The removal of PR itself presented the opportunity for redrawing electoral divisions and ward boundaries for local elections, many of which, under the pre-PR system, had been fixed in the 1840s. Population changes since that time had created enormous discrepancies in representation. However, the Schedule laying down the guidelines for the arrangement of electoral divisions required that attention be paid to rateable valuation as well as population. Whether or not the redrawing of boundaries was based predominantly on sectarian considerations within these criteria (and they clearly were in Derry and some of the border areas), the property provision would guarantee Unionist bourgeois ascendancy given their historical control of land, commerce and industry. It is a perfect example of class principles having sectarian application and is the basis from which several Unionists attempted with extraordinary self-righteousness to justify 'electoral imbalances' to the Cameron Commission almost fifty years later.[4] In fact, the importance of the rateable valuation criterion was to increase in future years when it was occasionally used to restrict the franchise. One such occasion was the first local government elections to be held after the scrapping of PR. The *Local Government (Franchise) Act* of 1923 was designed to disenfranchise 'a very large number of irresponsible people' who, while not qualifying for a local government vote under the householder qualification, were nonetheless eligible by virtue of ownership or occupancy of land. The objection was to voters qualifying 'out of a bog plot that is not valued at all'. The Act restricted the franchise in this respect by limiting the vote to those holdings of land with a valuation of £5 or more.[5]

Details of the sectarian consequences of property voting qualifications emerged during the parliamentary debates on a Bill which introduced further restrictions to the franchise in 1946. Twenty-five to thirty thousand farmers and their wives were said to have lost the local government vote by increasing the land valuation limit to £10. Abolishing the lodger vote had more serious consequences, excluding an estimated 350,000 adults lodging with friends or relatives. Conservative estimates put the housing shortage at 100,000 dwellings at this time. As one Nationalist MP complained bitterly, 'first you deny the people houses, and then because by reason of your own failure they have no houses, you deny them votes' (HC Deb. V.29 c. 2021). Even with the vote, electoral divisions and ward boundaries were drawn in such a fashion as to nullify Catholic representation — the estimated effect of these factors being that one Unionist vote equalled 2.5 Nationalist votes.

While Britain and the Irish Republic had been democratising local government (the Republic introduced universal adult suffrage for local elections in 1935), the Unionist government was consolidating its grip on local politics by fixing ward boundaries, by distributing votes to the propertied and by disenfranchising the propertyless. The results of the 1924 and subsequent local elections demonstrated that, except for the odd urban and rural district council, NI was to be ruled by the Protestant ruling class from top to bottom, a rule that was unalterable through the 'normal channels' of bourgeois democracy. The abolition of PR and the reconstruction of wards and the franchise meant that, for the rural and county councils, elections were hardly necessary. The only question for the Unionists to resolve was who was to be chosen to serve on the local council. There was clearly no point in anti-Unionists contesting seats and, as Gallagher (1957) shows, the average proportion of uncontested seats for these councils from 1923 until the 1950s was over 90%. Council seats in urban areas and particularly Belfast were more often contested but with few unpredictable losses for the Unionists. Budge and O'Leary (1973) argue that the abolition of PR after the 1920 elections had two main consequences in Belfast: it reduced the number of contested seats and of greater importance, it allowed the Unionist party to concentrate resources in marginal seats 'to beat down the challenge of the NILP'.

The continuity of personnel and regime in the running of local councils which all this implies has been well-illustrated in the case of Belfast. The firmly established nineteenth-century practice of extending ownership and control of capital into the local political sphere in order to influence the organisation and development of municipal services continued at least until the end of the second war. The integration of business and politics inevitably gave rise to a number of public inquiries into contract-fixing and overpayment usually involving land and houses.[6] But, however widespread such practices were and still are, their exposure neither effected Unionist dominance of the Corporation nor became a serious basis for reform.

Protestant bourgeois patronage, operating through the local government system on the basis of carefully concocted electoral districts and a restricted franchise, was well fortified against the political and economic forces for change which emerged in the 1950s and 1960s.

The Crisis of Local Government Finance

In 1911, of the £547,000 raised to run the city of Belfast, £428,000 or 78% of the total was made up of rates (Collins Report, 1928). Ten years later, rates still accounted for nearly 75% of all local authority revenue in NI. But dramatic changes in the financial basis of local government took place between the wars, as illustrated in Figure 1, which shows the contributions of local and central taxation to the income of all local authorities from 1921 to 1939.[7]

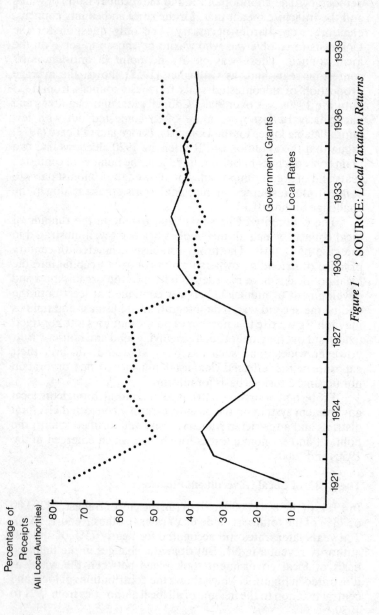

Figure 1 · SOURCE: Local Taxation Returns

Percentage of
Receipts
(All Local Authorities)

80
70
60
50
40
30
20
10

1921   1924   1927   1930   1933   1936   1939

——— Government Grants
.... Local Rates

The most obvious fluctuations of the graph can be tied to specific policy changes emanating from Britain. The immediate increase in central government support in the financial year 1922/3 was the result of nearly £¾m expenditure on criminal injuries arising from the repression and reaction in the first few years of the new state — a sum financed directly by the British exchequer. These payments continued until 1925/6. The de-rating legislation of 1929 provided for the total exemption from rates of agricultural land and buildings, the value of which amounted to 25% of all hereditaments in NI at that time. This reform was originally designed by Churchill as a way of improving the competitiveness of British industry abroad. A 75% exemption was granted on industrial and freight transport heriditaments. Not only did this constitute a sizeable subsidy to landed and industrial interests, it also removed the justification for the restricted franchise. The loss of revenue was made good by central government grants. The slight reduction in government grants just before the war followed the deliberate cutback of central government spending on education and the transfer of the cost to the rates. It was an imposition which Belfast Corporation resisted fiercely. The strained relations between the two levels of government within the North signalled the political consequences of the encroachment on local autonomy.

But the shift in the financing of local government from local to central taxation was a permanent and long-term process given the British commitment to a welfare state. At the end of the second war, local government in NI raised 42% of its revenue from the rates. As can be seen from Figure 2, from the end of the 1950s this local tax base steadily declined until rates made up just 25% of total receipts.

As rates fell, central government grants increased, reaching a peak of 63% of local government receipts in 1967. The Nugent Report (1957), observing the dependence of local government revenue on the central exchequer and alert to the political implications of this, suggested agriculture and industry should be re-rated, though not in a fashion which would prevent competitiveness with British production. This appeared to be the only option in revitalising the local tax base since the local government bourgeoisie had always pursued its class and sectarian interests by keeping the rates burden on domestic ratepayers as low as possible.

Local government was caught in a double trap. Autonomy

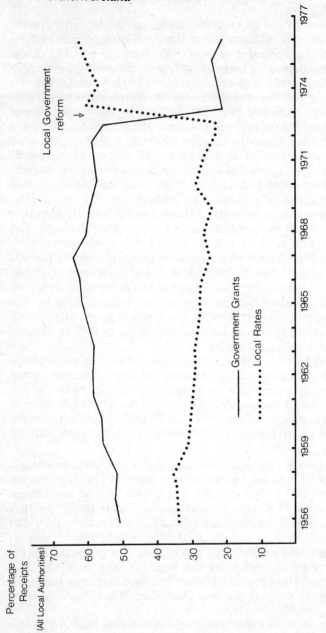

Figure 2   SOURCE: *Local Taxation Returns*

was undermined, as local taxation declined, and further weakened by the fact that expenditure of the dwindling local revenue was increasingly directed by Stormont, especially in areas such as education. Indeed, Nugent appears to have been rather dismayed by the inevitable erosion of autonomy which he saw as the explanation for councillors' lack of interest in, and enthusiasm for, a 'progressive' local government administration.

The crisis in local government finance took on differing forms both between different services and between different authorities. Rural District Councils, dependent on the County Councils for their rates revenue, were most heavily supported by government grants as a proportion of their total revenue, but were not restrained from engaging in some of the most blatantly sectarian housing allocation practices. Part of the burden of education expenditure, an increasing proportion of all local authority expenditure in the post-1945 period, fell to Urban District Councils who passed the revenue on to County Councils. Thus, a growing element of Urban Districts' revenue was spent by the Counties, on which they had no representation. As was claimed by the town clerk for Downpatrick,

> 'It is a source of considerable annoyance and embarrassment to Urban Authorities that they have no direct representation on County Councils, and therefore no say in the expenditure for which they are required to pay through the county demand. County Council chairmen are regularly reported at the annual estimates meeting, deploring the rising cost of education, health and welfare, and calling on those committees to economise. The committees concerned might justly reply that they do not set the minimum standards, that there are certain nationally recognised standards such as the ratio of teachers to children, the size and design of buildings, the school-leaving age . . . All this means that education committees have very little room in which to manœuvre' (Hayes 1967: 88).

By the mid-1960s, education accounted for 40% of total local authority expenditure. A government report of 1964 observed that, particularly after the restructuring of education finance in 1953,[8] the Ministry had come to assume a much higher responsibility for the cost of education than was the practice in Britain. If the Ministry had not provided its backing of over 75% of all educational expenditure as costs increased after 1944, 'the average charge to the rate-payers today would be higher by almost 4/- in the pound' (*Educational Development in Northern Ireland* 1964: 26). The clear implication was that local government finance would have collapsed under the strain, or else ratepayers would have rebelled.

If the Ministry of Education, or ultimately the British exchequer, had not forestalled the local taxation crisis, it would not have been possible for the Nugent Report to frame its recommendations on local authority finances in such general terms.

Local Government for 'Development'.

While Nugent argued for re-rating, the regional economic planners were saying quite the reverse. Both the Hall and Wilson Reports (1962 and 1965) suggested that continued *derating* would add further to the attraction of NI as 'an investment region'. The economic planners had little respect for traditional institutions which stood in the way of 'regional development'. The reorganisation of the state which the planners proposed was taken as a direct threat to the traditional locale of Unionist power, historically constituted and ingrained in the local government system.

The starting point for state planning was Isles and Cuthbert's survey published in 1957, which, having mapped the structure of local economic activity, went on to discuss the most suitable political and administrative institutions to provide services for in-coming capital. Greater autonomy for Stormont had the danger of 'alienating' British investment. Closer links with Britain through political and financial institutions, and the rationalisation of administration within NI, was what the industrialist required. The working class could make their 'contribution to prosperity' by accepting lower wages than other workers in the British Isles, thus improving the North's chances in the international scramble to attract investment.[9] All the development reports of the early 1960s shared these basic assumptions and a certain optimism that the state could be transformed reasonably smoothly for the task of modern government. There were motorways to be built, populations to be moved, skilled and professional workers to be produced, harbours and houses to construct and drains to be laid.

Most of the reports were produced by teams of academics or industrialists, often British, whose understanding of NI politics was to see it as an expression of an outmoded parochialism, laced with archaic religious and cultural attachments. Progress rested on an acceptance of the secular criteria of British social democracy; sectarianism in politics and administration could be an impediment to economic advance. The Matthew Report (1963) which dealt with the organisation of physical development within what was now called the Belfast Urban Area, a new unit defined by the ecological concerns of Town Planning, cited the irrationality of state administration:

> 'There are some 34 local authorities in the area with which this Report is mainly concerned; 19 of these are planning authorities: 30 have responsibilities for the provision of housing, water and sewerage, parks and playing fields; 22 have responsibility for roads... The obvious general comment must be made that this multiplicity of small units operating a variety of powers bearing on physical development is unsuitable for any form of integrated planning'.

Furthermore, Matthew (1963: 15 and 46) doubted the expertise of elected local councils to handle the sorts of decisions which modern planners needed to make. If monopoly capital was to be attracted to the North, the state would need to gear up its activities particularly with respect to the provision of infrastructure and labour reproduction.

The recasting of local government as an agency of regional economic development required submitting the state's activities to examination according to criteria of industrial efficiency — discussing urban/rural areas as 'economic units' of government, and relating rural to urban zones as 'economically integrated areas' (see Simpson 1966). Later, the more autonomous rhetoric of management science and the communications industry would cloud debate and committee proceedings; already the notions and language of corporatism were seeping into the thinking of planners. For example, the Lockwood Report (1965: 110) on higher education stated 'we consider that for the future some arrangements should be made by the government to ensure that each is aware of the other's problems and intentions, and that development proposals of individual institutions are adequately associated with development intentions in higher education generally'. There were few, however, within the Unionist state who saw 'development' in such unambiguous terms. By the early 1960s it was clear that the existing structure of local government was under attack and in the spring of 1966 an inquiry into the reform of local government was formally announced.

The Politics of Reorganising the Unionist State

The recommendations of *The Reshaping of Local Government: Statement of Aims*, published in 1967, represent the first attempt by Stormont to construct a Unionist consensus on the pending reform. The discussion paper put considerable emphasis on appeasing local councillors and indicated that administrative reform was compatible with reconstituting 'local interests', albeit within a framework of new spatial, financial and administrative responsibilities. Various statements confirmed the cohesion of the Unionist state at all levels: a 'special relationship' was said to exist between central and local government, ministers and their civil servants being known personally to councillors and senior local government officials — 'contacts are frequent, easy and informal'. The need for the 'greatest degree of integration' was asserted in order to give 'adequate expression to more localized interests and aspirations'. In fact the three tests of good local government had been, and would remain, 'efficiency, economy, and the effective representation of local aspirations, all in harmony with public policy as a whole'. Above all, it was the government's self-professed aim to achieve a 'healthy and vigorous local authority system' (*Statement of Aims* 1967: 4-5).

But the most obvious attempt to convince local authorities that reform and the continuation of Unionist hegemony were possible came in two ways: firstly, in the form of one of the few defiinite promises of this initial discussion paper; and secondly, through what was absent from it. And so it was announced that one of the powers traditionally regarded as vital for territorial and therefore political control would not be taken from local hands — 'housing administration in all its form will remain one of local government's most urgent concerns'. The other crucial mechanism for reproducing Unionist domination of local government, the restricted franchise operating in conjunction with gerrymandered ward boundaries, is not mentioned anywhere in this statement of aims. Clearly, the 'responsible people' who were drawn into 'active participation in local administration at each recognised centre of local life' were not those who had been systematically excluded from public housing and were lodging with parents or relatives, and not those who were farming small plots of the worst land rated too low to earn them the vote.

There was some risk in reform. Local politics was one force to be reckoned with but the dynamic for reform — 'regional development' — demanded state services, provided efficiently and on a scale appropriate for the type of investment already committed to the North. At the same time the overall level of expenditure by the British state was beginning to be called into question by Britain's creditors. By Maud Commission criteria, the whole of NI was hardly a 'viable administrative unit' and, as the Macrory Report pointed out in 1970, NI

> 'is smaller than Yorkshire and has a population of 1½ million . . . the rateable value of the entire province is only £14m. In contrast the rateable value of the City of Leeds alone . . . is nearly £22m; and many of the proposed unitary authorities in England will have rateable valuations of £20m, £30m and even £40m'. (Macrory 1970: 24)

Although Stormont was not considering abolishing local government, it had to accept that the existing units of administration were far too small. Thus there would be fewer councils, but each would nonetheless represent

> 'an area of recognisable identity and traditional local sentiment in which people knew the leaders of their community and were accustomed to work together in various social organisations'. (*Statement of Aims* 1967: 9)

The political problem was to ensure that in some system of area councils, based on 'historic towns', amalgamations of existing authorities could be allowed 'to emerge through discussion' which reproduced the same degree of Unionist control as had existed for the last forty years.

In fact, 'reform' as constituted and promoted by the modernisers at Stormont looked very much like business as usual for the sectarian state. It is at this moment that the seemingly separate trajectories of the politics of administrative reform and the growing extra-Parliamentary anti-Unionist Civil Rights movement intersected. The transcendence of the Unionist state and the reform of local government merged as a single political issue. It appeared to Civil Rights activists that reorganisation would result in continued allocation of jobs and housing by Unionist local authorities and in no improvement of the Catholic population's chances of political representation. Moreover, it looked as if the state was lining up for yet another round of boundary gerrymandering. The slogan 'One Man (*sic*) One Vote' captured all the immediate issues and had, in its manifest justice as a single issue, a mass appeal. The Unionist state took the protest for what it was — a peaceful but provocative threat to the state — and responded, as in the 1930s, with repression (or 'over-reaction', as the technocrats of civil disorder later described it). This was not 1932, however, and the radical reformers (e.g. Currie, Devlin, Farrell, Hume, McCann) were at their core educated, organised, articulate and determined.[10] The first sign that banning marches and batoning marchers could not be the only response of the Unionist government came in November 1968, when O'Neill (the Prime Minister) announced a package of reforms designed to mediate the specific revolt of Derry and to take the sting out of the whole Civil Rights campaign. Derry would be run by a Commissioner, thought would be given to reforming the *Special Powers Act*, the multiple company vote was to be abolished, and housing authorities would be encouraged, not forced, to base their allocations on a model points system. Farrell summed up the package:

> 'it was too little, too late. It was enough to outrage the Loyalists without satisfying the Civil Rights movement at all. The whole campaign began to centre around 'One Man, One Vote' — effectively around who controlled the gerrymandered councils. O'Neill wouldn't concede it — it would have split the Unionist Party. The Civil Rights movement wouldn't be satisfied without it'. (1976: 248)

Britain's relationship with the North inevitably became more public than it had been since the war. Wilson asserted the British government's support for O'Neill's administration early in November 1978. Wilson was backing O'Neill but not without bringing pressure to bear for certain reforms, including the local government franchise. He announced on 12 December, 'we do not feel there is any justification for the prolonged postponement of "One Man, One Vote" in Northern Ireland despite the long-term propositions that have been made'. Six months later, British troops were patrolling the streets of Derry and Belfast.

By the winter of 1968/9, the Unionist leaders at Stormont were openly struggling with a number of contradictory pressures surrounding the reorganisation of local government. Firstly, there were the basic demands of economic and physical planners, and civil servants for technocratic efficiency in the administration of local services, demands which had triggered the reform proposals initially.

Secondly, the Unionist Party at all levels had to be reassured that reorganisation would not involve a significant erosion of bourgeois Protestant power. An important indicator of this in practice would be the organisation and maintenance of the sectarian-spatial status quo in any newly-devised local council areas. As already noted, a major gesture in this direction had been made in the 1967 discussion paper which confirmed the new local authorities' control of housing. It was now necessary to guarantee Unionist majorities in as many councils as possible, a task complicated by the British insistence on a universal franchise. The latter was conceded in May 1969. In July, Stormont produced its plan for 17 Area Councils, few of which were simple amalgamations of existing council territories (*The Re-shaping of Local Government: Further Proposals*). The document went to great lengths to demonstrate the part played by all sections of the Protestant community in constructing the proposals. It was reported that extensive consultations had been held with interested parties which included as a matter of course the Orange Order, and that

> 'most councils placed very great emphasis on the fact that large-scale administration was not the sole objective. They urged that local feeling, local pride, historical association, cultural links, the local newspapers that people read — were all factors that entered so strongly into local loyalties that they clearly ought to be reflected in the pattern of administration' (*Further Proposals* 1969: 2).

The suggested new council areas were a general response to these local demands. Where populations were finely balanced in terms of sectarian composition as in County Fermanagh, an apparently minor revision of old boundaries to include two small Protestant communities was evidently designed to increase the probability of a Unionist-controlled council irrespective of changes in the franchise and ward boundaries. In other areas, predominantly Catholic districts were to be amalgamated with Protestant strongholds as a means of nullifying Catholic votes. Where Catholic majorities appeared unavoidable as in Strabane or Newry, powers might be effectively minimised by making the Area Council and its budget as small as possible.

The third problem for the Unionist leadership was to act as if it were not responding to civil rights demands and to the interventions of the Wilson government. Plans for reorganisation thus continued as if there were no mass movement on the streets, no widespread 'law and order' problem (although the Cameron Commission had been announced in January 1969) and no pressure from Westminster for more extensive reforms.

The *Further Proposals* White Paper was quickly buried in the turmoil of political events. Units of the British Army moved into Derry on 14 August, ending the RUC's siege of the Bogside following the riots which had accompanied an Orange parade two days earlier. After a night in which the RUC attempted to control the tension by machine-gunning the Catholic Divis Flats in the lower Falls, the Army was deployed in Belfast the next day. Four days later, Wilson and the new Unionist leader Chichester-Clark issued a joint declaration from Downing Street which, in addition to affirming the UK's 'ultimate responsibility' for law and order in NI, stated that 'both Governments have agreed that it is vital that the momentum of internal reform should be maintained'. On 29 August, another joint statement, made during Callaghan's visit to Belfast, announced the creation of two Joint Working Parties to investigate the allocation of housing by public authorities, the employment policies of public agencies and the possibility of setting up a NI community relations programme (see Chapter 6). Clearly, Stormont's plan to leave housing under the control of local government was being questioned. By October 10, the same day on which the Hunt Report on the reform of the police was published, yet another joint communiqué announced that housing was to be taken from local government and placed in the hands of a central housing authority. If there had been any rationale for the number and size of the proposed Area Councils connected with their responsibilities as housing authorities, this no longer existed. Plans for reorganisation would therefore need to be revised.

The 'Depoliticisation' of Reform: The Macrory Plan

The Cameron Commission (which reported on 12 September 1969) was not unaware of the sectarian history of local government, but it employed a 'rotten apple theory' in seeking some judgement of the issues. A few local councils were bad apples in an otherwise sound apple barrel — the NI state. Given other legislative and administrative reforms, the Commission was convinced that local government reform

> 'would be a major step towards healing the communal divisions which lie so close to the root of these disorders and towards promoting not only a greater sense of unity within the community but also as a probable consequence, *an increased measure on all sides of loyal acceptance of the Constitution of Northern Ireland*'. (my emphasis) (Cameron Report 1969: 58)

In December 1969, Faulkner (as Minister of Development with overall responsibility for local government) appointed

Patrick Macrory to conduct a review of local government reorganisation.[11] Macrory's task had already been 'depoliticised' to some extent by the decision on housing, and by commitments to the abolition of plural voting[12] and the introduction of universal adult suffrage.

The future of local government would be further discussed, Macrory asserted, according to technical, not political, considerations. As his report pointed out, past proposals for reform had made no attempt to achieve uniformity in size, population, or financial resources among the new councils. Paramount attention had to be given to specifying the 'optimum management unit' for modern administration:

> 'there is no room here for petty jealousies, departmental feuds, or administrative warfare, and no time for barren controversy. We have therefore refused throughout to adopt doctrinaire attitudes on the merits or demerits of elected local councils, appointed boards, centralisation and other vexed issues, nor have we let ourselves be drawn into political argument or debate on the past record of local government in Northern Ireland. On the contrary, we have tried to look to the future and to recommend the system which in our view will best meet the requirements of economy, efficiency and local involvement'. (Macrory 1970: 58)

The Macrory plan attempted to distance the question of administrative reform from the politics of civil rights and the imminent collapse of the Unionist government. Inasmuch as Macrory sought local opinion, it was from those sections of the civil service which supported the centralisation of services and which were able to present the case for reorganisation in the language of technocracy. The main precedent in this respect came from those engaged in the reorganisation of the health service and personal social services, whose recommendations were distilled in the Stormont Green Paper of 1969 (Ministry of Health and Social Services 1969). The Green Paper proposed a system of Area Boards, directly responsible to the Ministry, which would plan and discharge all health and personal social services. The Minister would appoint social work, medical and administrative experts to serve on these Boards, although a minority of seats were reserved for elected local councillors. Between three and five Boards were thought to be appropriate given the size and geography of NI. This type of structure was put forward to Macrory by the Ministry of Education once it became clear that County Councils (the education authorities) would be abolished.

Macrory adopted the Area Board system, arguing that a majority of appointed experts and 'public spirited individuals', and a minority of elected councillors was a suitable combination of professionalism and popular representation. But the dominant theme of the Macrory recommendations with respect to the distribution and control of services between Stormont and local government was to emphasize the role of service professionals and experts, since 'sensible' and 'spontaneous' social democratic politics were absent.

In a similar vein, Macrory drew a distinction between 'politics' and the criteria for efficient government from which he re-composed the remnants of the local government system. The highly controversial question of ward and council boundaries was passed on to a Boundary Commission, Macrory having decided on 26 District Councils based on the main centres of population. It was thus unclear how many of the Districts would be controlled by Unionists. Some years later in a radio interview, Macrory claimed disingenuously that the question of sectarian control had never entered his head when deciding on the number of councils — it was a purely technical decision! His mind appears to have been on a similar track when asserting in the Report that PR was 'a separate issue' from the reform of local government.

If local government reform had received any political impetus from the Civil Rights movement and what had now become 'the troubles', this had been defused and fragmented by the British state through the agency of Macrory.

The Relegation of Local Government

After considerable delay and the assumption of Direct Rule, local government was finally reorganised during the winter of 1972/3. The Boundary Commission had produced 'as fair a division of the sectarian spoils as Northern geography permits' (*Irish Times* 27/6/78), and Macrory's 26 Councils began to administer their restricted services and adjust to their relegated status. The British changed the voting system to PR and this was used for the first District Council election in the spring of 1973.

The new areas, franchise and voting system clearly enable minority parties to win more seats than under the old system and have greatly intensified the electoral contest. In the 1977 elections only two of the 98 district electoral areas were filled without contest (Elliot and Smith 1977: 4). The proportion of Councils with Unionist majorities has fallen to under 70%, although the

Official Unionist Party enjoys a clear majority in one District only. The main Catholic party, the SDLP, with 22% of all councillors, controls no council in this way and must rely on Nationalists, Independents and the cross-sectarian Alliance Party to secure a majority. Even though over 85% of councillors can generally be split into Unionist and anti-Unionist camps on most issues (Alliance have 13% of all councillors), coalition government is the rule rather than the exception. The reforms have therefore given rise to a greater expression of political tendencies than was possible in the past. Notable on the Unionist side is the emergence of Paisley's Democratic Unionist Party with 14% of all councillors and outright control of Ballymena District. The Republican Clubs, banned under the old regime, currently hold three seats in Belfast.

Occasionally, elections have resulted in equal numbers of Unionist and anti-Unionist members. In the case of Fermanagh District in 1973 the new council was inoperative for several months, being unable to agree upon a chairperson. Disputes of precisely this type are rare, although the more general issue of consensus government and power-sharing which lies beneath them emerges more regularly, often in the form of disagreements over whether or not the tenure of Mayorships and committee chairs should be rotated.

Whatever the developments in party politics at the local government level in the 1970s, it could be argued that these are of little significance. To take the argument further, it could be asserted that in view of the former centrality of local government in the maintenance of Unionist hegemony, the relegation of the system represents a substantial invasion of the Unionist state. The new District Councils, with scarcely ten per cent of the budget of the pre-1973 local authorities, are by no means the keystone of contemporary state activity. There are far fewer councillors — 526 as compared to over 1200 previously — to meddle in state administration.

This interpretation of the reform of local government is misleading in a number of ways. Firstly, the political forces observable in the composition of councils are not primarily the *product* of changes in the political system. The rise of the DUP (formed in 1971), the SDLP or Alliance (both formed in 1970) .can be explained only with reference to the history of class and sectarian struggles and the material forces which have shaped those struggles. These political groupings have a constituency and influence well beyond the restricted sphere of the official responsibilities of District Councils. Councillors themselves are active and successful lobbyists on many issues over which they have no formal control, notably housing but also repression, employment, planning and so on.

Secondly, the resources and powers which District Councils *do* control and exercise should not be underestimated. Councils remain sizeable employers and there are few indications of a willingness to change sectarian practices. The majority of councils still refuse to sign the Fair Employment Agency's declaration of intent to implement the principle of equality of opportunity (FEA 1980: 9) and indeed call for the abolition of this body. It is said that discrimination in local authority employment is not only widespread but also a natural and inevitable part of one's duty as a Loyalist councillor:

> 'You see, when people find out you're on a selection board they chase you up no end . . . and say, "Look. I'm in Lodge so-and-so and I'm in for that council job — you'll not forget now. That other fellow isn't one of us you know" . . . Now, I wouldn't deny a man a job because of his religion because that's not right . . . But then if Catholics get in at all, your own people come and hump at you and say, "huh, you're not looking after your own" . . . A lot of councillors say they're not going to come in for that sort of abuse so they just vote for the Protestant candidates'. (*Irish Times* 18/3/78)

Sectarianism laced with Protestant fundamentalism is the very core of politics in the Districts surrounding Belfast — in sharp contrast to the border areas, where cross-border discussions on the joint planning of services is increasingly evident. In the case of the former, particular issues recur — for example, Sunday opening of leisure facilities, housing developments, security resolutions and the planning applications of the Gaelic Athletic Association. To take an example of the latter, when a community group tried to lease a disused dump from Craigavon council with a view to creating a sports ground, the deputy mayor proclaimed:

> 'the Gaelic Athletic Association is a body which practises discrimination and we should have nothing to do with it. We will not help an organisation which discriminates against the British Army and the Royal Ulster Constabulary who are being shot at and murdered'. (*Sunday News* 19/11/78)

At times these councils are extraordinarily petty — for instance, denying Catholic areas Christmas trees on the grounds of vandalism. In one case the community asked for a tree to be erected outside a police station to meet this criticism but was still refused.

District Councils, therefore, are an important platform from which Unionists ideologically declare the essential relationship of Protestants and Catholics to the state on a whole range of issues which are certainly not confined to prescribed council duties. In terms of the fundamental question of shifts in political relations, anti-Unionists who were denied a relative share of representation and power throughout the life of the Stormont government have benefitted little from local government reform. While their chances of election and council control have been increased, it is a hollow victory to be in command of a minimal budget and relatively inconsequential services.

NOTES

1. *Under the 1898 Local Government (Ireland) Act* there were four main types of local authority — County Boroughs (Belfast and Derry), County Councils, Rural District Councils and Urban District Councils (in addition to the Poor Law Boards and Town Commissioners). Before the *New Towns Act* of 1965 and the implementation of the *Local Government (Northern Ireland) Act* of 1972, 73 local councils existed. Reorganisation established a single-tier system of 26 District Councils.

2. Booz, Allen and Hamilton, consultants for the management 'revolution' of Stockport Borough, drew up Northern Ireland's NHS reorganisation plans which integrated the social work service and the Health Service. Travers, Morgan & Co have been involved in the planning of Belfast from the early 1960s. Their many projects include the Dublin traffic plan, a study of Bradford's bus system undertaken for the West Yorkshire Metropolitan County Council, the Cambridge transport study, and the drawing up of proposals to redevelop East London's docklands commissioned by the GLC.

3. Compiled from *Local Taxation Returns* and *Northern Ireland Digest of Statistics*. In 1955 the Irish Republic spent five times the North's expenditure on roads. Five years later both states spent the same. See O'Loghlen (1969).

4. This Commission was set up in 1969 to inquire into and report on the violence and civil unrest since October 1968.

5. Before this Act, anyone occupying land or premises — whether rated or not — could be registered for a local government vote. The Debates include stories of people qualifying for the vote by virtue of tenancies for 1 sq. yd. of land for a bee-hive, for hen-houses, and for stalls at the back of a chapel where the congregation tied up its horses (see HC Deb. V.3 c. 867-870).

6. 1926 *Inquiry into the Housing schemes of the Belfast Corporation* (Chairman R.D. Megaw).

1941 *Inquiry into the Finance and Administration of Whiteabbey Sanatorium* (Chairman J. Dunlop).

1954 *Belfast Corporation Housing Allocations Inquiry* (Chairman T.A.B. McCall, QC).

1962 *Belfast Corporation Inquiry* (Chairman R.L. Lowry).

7. Receipts from gas, electricity and transport undertakings have been excluded from the calculations.

8. The so-called 'Pollock shilling', introduced as an education tax imposed on rate-payers in 1935, was dropped. Pollock was Minister of Finance at the time. See *Educational Development in Northern Ireland*, Cmd 470.

9. See especially Chapter XIII: 'Owing to the extra costs involved in being located on the outskirts of the economy, Northern Ireland cannot sustain (at full employment) the same average level of earnings for its workers as GB unless its industries, taken as a whole, can produce a bigger average net output per worker... Otherwise, a general attempt by workers to obtain wage rates high enough to yield average earnings on the scale in GB, could only have the effect of forcing down the rate of profit on capital below the rate in Britain, and so drying up the supply (of capital) and promoting unemployment'.

10. Bernadette Devlin (now McAliskey), Eamonn McCann and Michael Farrell have all produced books which cover this period. See Bibliography. Farrell's book provides a useful roll-call of civil rights activists. Austin Currie and John Hume are now key figures in the SDLP, Hume as leader of the Party and one of the three NI Euro-MPs.

11. Macrory was with Unilever from 1947 and became a Director in 1968. His other Directorships include the Bank of Ireland Group (since 1971) and Rothman Carreras Ltd. (since 1971). He was a member of the Northern Ireland Development Council from 1956 to 1964.

12. Plural voting refers to the practice whereby registered companies could cast up to six votes, depending on the level of rates paid.

5

Housing, the State and the Politics of Segregation

The Legacy of Unionist Rule

The political economy of housing in Britain has received much attention in recent years; as a consequence we have a better understanding of how the capital-labour relation is historically constituted in the state's mediation of the housing question. This is of direct value to the analysis of housing in NI because of the North's dependence on the British state for its repertoire of housing policy. But the British framework of housing policy has been used in NI to reproduce labour power and relations of production in a specific form. Under Unionist control, housing policies confirmed the constitution of the state and the subordinate position of Catholics within it. Hence housing struggles typically appear as sectarian struggles over territory, property and other housing resources. This is recognisable in the pattern of segregated Catholic and Protestant areas which are to be found throughout the North, signified by appropriate graffiti, coloured curb stones and wall-paintings.

Since the partition of Ireland, Unionists have attempted to reconcile the inherent instability of the North with the need of a capitalist state to facilitate the housing of the working class. Housing policies were rarely represented in terms of the universalistic ideology of citizenship rights associated with the British welfare state, but were essentially a matter of reacting to political forces and particular interests in the housing complex (landowners, builders, estate agents etc.) in order to perpetuate Unionist power. The result is that working class housing in NI is amongst the worst in Western Europe.

The three principal forms of tenure — public renting,

owner-occupation and private renting — structure housing struggles and state intervention to a large extent (Ginsburg 1979:113). Just as in Britain, there have been dramatic changes in the proportions of NI households in each tenure category (see Table 1). Statistics are not available to trace these developments prior to 1961, but it seems that the relative decline of private landlordism has been much slower in NI (Birrell *et al* 1971; Byrne 1979).

Table 1: Housing by Tenure, NI and Belfast

Year	Public rented '000s	%		Private rented (and miscellaneous) '000s	%		Owner-occupied '000s	%		Total '000s
NI:										
1961	79.3	21	(25)†	138.5	37	(31)	155.0	42	(44)	372.8
1971	147.9	35	(29)	84.2	19	(19)	195.4	46	(52)	427.4
1974	153.5	35	(29)	72.2	17	(15)	212.2	48	(56)	437.9
Belfast:**										
1961	12.9	11		66.0	57		37.3	32		116.2
1971	31.7	25		39.6	32		54.1	43		125.4
1978*	32.2	30		25.9	23		50.5	47		108.6

* excludes vacant dwellings.

** figures for Belfast are not strictly comparable. The 1961 figures refer to Belfast County Borough and those for the remaining years to Belfast District Council (a larger area).

† equivalent percentage for Britain.

SOURCES: *NI Census of Population 1961* and *1971*; *NI Housing Condition Survey 1974*; *Belfast Household Survey 1978*; Ginsburg 1979.

Table 1 shows that in Belfast 57% of households rented dwellings from private landlords in 1961. This means that until very recently the late 19th and early 20th century housing stock was of major importance in housing the working class. The state's commitment to council housing was minimal from 1920 to the late 1940s. Under the Irish version of the *Addison Act*, local authorities built only 1,657 dwellings,[1] adding a further 1,700 under subsequent Stormont legislation. The first Stormont *Housing Act 1923* imitated the *Chamberlain Act* provisions for gearing subsidies towards private as opposed to local authority building (but with minimal controls on standards); this was the chief instrument of Unionist policy for the inter-war period. This policy, suspended in 1937 but re-enacted in 1946, directly expressed the inflence of Belfast Corporation's housing committee, which was mainly composed of estate agents, landlords and developers (see Byrne 1979; Buckland 1979:164). It is likely that the number of private tenancies increased in the 1920s and 1930s, confirming private landlordism as the central social relation between the production of housing and its consumption by the working class. No slum clearance was carried out during this period.

Stormont's legal regulation of private landlordism from 1920 to 1972 was aimed primarily at increasing rents (under Acts of 1920, 1925, 1951 and 1956) and permitting 'creeping decontrol'.[2] Not until the 1978 Rent Order was there any statutory obligation on landlords to supply a rent book, or a permanent tribunal system to which tenants might appeal against rent levels. This legislation is another example of landlord interests prevailing over those of tenants. It has resulted in substantial rent rises for what are now called 'regulated' tenancies and makes no provisions governing rent levels or security of tenure for furnished tenancies (which have expanded rapidly in the last 20 years).[3]

Thus the main changes in the pattern of tenure occurred after 1945. War damage and a new leadership of the Unionist Party contributed to the increased production of council housing in the immediate post-war years.[4] Furthermore, the levels of financial support from Westminster were being re-negotiated and this involved Stormont in its first major assessment of the existing housing stock.[5] The Planning Advisory Board (1944) adopted extraordinarily low standards for estimating housing needs. For example, a dwelling was regarded as fit providing there was i) a water supply within 50 yds or 100 yds (urban and rural respectively) of the house, ii) a dry closet within 80ft of the house and iii) a mains supply of gas and electricity within 'reasonable' distance of the house. Even so, a building programme of 97,500 dwellings was still said to be necessary. Stormont, with little political acrimony, established a new central government housing agency, the NI Housing Trust (NIHT), recognising that the state could not rely totally on local councillors in expanding public sector housing.

The record of post-war building is one of periodic revisions upwards of estimated requirements and a failure to meet the targets set. The new housing built from 1944 to 1971 is detailed in Table 2.

Table 2: New Private and Public Housing 1944-1971

	Local Authority	NIHT, Development Commissions and others	Private subsidised	Private no subsidy	Total Public	Total Private	Total
No.	73,153	55,288	61,560	8,801	128,441	70,361	198,802
%	37	28	31	4	65	35	100

SOURCE: *Housing Return for Northern Ireland.*

Most of the private building was subsidised and 90% of the total private output was for owner-occupation, although 5% was for private letting and a further 4% for letting to farm workers.[6] But this new private housing accounts for only 32% of total owner-occupation in 1971 listed in Table 1. The bulk of the remainder is made up of rural properties purchased under the Land Acts in the few decades before partition, and many of these properties are occupied by retired farmers or farm workers with very low incomes.[7] Thus the 1974 Housing Condition Survey found 24% of owner-occupied housing 'substandard' and that the owner-occupied sector accounted for 40% of all unfit dwellings. (54% of unfit dwellings were in rural areas.)

In terms of design, space and facilities, the new public housing was generally inferior to British council housing of the same period, although local authorities avoided multi-storey units until the late 1960s and relied largely on local building firms. This was not the case with the NIHT, however, which from its inception depended heavily on the patented building systems of British-based construction companies (e.g. Laings and Farrans). The NIHT therefore led the local field in flatted and multi-storey accommodation especially after the changes in the structure of British subsidies in the mid-1950s towards slum clearance and high-rise developments. Much of the public sector dwelling stock is therefore of low quality, contrary to the impression given in the Housing Condition Survey. This survey does, however, show the poor condition of the total housing stock, as well as allowing a direct comparison with Britain to be made, as in Table 3.

Table 3: Housing Conditions in NI and Britain

Percentage of total dwellings:

	Unfit	Without internal W.C.	Without fixed bath	Lacking at least one basic amenity	Lacking four basic amenities
Britain (1971)	7.3	11.9	9.5	16.8	7.7
NI (1974)	19.6	24.1	23.5	26.2	22.3

SOURCE: *Housing Condition Survey 1974*

The available information on housing by socio-economic group and nominal religion, though limited, suggests that Catholics are more likely to be public sector tenants than Protestants, but slightly less likely to be owner-occupiers or private tenants (see 1971 *Census* and *Household Survey* 1975).[8] The significance of this dependence on the public sector for Catholic politics was strongly underlined by the Civil Rights agitation on housing and by the early 1970s anti-internment rent strike, as we shall see.

In spite of the deplorable condition of the housing stock, the politics of housing prior to the fall of Stormont predominantly concerned two other issues — the location of new housing and the allocation of public housing. The first of these is closely linked with the politics of factory location and the provision of employment. This is because the relationship of male and female, Catholic and Protestant workers to employment has been vital in structuring housing opportunities — both in terms of rents which can be afforded and stated locational preferences when joining the queues for public and private housing.

The Location of New Housing 1944–1971

As Chapter 2 shows, one of the political concerns of the state's regional policy was to provide employment for Protestant workers, given the continued decline of the shipbuilding and engineering industries. In terms of maintaining an all-class alliance during the politically hazardous period of mounting unemployment for skilled Protestant workers in the late 1950s and early 1960s, it made no sense for the state to concentrate infrastructure in the underdeveloped west or in Catholic areas of high male unemployment in the east. Similarly, as new investors sought the most highly trained and disciplined labour, good communications and necessary reproductive facilities for their workers, they had no general reasons to locate other than in the Protestant heartland of the Belfast region. The Unionists' housing policy was thus intimately tied to the labour needs of capital. The spatial implications of this for the building programme are brought out in Tables 4 and 5, which together cover the period 1944-1971. This period has been divided in two because 1959 marks the official change in policy from general building towards slum clearance. In both Tables, official estimates of the new housing needed in the different areas at the beginning of the period are given, and it is evident from this that 'need' was not the determining political force behind the location of new dwellings.

Table 4: New Housing 1944-59
and Official Estimates of Housing Needs 1944

	Local Authority	NIHT	Local Authority & NIHT	Private	Total Completions	Estimate of Housing needed
	%	%	%	%	%	%
Belfast City	23.1	1.5	14.2	18.9	15.9	24.2
Belfast environs*	27.7	72.7	46.2	53.0	48.6	29.5
Derry City	5.7	3.7	4.9	.6	3.4	3.9
Rest of NI	43.5	22.1	34.7	27.5	32.1	42.4
Total	100.0	100.0	100.0	100.0	100.0	100.0
Number	29,922	20,995	50,917	28,283	79,200	97,501

* 'Belfast environs' is a similar area to that used in Chapter 2, Map 2, except that here it comprises local council areas, and excludes Ballynahinch, Banbridge, Downpatrick and Newcastle in the south, and extends only as far as Ballymena and Larne in the north.

SOURCES: Compiled from *Housing Return for Northern Ireland*; *Housing in Northern Ireland*, Cmd. 224, 1944.

The building programme as a whole was heavily weighted towards the environs of Belfast. In both periods, the NIHT concentrated nearly three-quarters of its building effort in the area surrounding Belfast. Indeed, the major function of the NIHT was to house workers for the new industries locating on the periphery of Belfast, notably at Newtownabbey and Lisburn. Of the houses built by the NIHT in the environs of Belfast, 55% were situated in just three areas (for both periods)—Castlereagh,

Table 5: New Housing 1960-71
and Official Estimates of Building Needed to Replace Slums

	Local Authority	NIHT	Local Authority & NIHT	Private	Total Completions	Unfit	Estimate of Building needed to replace slums
Belfast City	15.6	2.3	10.0	10.3	10.1	25.8	48.8
Belfast environs	35.2	73.8	50.7	66.3	56.5	28.9	26.0
Derry City	1.1	4.7	3.2	1.3	2.5	7.6	9.0
Rest of NI	48.1	19.2	36.1	22.1	30.9	37.5	16.2
Total	100.0	100.0	100.0	100.0	100.0	100.0	100.0
Number	42,231	26,973	72,281	42,078	114,359	71,496	32,303

SOURCES: Compiled from *Housing Return for Northern Ireland*; *Proposals for Dealing with Unfit Houses*, Cmd. 398, 1959.

Lisburn and Newtownabbey. The private building was a little more dispersed with respect to the environs of Belfast, with 47% of new housing concentrated in the three areas mentioned. Private building catered for the growing sector of white-collar workers in the commuter settlements such as Bangor (11% of output).

NIHT's 'flexibility' as a central government agency allowed it to be highly responsive to the needs of individual capitals. On at least three occasions it launched housing projects to cater for the specific requirements of multi-national companies. It provided dwellings, for example, for Chemstrand at Coleraine in the late 1950s, for GEC at Larne in the mid-1950s and British Enkalon at Antrim in the early 1960s. NIHT apparently had no difficulty persuading Stormont to produce extra subsidies for busing building workers to and from these tailor-made projects.

The original intention that the NIHT should work alongside local authorities met few objections in the area surrounding Belfast. These Protestant strongholds had little to fear, for example, from the expansion of industry and population in Newtownabbey, or from the few Catholics who were offered NIHT housing there. Similarly, outside this area, most of the Unionist-controlled councils were content to see NIHT adding to their dwelling stock in small quantities: NIHT helped to relieve local housing problems without putting pressure on the rates or undermining electoral majorities. As the planning authorities, local councils could control the location of NIHT developments and the NIHT occasionally expressed frustration at delays in the development of infrastructure and the refusal of planning permission, notably concerning schemes in Dungannon, Enniskillen and Derry. After the *1956 Housing Act (NI)* (requiring local authorities to prepare slum clearance schemes), however, the contradiction between the preservation of Unionist control of local councils and the state's housing of the working class became more acute.

The major slum clearance schemes were in Derry and Belfast. Before the plans were drawn up in 1959, Derry Corporation had built two-thirds of the total public sector housing in the city, but the low combined output of NIHT and the Corporation was of increasing concern to the state in the 1960s. Referring to housing in the Derry area, the NI Economic Council (1966:12) complained, 'the visiting industrialist is unlikely to feel confident of being able to establish a new undertaking successfully in a centre where there is acute shortage of houses'. The Council warned that

> 'any area seeking new industry must firmly decide that, however long is their waiting list for housing, or however much hardship is being suffered by those at present without houses, absolute priority will be given to the key workers required to start up a new industry'.

NIHT was keen to build but the Corporation and surrounding rural district councils were anxious about the probable effect of greenfield development and urban redevelopment on the engineered Unionist council majorities. In Derry City, the 40% Protestant population elected 12 councillors compared to the Nationalists' eight. Of particular distaste to the Corporation was the state's designation of the Catholic Bogside as ripe for redevelopment. NIHT took on this task but with considerable delays as the Corporation altered the layout of roads and refused approval of NIHT sites and building designs. The Corporation drastically cut its own building programme in the 1960s, producing only 448 dwellings (c. 25% of its 1950s output) compared to NIHT's 1,255. But NIHT activity in the city did not threaten the sectarian spatial status quo as anticipated, since all of its building was confined to the South Ward (overwhelmingly Catholic). The Bogsiders were not dispersed because in principle NIHT preferred to rehouse 'slummies' (its term) *in situ*. It clearly drew the distinction between 'the roughs' and 'the respectables' assuming that the roughs would contaminate a 'good' estate if housed in significant concentrations.

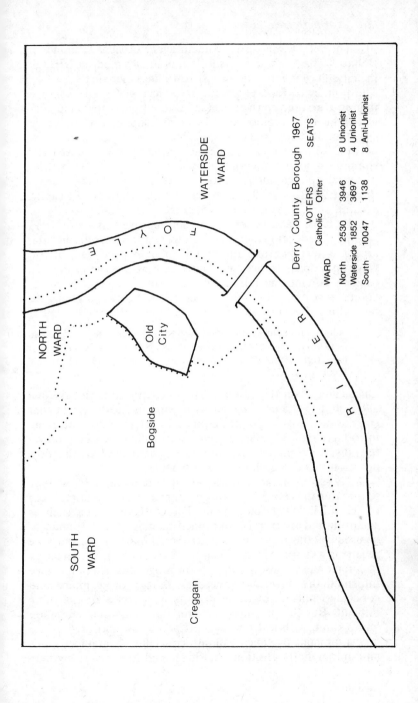

Derry County Borough 1967

| WARD | VOTERS | | SEATS |
	Catholic	Other	
North	2530	3946	8 Unionist
Waterside	1852	3697	4 Unionist
South	10047	1138	8 Anti-Unionist

WATERSIDE WARD

NORTH WARD

SOUTH WARD

FOYLE

RIVER

Old City

Bogside

Creggan

The NIHT was also the main agent of slum clearance in Belfast.[9] This was the first substantial involvement in NIHT in the city, since it had built only 320 dwellings there in the 1950s.[10] The politics of redevelopment in Belfast were more complex than in Derry, given the centrality of the Belfast region in post-war industrial development. The redevelopment of the inner-city's pre-1870 housing was highlighted by the need to develop a network of roads and urban motorways to service industry and commuters in the environs of Belfast. Transport and housing were welded together as the focus of debate within the state over the restructuring of the 19th century physical basis of capital accumulation. (See Wiener 1975; O'Dowd and Tomlinson 1980).

By 1963, Belfast Corporation had approved a massive NIHT scheme to redevelop the Catholic lower Falls. It was through this area and the adjacent Protestant Shankill that a six-lane motorway was to pass. Twice the council redrew the line of the new road — forcing the NIHT to redraw and resubmit plans. In addition, vesting and slum clearance were being delayed by the difficulties of tracing landowners and leaseholders:

> 'The ownership of the land has to be ascertained and in old built-up areas this can be a very slow process if owners and their legal representatives display no sense of urgency'. (NIHT Annual Report 1964/5)

Uncertainty over the motorway plans continued during the late 1960s and the decade ended with parts of the scheme under consideration at a public inquiry. Fourteen years after the introduction of subsidies geared towards slum clearance, only a few dwellings had been completed, among them the now notorious Divis complex (a NIHT scheme).

Those very areas in which the functions of the NIHT seemed to threaten the control of local government were the prime focus of the Civil Rights movement. Direct action tactics such as squatting and interruption of council meetings were beginning to be used by housing groups and activists in March 1968, and were receiving widespread publicity (see McCann 1974). The sectarian location of new housing and the slow progress on slum clearance informed the new agitation, even though the complex and concealed politics of these matters made mass campaigning difficult. But the practice of discriminatory housing allocation had a direct political vitality: to Catholics it appeared as the crucial practice by which Unionist councillors guaranteed votes and automatic re-election, and it seemed to explain why they themselves were so badly housed. In Derry, struggles over housing and the related Civil Rights revolt forced the state to replace the Corporation and the neighbouring councils with a Development Commission.

Housing Allocation

It was the allocation practices of the local authorities rather than NIHT which attracted the attention of the Civil Rights campaign, although there was some criticism over the Protestant control of NIHT. Discrimination in the allocation of council housing bolstered the delicately composed local government electoral divisions and it was assumed that NIHT had no specific political interests of this sort to pursue. In many cases, the allocation of a council house meant the enfranchisement of the new tenants for the first time. If the appearance of democracy within a Protestant state was to be maintained, it was essential to create as many Protestant voters as possible and to confine new Catholic tenants to areas or wards where Catholic majorities were already unavoidable.

Few of even the largest authorities felt compelled to organise the housing queue by means of a points-system. When they did, as in the case of Belfast Corporation, the system was geared towards reproducing the sectarian spatial status quo and towards housing ex-servicemen. In this particular system some attention was paid to need, as is shown in the loading for tuberculosis. A TB certificate served almost as a passport to rehousing. Hence, certainly in the 1950s, there was a thriving sideline for some doctors and their assistants in selling such certification (see *Belfast Corporation Housing Allocations Inquiry* 1954).

The allocation practices of the NIHT, albeit based on a points-system, were also significant, however, in maintaining Unionist power at the local level, as we have already seen in the case of Derry. The NIHT selected its tenants carefully, not on the basis of 'discrimination' *per se*, but through price and through forming 'a sound opinion as to the merits of the case'. Women and families with men working outside of NI were excluded altogether as applicants for NIHT housing. In the late 1940s and early 1950s the NIHT aimed to provide a three-bedroom dwelling at a standard rent of 14/–. It had a clear notion of what proportion of a wage-earner's income could 'reasonably' be taken in rent and the standard rent meant that substantial sections of workers were ineligible for NIHT housing. In 1956 it was revealed that two-thirds of NIHT tenants were either white-collar or skilled manual workers, predominantly married couples with young children. Among its tenants fewer women were employed than in the population as a whole and there was considerably less male unemployment (4% as compared with 8%). The majority of families, up to 70% for some estates, had previously lived in a district adjacent to the new estate (NIHT Annual Report 1955/6).

The NIHT's housing management was explicitly based on methods pioneered by Octavia Hill. It saw its main objective as providing a framework within which 'a wholesome family life should be easy to develop'. To this end, housing managers would conduct periodic internal maintenance inspections (on top of weekly, later fortnightly, visits to collect the rent) and teach new tenants how to 'adjust' to 'unfamiliar modern equipment' and unfamiliar rents. Deviant estates were identified on the basis of rent arrears (always below 0.1% of rental income for the 1950s and 1960s), best-kept estate and gardens competitions. Furthermore, housing management was seen as a job for 'Ulster girls' who were said to have the necessary sensitivity especially when it came to managing the process of slum clearance and redevelopment:

> 'The Housing Manager is sometimes faced with considerable opposition from the community... and it is *her* job to provide sympathy, understanding and permanence in a period of upheaval and transition'. (my emphasis) (NIHT Annual Report 1957/8)

Thus in the case of local authorities *and* the NIHT, housing allocation tended to be biased towards some sections of the Protestant working class and against the Catholic working class, whether or not a points-system was used. In their different ways, local authorities and the NIHT did more than reproduce Unionist-controlled local councils, since their housing policies served to cement existing bourgeois alliances and reinforced the respective relationship of the sectarian fractions of the working class to the state. Indeed, the failure of some local authorities to use a points-system was not entirely at variance with British allocation practices. As Merrett (1979:205) states, housing management in Britain is highly independent and discretionary:

> 'in this field local authorities operate with a minimum of legal control, the legislative framework being phrased in such a way as to allow considerable freedom in deciding who should be housed, when and where'.

Thus the 'merit system', whereby individual councillors select tenants and allocate houses, still predominates in certain areas, notably Wales. Nevertheless, the replacement of these practices by a points-system was one of the main reforms advocated by the Civil Rights movement and a prominent concern of the British state in 1969.

The Reform of Housing Administration

The burgeoning politics of housing in the latter part of the 1960s were inseparable from the central political struggles rattling the door of the Orange state. There was a shift in Catholic politics away from the more conservative tendencies of Nationalism towards a cocktail of labourism, libertarianism, socialism and tempered Republicanism; that shift coincided with the emergence of militant loyalism and the splintering of Unionism. Catholic and Protestant class alliances were in a state of flux; the post-war acquiescence of the Protestant and Catholic working class, punctuated briefly by the 1950s IRA campaign, was no longer something to be guaranteed.

Relations to the state and among the class fractions were becoming more and more dependent on the momentum of reform and the deployment of repression. The crisis of state legitimacy rapidly emerged in the form of rioting and neighbourhood defence — 'no go' areas. A major 'sort out' of mixed areas was set in motion as people sought the security of their respective sectarian ghettos. Elected representatives struggled to maintain their grip while all branches of state administration collapsed in large areas of Belfast and Derry. Community groups, tenants' associations, vigilante committees and paramilitary groups became the local units of social organisation. It was in this situation that the British established a single centralised housing authority, the NI Housing Executive (NIHE), in place of the NIHT, the Development Commissions and the 67 local housing authorities. The Cameron Commission had put 'housing griev-ances' high on the list of causes of the disturbances in Derry and elsewhere in 1968 and 1969. The problem was partly defined as the product of

> 'a rising sense of continuing injustice and grievance among large sections of the Catholic population . . . in respect of i) inadequacy of housing provision by certain local authorities ii) unfair methods of allocation of houses built and let by such authorities, in particular, refusals and omissions to adopt a "points" system in

determining priorities and making allocations iii) misuse in certain cases of discretionary powers of allocation of houses in order to perpetuate Unionist control of the local authority'.

Although at the time the housing problem was described as an emergency, the real emergency of concern to the state was the breakdown of law and order. Where housing fitted in was that it provided the Catholic working class with an admittedly legitimate grievance, legitimate in the sense that Catholics were denied the full exercise of citizenship rights associated with post-war British social democracy. Removing the grounds for complaint would destroy the basis of disaffection, lead to the restoration of order, and finally, the withdrawal of troops.[11] As Kennedy and Birrell (1978:99) put it, NIHE

> 'represented an essential feature of a social reform programme towards the elimination of grievances and of a strategy that might help remove the underlying factors behind violence and ensure future viability and well-being'.

The NIHE was to be equipped with the financial and professional resources to launch the major building drive advocated by the 1970-75 Development Programme and was not to be inhibited by delays in the release of land or in the production of infrastructural facilites. The rationalisation of rent levels, the introduction of rent rebates and the adoption of NIHT management methods including, of course, a points-system of allocation, were seen by housing administrators as the major benefits of the reform. In parallel with trends in Britain, however, NIHE's new building programme fell sharply in the early 1970s, recovering temporarily under the Labour government in 1975 and 1976, but hitting an all-time low in 1978 (Table 6). The Tories have cut the planned starts for 1980/1 by 33%. (See *Belfast Telegraph* 16/4/80).

Table 6: NIHE Housing Starts 1969-1978

1969	8,910	1973	4,196	1977	4,670
1970	7,826	1974	4,126	1978	2,841
1971	9,093	1975	6,218		
1972	6,087	1976	9,274		

The basic posture of the British state has been to set itself above the social relations in housing. This may be seen as part of a broader ideology of dissecting the 'NI problem' as a whole into a number of separate elements to be treated individually on the basis of consultation with those having a 'legitimate' concern. In general, the local state has worked less hard at the problem of mediating changes in British housing policy in the last ten years — the retreat from slum clearance and new building, the selling of council houses, real increases in rents, the temporary expansion of rehabilitation expenditure — than at severing the connection between the housing problem and constitutional politics, sectarian conflict, and the breakdown of law and order. The NIHE has attempted to police a concept of a 'normal', if severe, housing problem by arguing that its efforts are constrained by factors beyond its control. The ball is put firmly in the court of the working class, not the state:

> 'A more approachable and comprehensive housing service cannot be provided if as a result of continuing social disorder staff time is diverted to coping with rent strikes, squatting, homelessness and intimidation . . . At times it appears as if our efforts may be crushed between the upper millstone of civil disorder and the nether millstone of unrealistic expectations . . . We will begin to solve the major housing difficulties which confront us when we face up to the fact that we cannot afford the dissipation of our energies, our resources and our finance, which results from civil disturbance, wanton vandalism and continued violence'. (NIHE Annual Report 1973)

The Politics of Civil Disorder

The early years of the NIHE were dominated by the politics of civil disorder. Between 1969 and 1974 an estimated 60,000 people or nearly a quarter of all households in Belfast moved house. Many left NI altogether, fleeing either across the border or to Britain. As Darby (1976:43) records,

> 'It seems doubtful that anything in the past came even close to the population movements that have taken place since 1969. In August and September of that year more than 3,500 families were forced to leave their homes, 85% of them Catholic. Two years later, during three weeks in August 1971, a further 2,069 recorded families left their homes. Between and after these two periods of exceptional violence, a less spectacular but steady flow of families abandoned their homes from fear or intimidation . . . between 8,000 and 15,000 families in the Greater Belfast area alone'.

The state appeared both reluctant and incapable of controlling the immediate causes of the moves and the movements themselves (Darby and Morris 1974). This presented a challenge to the legitimacy of the official (now reformed) allocation system since unofficial allocation became a common practice. The allocation issue was inextricably linked with intra-working class intimidation and the increasing sectarian polarisation of housing estates. The NIHE saw that its image as a 'fair administrator' was being undermined by the process of segregation and declared,

> 'We believe that most people in the community share our aims. They would like to see us provide well designed houses, operate a fair system of housing allocations and encourage religious integration'.
> (Annual Report 1973)

There was some support for this policy of integration. It was suggested, for example, that mixed estates could be created and maintained through the financial incentive of adjusting rent levels according to the degree of segregation — the correct mix attracting lower rents (NI Community Relations Commission 1972) — or by getting tenants to sign a covenant of non-bigotry and good behaviour towards their neighbours, backed up by 'the necessary extra precautions and protection' (Darby 1976:47). But, as the political parties recognise, intimidation and polarisation are issues which belong in the realm of power and struggle over the state. Although the Official Unionists (1973:12), for example, have firmly stated their support for integrated housing, the matter cannot rest there since they must blame Catholics for the general insubordination which they (the OUs) identify as giving rise to the problem in the first instance:

> 'formerly mixed estates like Suffolk and New Barnsley have seen an almost total out-flux of Protestants, while some suburban estates have seen large reductions in Catholic population. The Lenadoon and New Barnsley confrontations show clearly the emphasis the Provisional IRA puts on using modern planning as a weapon in its campaign'.

The polarisation in relations, of which the almost complete segregation of working class areas is a part, was not mediated by the NIHE through experiments in integrated estates. Instead, the NIHE launched an attack on one manifestation of the segregation process — unofficial allocation, or squatting. Catholics, who formed the majority of those involved in the population movements, crowded into West Belfast, where competition for dwellings was already intense. It became commonplace for squatters to move into partially completed new dwellings; by 1977, the NIHE was attempting to deal with over 6,000 squatters. NIHE's policy has shifted from the partial 'legalisation' of squatting towards one of criminalisation, a change which is directly related to the increased military stabilisation of Belfast and the cessation of widespread intimidation forcing families to move.[12]

In the early 1970s, squatting was to some extent recognised by the NIHE as an expression of emergency need and so many squatters were given rent books providing their case was 'genuine'. The policy was less 'rational' than this suggests, however. In most instances, it was impossible to enforce eviction orders and the NIHE had little option but to accept squatters as legitimate tenants. Gradually, the policy towards squatters has been refined, with a corresponding increase in the use made of the squatting issue to manage the housing shortage in Catholic West Belfast. The ideology at present is that squatting 'in the majority of cases is carried out by people with *no real housing need*' (NIHE Annual Report 1979). Two major strategies have been developed, the one relying on the bureaucratic and legal form, the other on community groups and politicians.

Squatters are charged rent, but the NIHE refuses to accept payment. As people are progressively fined for illegal occupation, they are faced with the choice of accumulating huge rent arrears (eventually handled by the debt collection apparatus) or squatting elsewhere. They are, of course, ineligible for rent rebates. The other strategy involves winning over 'respectable' community groups so as to condemn and resist squatting. The means of persuasion is to cease construction work and redevelopment whilst squatting continues. The policy has found favour at least with (Official) Sinn Fein – the Workers' Party, who have loudly branded squatters as 'housing pirates':

> 'squatting is a cut-throat practice and those who indulge in it mindlessly should be ostracised by the community'. (*Belfast Telegraph* 26/9/78)

This attack expresses the growing conflict between NIHE and unofficial allocation which results in tenants allocated dwellings through the points-system preparing to move, only to find the premises appropriated by someone else.

Squatters have been made a scapegoat in the management of housing in West Belfast. It is made to appear that nothing can be done about the shortage until squatting ends, even though squatting is unlikely to end until housing provision is greatly improved. Concluding its housing proposals for West Belfast drawn up in May 1978, the Department of the Environment (1978:9-10) states:

'While the Government and the Housing Executive will do everything possible to carry out the programme successfully, the improvement of the housing conditions of those in greatest need cannot and will not be achieved if squatting persists and if rent payments are not regularised... The job can only be done successfully and on an acceptable time-scale if there is a partnership between Government, Housing Executive, community leaders and the people themselves'.

Thus the Civil Rights politics of housing allocation were largely diverted into the politics of squatting and its management. The points-system serves the NIHE's ideology of fairness and impartiality, in spite of the way in which segregation restricts housing opportunities and in spite of the division of the housing queue by area and nominal religion. The 'respectable' politics of housing allocation are now confined to discussions between the NIHE and the Housing Council (an advisory body composed of district councillors) over the points weighting for applicants' stated area preferences.

The shift in the management of the rationing of public housing is associated with one of the strategies of the 1974-9 Labour government for controlling opposition to changes in the housing programme in Britain. There was an attempt to restructure the process of decision-making by encouraging local authority tenants to take part in 'tenant control', 'tenant consultation' and so on (CSE State Group 1979:82). But in NI, the policy took on a particular form of giving recognition only to 'responsible and representative' tenant organisations:

'It has been suggested to us that some bodies claiming to be representative of local communities or of tenants are merely "front organisations" for illegal organisations. Whilst no specific evidence along these lines was submitted to us, we recognise the possibility of this situation arising, and of *a respectable community or tenant body simply bcoming a mouthpiece, over a period of time, for an illegal organisation*'. (Department of Environment 1976:8)

The merest suspicion of 'paramilitary entryism' is therefore sufficient to discredit the demands of a tenant group. In practice, such ideologies are directed exclusively at the Catholic working class. Although rhetorically less blunt, they are in essence the same lever as that operated by Unionist spokesmen when dismissing Catholic campaigns for housing.

The polarisation in social relations since 1968 has brought the distinction between Catholic and Protestant housing into sharper relief. The state came to recognise the distinction explicitly and of course at one level it can hardly do otherwise. The state's regulation of these relations, however, particularly involved the Catholic working class as can be seen in the case of the anti-internment rent strike which began in 1971.

Internment and Rent Arrears

The traditional personification of housing authorities in working class areas, the rent collector, was withdrawn from many areas in the early 1970s. The antagonism of the Catholic working class towards housing officers stemmed from the state's response to the Catholics' strike of payments to government agencies (principally rent and rates) organised in opposition to internment. Stormont passed the *Payments for Debt (Emergency Provision) Act 1971* (PDA) giving the state very wide powers to recover arrears (see *Belfast Bulletin* 1979). Initially this Act was aimed at 'political rent strikers' only, allowing deductions to be made at source from any social security benefit and from the wages of those in state employment. The effect of the PDA can be gauged to some extent from the figures presented in Table 7. Rent arrears had been an insignificant issue before 1971.

Table 7: Public Sector Housing Arrears

Date	£ Millions	Percentage of rental income	Numbers of tenants in arrears
1971/2	.9	27.1	
72/3	2.3	15.3	
73/4	3.1	19.6	
74/5	3.8	22.3	
75/6	5.1	22.8	
76/7	5.7	19.7	
77/8	7.0	18.0	41,535
78/9	8.9	16.0	42,560

SOURCES: *Digest of Housing Statistics*; *NIHE Annual Reports*

There appears to have been an immediate drop in the proportion of total rental income outstanding through arrears following the introduction of the PDA. But from 1973 this rises to the peak figure of 22.8% in the spring of 1976. Ginsburg (1979:156) points out that 'since the payment of council rent involves the appropriation of value by loan finance, there is inevitably a class conflict of interest between tenant and landord, and although this rarely comes to a head collectively, rent arrears

ANTI INTERNMENT MESSAGE

THE UNIONISTS HAVE BEEN ASKED TO DISCLOSE THE FACTS ABOUT THE RENT AND RATES STRIKE . . .

They have refused!

YOUR COMMITTEE GIVES YOU THE FACTS (from a reliable source).

At 26th November, 1971, Local Authorities and Housing Bodies had registered 14,000 applications for collection of Rent and Rates from Social Benefits.

At the present rate Civil Servants estimate that by 30th December 1971, 30,000 applications will have been made.

Thousands of pounds have been spent on advertising aimed at breaking the campaign.

RESULT! Less than $\frac{1}{4}$ of one per cent. (only 80 people) have started to pay.

BRADFORD HAS FAILED!

THE UNIONIST PARTY IS NOW A DEBT COLLECTING MACHINE . . . WE INTEND TO LET THEM COLLECT.

PAY NO RENT—PAY NO RATES

Unionism has a future for you . . . . . BEHIND BARS

and hostility to rent collectors and council officials are sympto-
matic'. This argument requires modification in the context of NI.
Because Catholics and Protestants relate to the state in different
ways, their withholding of rent elicits different responses from
the state. While it is evident that throughout the 1970s arrears
were increasingly an expression of material deprivation, they
were simultaneously an expression of sectarian relations.
Politically this can be recognised in the argument which explains
arrears in Protestant areas as a conscious attempt to pressurise
the British government into clamping down harder on Catholic
civil disobedience. The latter is represented as the true source of
the problem:

> 'the lack of determination by the Department of the Environment
> and the Housing Executive to seriously tackle the problem in the
> (Catholic) Twinbrook area is the main factor. More and more
> tenants in the law-abiding (Protestant) estates are completely
> frustrated with the double standards being applied'. (*Ulster Star*
> 26/5/78)

Following the logic of the 1974-9 Labour government's
'non-sectarian' policies, the PDA was extended to all rent debtors
in 1976. Ideologically the PDA was being universalised but
politically the move was anticipating threats of rent strikes by
sections of the Protestant working class against substantial rent
increases designed to bring NI rents closer to average UK levels.
In 1976 rents were approximately 60% of the average council
house rent in Britain. Permitted rent increases in Britain at the
time were based on the average level of wage settlements and the
Labour government was not only determined to apply this
guideline in NI but also to close the gap between Britain and NI.
Although precise comparable information is not available, it
seems that from 1976-9 rents in Britain rose by about 50% but in
NI by 125%. In the summer of 1979 NI's rents were rising at a
rate of 12.4% per annum compared to Yorkshire's rate of 4.9%
(Reward Regional Surveys). Justifying the rent increases in 1977,
in impeccable Thatcherite fashion, Ray Carter (1977) stated that
'the average Executive tenant spends only 7% of his income on
rent. In fact the average tenant spends more on alcohol and
tobacco than on rent'.

The rising cost of living and the associated arrears are
mediated by referring back to the anti-internment strike and thus
to Catholic political action and its imputed impact on the breakdown of social discipline and family budgeting. The rent strike

was one of the few peaceful means available to the Catholic working class to protest against the state's internment policy; it was met by the PDA, which forced many tenants to exist on incomes well below the official poverty line. The PDA began as an instrument for controlling Catholic protest but eventually was applied to the working class as a whole.

The Crisis of West Belfast

The main effect of the population movements was to aggravate further the existing housing problems of the Catholic working class. As regards Belfast, Protestants had a much wider choice of refuge in the estates of East and North Belfast, but Catholics were limited largely to the West. Table 8 shows that by 1978 the proportion of vacant dwellings in Catholic West Belfast was less than a quarter of that in the rest of Belfast City Council area.[13]

Table 8: Rates of vacant dwellings and overcrowded households in Belfast, 1978
Percentage of dwellings or households in each area:

	Vacant	Overcrowded
Catholic West Belfast	1.7	23.0
Rest of Belfast	8.5	12.4

SOURCE: Compiled from *Belfast Household Survey 1978*

In 1973 the Housing Executive started to plan a greenfield housing estate to relieve the housing crisis of West Belfast. It was to cater for Catholics only, 'regrettably', and was to be situated at the southern tip of the existing belt of Catholic housing and adjacent to the Twinbrook estate — as Loyalists saw it, 'on Protestant land handed down through many generations' (see O'Dowd and Tomlinson 1980). The original proposal was for a vast estate of some 4,000 dwellings, housing about 18,000 people; the estate would be under the jurisdiction of the staunchly Loyalist Lisburn Council, as far as recreational facilities and refuse collection were concerned. There was immediate and widespread opposition to the scheme which resulted in the Department of Environment (DoE) reducing it to 2,000 houses for a population of 8,000. This reduced scheme was then put to a public inquiry at which the DoE unconvincingly tried to demonstrate that demographic changes in the past eighteen months, and not political pressures, had necessitated the drastic revision in the size of the estate.

Not content with this, the main objectors at the inquiry,

Belfast and Lisburn Councils, attempted to show that new housing on that scale was unnecessary and could be situated elsewhere within the existing confines of Catholic West Belfast. Alternatively, Catholics could be forced to move to one of the growth centres or the new town of Craigavon. But the objectors central preoccupation at the inquiry was with the threat which Catholics pose to law and order and to the state itself: 'West Belfast is the largest single terrorist breeding ground in Ulster. The planners are proposing to increase it'. Poleglass clearly presented a major opportunity for mobilising an all-class Protestant campaign against the failure of the British to defeat the IRA and against the assserted willingness of British governments to pander to the minority community. As one objector put it:

> 'The trouble which we are experiencing now could look like a picnic by comparison with what might happen if the Poleglass scheme were allowed to go ahead. Poleglass is going to become the cockpit of conflict. If the British Government and the authorities want to take on the Loyalists in the North of Ireland on the whole issue of the breakdown of law and order and the sell-out in treachery to which Loyalists have been subjected during the past years then let it come. There could not be a better place to fight'.

Had the British really considered the strategic military problems which Poleglass raised?

> 'This land is in an elevated position overlooking Belfast and the Lagan Valley complex (which contains some of the most expensive properties in Northern Ireland). From a military point of view, it would be a very good stronghold and a very hard position to take. It would be opportune for them to have it'. (see O'Dowd and Tomlinson 1980)

As a vehicle for constructing consensus around areas of state intervention, public inquiries in NI are of limited value to the state. Indeed, the anti-Poleglass protest did not cease with the publication of the 'findings' of the inquiry, but gathered momentum. The campaign took to the streets in the form of marches and public rallies addressed by a coalition of all shades of Unionism, Protestant clergy and Orangemen. The high-point of the direct action came in October 1978 when the military and police were called out to stop a proposed march on Twinbrook.

Seven years after Poleglass was proposed, not a single house had been produced. It is evident that the Conservative administration is neither anxious to promote the scheme nor determined

DO YOU WANT POLEGLASS ?

THIS IS YOUR OPPORTUNITY TO SAY NO —

SUPPORT . . .

THE STOP POLEGLASS CAMPAIGN . . .

PARADE AND RALLY

(ORGANISED BY THE ANTI-POLEGLASS ACTION GROUP)

Saturday 23rd September

2.00 p.m. — Assemble at Wallace Park, Lisburn.

2.30 p.m. — Parade from Wallace Park, Lisburn to Kingsway Park, Dunmurry.

SPEAKERS AT THE RALLY IN KINGSWAY PARK DUNMURRY

JIM MOLYNEAUX
M.P.

IAN PAISLEY
M.P.

BANNERS, FLAGS & POSTERS MAY BE CARRIED

VEHICLE ENTRANCE TO CAR PARKING IN WALLACE PARK AT
MAGHERALAVE ROAD ONLY . . .

The Star 22 September 1978

to defend it from Unionist attacks. Lisburn Council, which continues to make deputations to the Minister responsible, appears to have won a major concession from the Tories:

> 'the Government would only be prepared to sanction each successive phase of housing development if it was satisfied that the Housing Executive had full control of allocation and management in the preceding phases. Squatting at Poleglass would undermine the objective of helping those in housing need in West Belfast and a situation in which the Housing Executive did not have full control of lettings and management would not be allowed to develop'. (Press release 9/8/79)

Although Loyalist threats of a war over Poleglass and what is euphemistically called a 'clean out' in Twinbrook have not materialised as yet, the 'paper tiger' thesis should not be carried too far. The anti-Poleglass campaign has succeeded in reducing the size of the estate and has mustered sufficient pressure to cast doubt on the future of the scheme after phase one. Lisburn Council is determined to ensure the misery of future tenants by not undertaking refuse collections and by not providing recreational facilities.

The reproduction of Catholic labour power through housing in West Belfast would seem to be one of the State's lower priorities. The history of the Poleglass estate is not the sole evidence of this. In the late 1970s, residents of the Divis complex began a campaign to have the flats demolished. Divis was in the final stages of completion at the end of the 1960s; thus it was ready for occupation by those burned out of inner-city streets situated at sectarian interfaces and those who were intimidated out of post-war estates on the fringes of the city. Its 'dreadful enclosure' status was confirmed from the outset. Like many of the high-density developments built at the time, Divis was the product of a state-assisted drive by the larger construction companies to raise their degree of monopoly in council house contracts. The state and big construction capital agreed that productivity could be raised by using industrialised building systems:

> 'The idea was to reduce costs by lowering the amount of on-site work required through the production of large standardised components in "factories". The subsidy system for council housing was adjusted to make it very attractive for councils to use any one of the multitude of industrialised systems provided by contractors. Industrialised systems do not have to be high rise but tower blocks represent the quickest, easiest and most profitable use of

industrialised methods for contractors'. (Direct Labour Collective 1978:80)

The high-rise boom proved to be a social and economic disaster with tenants and housing authorities picking up the cost of 'this failed venture in innovation' *(ibid)*. Yet generally speaking, the state diverted criticism away from the construction industry and on to tenants themselves. Damp, for instance, is attributed by the NIHE to the tenants' failure to heat and ventilate their dwellings properly rather than to skimped construction, 'bridged' walls, leaking flat roofs and inadequate insulation. In a few cases, the NIHE has responded to tenant action by adding pitched roofs to medium rise blocks, but more recently it has had to face the possible demolition of dwellings barely one-sixth of the way into their repayment period. Divis flats were among those considered by a working party on 'vacant and unpopular dwellings' in Belfast.

For several years, the NIHE took the position that the replacement of Divis was an impossibility. It acknowledged that conditions were appalling and that occupancy was twice the official maximum, but asserted that the shortage of space in West Belfast prevented rehousing. Under the Labour government, the decision was taken to rehabilitate the flats at a cost of £5m. The residents, however, were determined to see the flats demolished and to this end began boarding up and making unusable any flats which fell vacant (some members of the Demolition Committee were prosecuted for this). The residents' own survey of the flats reveal an average of 7.9 persons per flat, an unemployment rate of 67% and an occupancy density of 418.7 persons per acre.

In September 1979, the Tory Minister responsible for housing (Goodhart) committed the NIHE to the demolition of approximately 750 unoccupied maisonettes and flats in Protesant areas. He remarked that the decision was 'another victory for violence and vandalism', rather than representing it as a victory for the Protestant working class, who had rightly refused to be housed in this accommodation and who had options in other areas. The response to similar blocks in Catholic areas was complicated by high rates of occupancy and tenant agitation. In addition, members of the Unionist- and Loyalist- dominated Housing Council continued to assert that nothing should be done in Catholic estates, especially Divis, until squatting ended and rent debts were paid off. The political compromise was a commitment to demolish some of the flats in Turf Lodge (where a number of cases of dysentry had occurred) and to the partial redevelopment of the Divis complex. Again the Minister (10/9/79) qualified these decisions with warnings of how little the state can do in West Belfast. As regards Turf Lodge:

'I would emphasise that this will, of necessity, be a lengthy process given the high level of demand for homes in West Belfast. It is right that this fact should be stressed. I don't want to raise false hopes of easy, quick solutions'.

And the Divis plan attracted the following remarks:

'Success in this depends, of course upon the co-operation of the community. It is only realistic to recognise that squatting which is encouraged by para-militaries would undermine such a policy'.

'This plan will cost a lot of money — more than £7m. It can help a lot of families. It can also be sabotaged by wreckers. But if the plan is sabotaged, the people who will suffer most are the people living in these flats. The Divis families can best help themselves by working together with the Housing Executive in every way'. (Goodhart 17/1/80)

Conclusion

The administration of housing before the fall of Stormont was dominated by two political concerns: the need to supply dwellings to house workers for the new industries mainly situated in the vicinity of Belfast, and the preservation of Unionist power at the local government level. Stormont and local authorities made the most minimal commitment to housing the working class on the basis of need. On occasions and in particular districts, administration was overtly sectarian, ultimately becoming a major target for the Civil Rights movement. British intervention sought to place housing administration on what was thought to be a more secure social democratic footing.

The NIHE took office at a time when the collection of rents, the control of allocation and access to estates had been wrenched from the hands of the old housing authorities. Under the direction of British politicans, NIHE abstracted 'the troubles' from housing and began to use the problem of civil disorder as a means of controlling working class demands which rarely presented themselves, however, through a broad cross-sectarian front. In spatial terms, the British state went on the offensive in order to penetrate the ghetto. Localised community groups, tenants associations and housing action groups were in a position of competing for a limited volume of resources on the basis of historically determined housing conditions, sectarian space and relations to the state. But the state, in terms of the new ideology, defined the ways in which housing struggles could be conducted so as to exclude threatening issues, forms of action and political groupings, and to set the parameters of what could legitimately be done.

As is brought out clearly in the case of Poleglass, however, the constitution of class relations in sectarian territories constantly contradicts the consensual social democratic ideology of the British state. This ideology is forced into an accommodation with the dominant sectarian political forces in NI. Far from leading to a substantial improvement in working class housing, the evidence of the last decade is that British ideologies in the arena of housing have become a part of the Unionist state.

Footnotes:
1. Most of these were allocated to 'policemen, civil servants, journalists, teachers and engineers'. (Megaw Report 1926)
2. The tenancy becomes decontrolled on vacant possession.
3. The Porter Report 1975 which preceded the 1978 Rent Order took evidence from 24 landlords, numerous professional bodies, but only eight tenants. Representations by students for rent control and security of tenure for furnished tenancies were dismissed as not 'wholly representative or indeed sufficient as a base for firm recommendations'. (1975:51)
4. Belfast Corporation put most of its efforts into emergency housing, such as prefabricated aluminium bungalows, many of which are still in use.
5. Stormont spent only £2½m on housing between the wars.
6. The majority of private houses built with subsidy for private letting were constructed between 1947 and 1960 and 41% of them were built in one area alone — Newtownabbey.
7. The balance is accounted for by the owner-occupied housing built between the wars and tenant purchase of urban dwellings.
8. The former point has been used to suggest that discrimination in the allocation of public housing was negligible. For a discussion of this point see Darby 1976. 41% of Catholics and 33% of Protestants are public tenants (1971 Census) but these figures are unreliable since about 9% of households did not state religion in the Census return (about two-thirds of these are thought to be Catholic; see Compton 1978).
9. In the pre-1959 period the NIHT began a few minor slum clearance and redevelopment schemes in outlying towns, for example Armagh and Cookstown. But it was not given powers to designate

redevelopment areas under the 1956 Housing Act and had to await an invitation from the local authority concerned. This remained the case even after new legislation in 1961 which made redevelopment subsidies available to the NIHT.

10. NIHT had of course been rehousing people from the Corporation's waiting list.

11. This scenario is implicit in the Downing Street communiqué which announced the NIHE.

12. The Army is mainly stationed in West Belfast and it uses NIHE high-rise flats as observation towers and ground-floor units as sentry posts. As Kennedy and Birrell (1978:113) argue, the military presence has important implications for NIHE: 'It is easier to take a strong position against squatters and rent strikers in areas where the security forces have a relatively high degree of control than where this control is absent'.

13. The Catholic Cromac Ward, not officially regarded as part of West Belfast, has been included.

Raiding Parties

PROTESTANT TELEGRAPH 7

15-1-1977

The passionate determination of the papist element to have the Poleglass housing scheme implemented, and the vehement assertions that the estate is necessary for their requirements, make one wonder if a massive papist population explosion is devastatingly imminent and that we are to be treated to fresh armies of snotty nosed, stone-throwing little popeheads. The North Belfast area is a happy hunting ground for papists seeking new territory, and scarcely a week passes without an extension of their desmesne. Why then, are they so anxious to have and to occupy Poleglass? There is enough room after all in North Belfast to accommodate them when they compel the Protestants to move.

It is many years since attention was drawn to the papist steam roller which was and is — slowly and inexorably making its way through Protestant districts and leaving papist enclaves in its wake. The blame for this was allocated to spineless Protestant house owners and estate agents who were selling their property to papists for the sake of a little pecuniary gain. As one leading estate agent said "we can always get a bit extra from a papist customer."

6
Community Politics

Political struggle around 'community issues' is no new phenomenon, but in the 1960s and 1970s there was a growing awareness on the part of the state, academic researchers and political activists that the arena of the 'community' existed and had to be examined. The state's assessment resulted in an increasing intervention in the 'community,' beginning in the United States with the War on Poverty and in Britain with the Community Development Project. Researchers and activists reached two contradictory conclusions. These have been typified elsewhere (Rolston 1977) as 'euphoric' and 'fatalistic' as regards community politics. Both positions were a statement not merely about community politics, but also about class politics.

Those who were euphoric about community politics tended to be so because they saw the arena as a fresh one for political activity, offering opportunities for spontaneous and independent action by working people outside the co-opted, stultified and hierarchical area of class politics. On the other hand, the 'fatalists' saw the 'community' as less important than the workplace; activity in the community was necessarily more localised much less amenable to an organised, society-wide programme than the more traditional arena of class politics. In a sense, the 'euphoric' and 'fatalistic' positions were inverted images of each other.

The assessment of community politics has come a long way since then. Increasingly the validity of such politics in class terms has been demonstrated in both theory and practice. The rediscovery of the Marxist concept of social reproduction created theoretical space for the analysis of the community in class terms. And as proof that the discovery of such space was not merely theoreticist, there was the practical evidence that community politics were a potential working class threat to the capitalist state, both local and central. The nature of this threat was seen not just by researchers, nor by political activists eager to exploit it, but also by the state, concerned to manage the working class. This management of the community became an essential part of the reproduction of the capitalist mode of production, and the growth of the 'community intervention industry,' so excellently described by Cockburn (1977), became part of the state's 'gearing up to govern.'

Just as the British state was becoming involved in community politics in Britain, it was faced with another threat, the beginnings of war in NI. From 1970 on the British state became more and more involved in 'gearing up to govern' NI, and part of the governing required it to intervene in community politics. That intervention has gone through two distinct phases to date. In the first, 1970 to c.1974, the community was seen as an arena wherein 'sectarianism' could be confronted directly. The second phase was directed more specifically at the 'normal' reproduction of capitalist class relations. The problem of this latter strategy has been, as we shall see, that the class relations of capitalism in NI are simultaneously sectarian. These relations were reflected in and reproduced by the community as much as by other institutions in the society. The extent to which British reformism was able to manage these sectarian class relations in the community needs to be examined.

The British State and Sectarianism

Because of the re-emergence of sectarian violence in 1969, the British state began to intervene more directly in the internal affairs of the NI state. At first the intervention was mainly in the form of a 'peace-keeping' army, but very soon the soldiers were followed by bureaucrats, charged with introducing reforms. The initial reforms were often spectacular (such as the introduction of 'one man, one vote' and the disarming of the police) and were carried out by reluctant governments at Stormont. The old Unionist sectarian status quo was under threat.

Despite the changes in the last years of Unionist government there was much that had remained the same. Despite the celebration of the 'modernisation' of the 1960s, there was still the old ingrained ideology to explain away inequality and discrimination. A sectarianism emerged which was all the more insidious for being dressed up as liberalism. This is typified in O'Neill's incredible and well-known remark that, if you treat Catholics with due consideration, there is no reason for them not to behave like Protestants. In the same vein, William Fitzsimmons, Minister of Health and Social Services under the last Prime Minister of NI suggested that the real

> 'problem with the Catholics of NI was one of education. Catholics produced too many children and sent them to inferior schools; they were not fit for key jobs' (cited in *Sunday Times* 27/2/72).

In some ways government attitudes had changed little from the days of Brookeborough and Craigavon.

There was little reason to believe that the new generation of British bureaucrats and politicians should have had the same sectarian attitudes. Thus, there was no longer the active encouragement of sectarianism by government which had typified raw unionism. To many it seemed the base of sectarianism had been removed overnight. Where O'Neill's proposals for reform in local government, housing, etc. tore the Unionist bloc apart, these same proposals were implemented quickly under the watchful eyes of British politicians and backed up by British guns. Thus much of the base on which sectarian patronage had traditionally rested was changed.

Given the reform of major state institutions there remained only one area in which, according to the British political logic of the time, sectarianism could continue to operate — that is, the area of sectarian attitudes and utterances. It was seen as a somewhat residual area, but an important one all the same, requiring some management if the promise of the other reforms was not to be nipped in the bud by out-and-out rabble-rousing.

To British politicians confronted for the first time with NI, it appeared that a racial model more than adequately explained the continuance of such attitudes. (This racial model was not confined to politicians, but was the response of many researchers confronted with NI for the first time; see De Paor 1970, Moore 1973.) So, it was a logical move to translate this model into a set of policies derived from the British state's attempts to manage racism at home. In Britain the growth of racial tension after Enoch Powell's 'rivers of blood' speech in May 1968 had led to the establishment of anti-incitement legislation and the up-grading of the government-sponsored race relations body, the National Committee for Commonwealth Immigrants, which was renamed the Community Relations Commission in the process. Consequently both Incitement to Hatred legislation and a Community Relations Commission (CRC) were introduced into NI. The Acts establishing both were to all intents and purposes carbon copies of the equivalent British Acts, except that the term 'religious discrimination' was substituted for 'racial discrimination.'

Only one prosecution has ever occurred as a result of the *Incitement to Hatred Act* in NI, that of John McKeague for publishing the *Orange Song Book*; he was acquitted. It is perhaps just as well that there have been no more prosecutions, for NI was thus spared the anomaly which occurred in Britain, whereby legislation ostensibly to protect black people was used more against them than against whites (see Dickey 1972).

A CRC looked more practical. Although only a small part of British strategy, it was an important locus of its attempt to manage the more obvious manifestations of sectarianism.

Intervening in the Community: the First Phase

In the aftermath of the riots in Derry and Belfast in August 1969 James Callaghan, British Home Secretary, visited the two cities. As he stepped on the plane to return home after walking up the Falls Road and addressing crowds in the Bogside, he announced the establishment of a Ministry of Community Relations and a CRC. By December 1969 both bodies were in operation. The ostensible purpose of the Ministry was to administer the 'Social Needs' legislation, money for projects in areas of 'special social need.' The less ostensible, but more important, purpose, at least in the minds of some politicians, was to show that government 'cared.' David Bleakley, the second Minister of Community Relations, stressed this latter purpose.

> 'One of the things I insisted on was that if the Ministry gave a swing or a playground, a plaque was put there to say that this had been done with the co-operation of the Ministry of Community Relations... We must find a way to let the people know that the government are and can be compassionate.' (Assembly Deb. V.3 c.120)

As for the CRC, minutes of the early meetings reveal that the Commissioners were not at all sure of how to go about the task for which they had been appointed, namely, 'encouraging harmonious community relations.' This was a daunting task in a divided society, and one made all the more awesome by their complete subordination to the Ministry. This subordination was apparent not merely in the fact that the Commissioners were appointed by government on Ministry of Community Relations advice, but also in the fact that in the early days the CRC needed Ministry permission to spend sums greater than £20 (Griffiths 1974:9).

There were eight Commissioners — four Catholics and four Protestants of liberal background. In fact, the whole aura surrounding the first moves at community intervention was one of liberal benignity. The Minister of Community Relations was a relatively innocuous Unionist MP, Dr Robert Simpson, who had resigned from the Orange Order on his appointment as a gesture of good will. Simpson had personally chosen the first chairperson of the CRC, Dr Maurice Hayes, Town Clerk of Downpatrick, a Catholic who had recently organised a civic week in his town. Hayes was thus seen by the government as having all the right credentials to front a body which in effect, if not intention, admitted by its very existence that Catholics had real grievances. But, more than a general sympathy for his fellow Catholics, Hayes had some definite ideas on what was to be done. He had visited the United States where he had been impressed by responses to black violence. It seemed to him that similar responses were necessary in NI.

In the United States one major element in the liberal response to black violence was community development (CD). Hayes believed that a similar programme needed to be begun in response to Catholic violence in NI. He introduced the other Commissioners to the idea, and while they might not have shared his enthusiasm, they at least shared his sense of urgency that the CRC be seen to be doing something. Consequently, within a year of coming into existence, the CRC had appointed Hywel Griffiths, ex-provincial Community Development Officer (CDO) with the Zambian government, and more recently a lecturer at Manchester University, as head of a CD team.

The philosophy of CD took on a specific variation when applied to NI. There is in all CD an emphasis on community action as therapy. This emphasis has particularly conservative connotations when the communities to be managed by community developers are violent. Hence, part of the pedigree of CD is in counter-insurgency work in British colonies. In NI a similar concern with CD as control was apparent, as this statement from Hayes reveals.

'Harmonious relations are the product of life in a well-functioning community with which the individual can identify and in which he wants to participate. This suggests an approach by way of CD — of helping to produce in local areas such healthy communities.' (Speech to conference of voluntary organisations, Belfast, 22/11/71, mimeo.)

For this reason the CD programme initially met with little opposition from Stormont; the CRC was no revolutionary body, not even in the very narrow sense in which Unionist poliicians may have defined the word. That is not to say, however, that there were not tensions between the Commission's commitment to liberal management and certain aspirations of sections of unionism. The CRC was a creation of the newly-interested British government, and that interest was resented by many Unionists. This resentment therefore partly determined the response to the CRC. To put it simply: many loyalists were suspicious of the CRC, seeing it as one more sop towards rioting Catholics. Loyalist elected representatives, even more than other elected representatives, were openly antagonistic towards the CRC.[1] They shared with other elected representatives a dislike of a government-backed body encouraging community politics outside of local democratic politics. But more, they realised that a disproportionate number of such groups could well be Catholic community groups.

Community groups had emerged as part of the Civil Rights movement. Two of the most active groups in Derry in the late 1960s were the Housing Action Committee and the Unemployed Action Committee (see McCann 1974). Working class Catholics, confident that Stormont cared little for their plight, had no hesitation in organising self-help groups. Furthermore, when the CRC's CD programme was actualised, Catholics had little initial problem relating to the CDOs. Thus, the Dungannon CD team found no difficulty in organising Catholic community groups, but had little success with Protestant groups.

'Social consciousness and motivation appears to be either more readily available or is expressing itself more in Catholic groupings (sic) in our area. We feel we will need to be aware of this and to make an effort to stimulate awareness in the Protestant groups. It would be all too easy to unconsciously work solely with those who show initiative.' (*Foundation Report* 1971, mimeo.)

Loyalist groups were quick to dub the CRC the 'Catholic Relations Commission' and to accuse it of being a 'front for RC propaganda' (*Newsletter* 9/8/73). Their suspicions were not totally unreal. The CRC *was* part of the British state's acknowledgement of Unionist discrimination. The majority of CDOs *were* Catholic[2]. The liberal notions underpinning the CD programme *were* part of the changed times of managing Catholic grievances by admitting their substance rather than dismissing them as Republican propaganda.

Despite Protestant fears, the proponents of CD believed that it would ultimately bring the Protestant and Catholic working class together. The rift would be bridged in two stages. Firstly, CD in local areas was to be encouraged, and on the basis of the self-confidence that would thus merge, it was argued that the second stage would occur: the coming-together of community groups across the sectarian divide to agitate on issues of common interest and concern. In short, 'the policy therefore of the Commission's professional team is to seek an improvement of community relations through CD.' (Hywel Griffiths, speech to North West Council of Social Services, Derry, 24/11/70, mimeo.)

The CDOs were ill-prepared to carry out this monumental task. They had no professional training; only one had been a CDO before, in Africa. Many of them were teachers, social workers, or from similar lower professional backgrounds (see Rolston 1975). A brief training programme *in situ* did little to help prepare them for the job, yet they entered their task with gusto. The fact that they were initially more successful than might have been expected was due less to their expertise than to circumstances beyond their control. Violence erupted in the local areas in which they had been working in August 1971 after the internment operation. A massive forced population movement within the greater Belfast area occurred, and in the midst of all the disruption, the statutory social services were slow to respond. The CDOs suddenly found themselves organising emergency services. Paradoxically they emerged from a period of doing straightforward relief work convinced that they were now better prepared to continue with CD work. They were adamant not only that CD could lead to improved community relations, but that it could only do so with them at the helm.

> 'The Commission has a valuable role to play. We can keep open lines of communication. Unless things become really bad we must keep trying. If we can't do this, no one else can.' (Hywel Griffiths, at CD team meeting, minutes 28/9/71)

So, in November 1971 both Griffiths and Hayes put in separate requests to the Ministry of Community Relations for an expansion of the CD programme. Griffiths was the more specific. He envisaged 30 project areas throughout NI and a staff of 110 CDOs (not counting research and administrative staff) under the CRC's direction (Griffiths 1971). It was to be a massive programme, placed under the control of a semi-autonomous body. And at the best of times the Ministry would have displayed a typical bureaucratic caution in the face of such a request. But, in the light of the weak position of the Ministry itself, the request became even more threatening. The Minister, Basil McIvor, wrote to Hayes:

> 'It is clear that if your proposals were adopted in their entirety they would very much reduce the present functions of the Ministry, to such an extent as to call in question the continuing need for a separate Ministry of Community relations at all.' (14/1/72)

So the Ministry procrastinated, neither granting nor refusing the proposed expansion. But McIvor's letter made it quite clear that no expansion was forthcoming. Consequently, in February 1972 Hayes resigned, to be followed two months later by Griffiths.

Looking back on these events, Griffiths has explained the impasse that led to his and Hayes' resignations in terms of the empire-building manoeuverings of the Ministry of Community Relations and its Assistant Permanent Secretary; it was too small a Ministry even to have a full Permanent Secretary (Griffiths 1974:21). It is true that at the time of Griffiths departure the Ministry had less than 30 members, Assistant Secretary included, that to survive it had to expand and that therefore its interests lay in preventing the expansion of the CRC. But this is only part of the story. An explanation which rests there relies too much on the intentions and idiosyncracies of a number of Ministry officials. It must be realised that the interests of individual bureaucrats fitted into the wider needs of the state at the time. The officials were expressing not merely their own opinions, nor even the reactionary protectiveness of a small Ministry, but the tendencies of the expanding reformist and repressive state.

At the time of Griffiths' and Hayes' resignations the Ministry had already begun to expand beyond merely administering 'Social Needs' money. The first new area of responsibility given to it was an interesting one, the administering of the 'civil liaison' scheme. The origins of the scheme are in Brigadier (now General) Frank Kitson's *Low Intensity Operations* (1969), a work of counter-insurgency theory. Here Kitson urges unified planning, centralised control and a single point of responsibility in any counter-insurgency campaign. This requires civilian-military liaison committees at central and local level in the society at war. He developed his theory in Malaya, but it was in NI as Commander of 39 Brigade in Belfast that he had a chance to put his ideas into practice with the Civil Liaison Officers (CLOs) of the Ministry of Community Relations. These civil servants, based in police stations, were to chair local Community Development Coordinating Committees, which were to bring together police, army and CDOs. The CLOs were also to act as go-betweens between community groups and government departments. In fact the scheme never lived up to the Kitsonian promise. The number of officers was small, never more than 20, their contact with community groups was minimal and their Co-ordinating Committees for the most part operated without the CDOs in attendance. But it is noteworthy that in NI even as ostensibly reform-oriented a body as the Ministry of Community Relations could not avoid also being oriented in the direction of repression.

From April 1972 onwards the Ministry's specific functions grew, and so did the Ministry itself. The state's intervention into the same areas in which the CRC was, or sought to be involved, increased, and with it the likelihood of the CRC's expansion decreased. In fact, it can be said that April 1972 saw the end of the CRC, but that it took it two more years actually to die. Those two years were a time not merely of increasing friction between the Ministry and the CDOs, but also of internal friction among CDOs and between the CDOs and the Commissioners.

Meanwhile, things had changed on the wider political front. Stormont had been prorogued and Westminster was directly governing NI. Darlington and Sunningdale occurred and the basis of the power-sharing experiment was laid. During all this time there was a great deal of confusion in all areas of government in NI. Bureaucrats and administrators were unwilling to take any decisions that had long-term consequences. So there was extra incentive for the Ministry to oppose expansion, at least until the power-sharing Assembly took over. It refused to act positively in the interim period.

As a result of growing demoralisation within the CRC a number of CDOs left and the Ministry would not replace them. The suspicion of the remaining CDOs was that the Ministry people had at least a conviction — and at most an assurance —

that the arrival of the Assembly would see *their* expansion and the CRC's demise. They were in fact correct.

The power-sharing Executive took over the reins of government in January 1974 and Ivan Cooper, SDLP, became Minister of Community Relations. Within two months of taking office he had expanded the functions of the Ministry and its size. It now had responsibility for sports provision; its responsibility for the building and running of community centres was widened; its brief for the first time was to cover rural as well as urban areas; and the number of staff was increased from 30 to 86. The scale and scope of the Ministry's activities is shown in the breakdown of money requested by Cooper for 1974/5 (see Table 1).

Table 1: Ministry of Community Relations
Estimates, 1974/5

	£s
Salaries	259,000
Operation 'Spruce Up'	750,000
Social Needs	989,000
CRC	289,000
Sport and Recreation	2,342,000
Leisure Centre in Derry	250,000
Housing Executive	30,000
Total	4,909,000

SOURCE: Assembly Deb. V. 3 c.63-86

This was certainly a much different-looking Ministry from that of three years earlier — not only more powerful in itself, but more integrated into the increasingly reformist state. It was no coincidence, therefore, that on the same day that he sought and received money to carry out his Ministry's programme, Cooper announced the disbandment of the CRC. The CRC, said Cooper in a long speech, was set up in 1969 and began to do CD work. 'Government itself could not perform this role, since government were a party to the conflict' (Assembly Deb. V.3 c.74). But, circumstances had changed. There was now a power-sharing Assembly. So, 'there is no longer any need for any section of the community to feel excluded from government or to fear that government may be unsympathetic to them' (*ibid*).

So the CRC was to be terminated and its functions would be divided up. CD would go to either the newly-instituted Area

Boards or the local councils. The research role of the CRC was to be taken over by the Ministry (now renamed the Department) of Community Relations. The Department would also increase its field ('Social Needs') programme, and the future of the Department would lie in a wide commitment to sporting, recreational and communal facilities.

One month after this announcement the Assembly fell, brought down by the UWC strike, and the governing of NI returned to Westminster. Some of the CDOs now felt that there was hope for reconstituting a more independent CD programme outside the confines of a CRC. Surely, their argument went, the British government, which had established the CRC in the first place, would now come to its rescue when it was threatened by narrow-minded local politicians and empire-building bureaucrats. But such CDOs read the situation wrongly. In August 1974 Lord Donaldson of the NIO made an announcement which not only failed to re-establish an independent CD programme, but took one more step towards the centralisation and technocratisation of community intervention. The Department of Community Relations was to be closed down and its functions, along with those of the CRC, were to be divided up among different government Departments. The re-shuffling of functions continued for a few years after Donaldson's announcement, and by the time it was complete the Department of Education had been given responsibility for administering what had been previously the major function of the Department of Community Relations, that is, grant-aid to areas of social need. This grant-aid was to be channelled through newly-established community services departments in each local council, even if the money was eventually to end up with a community group. The local councils were also given responsibility for what had been previously the major concern of the CRC, the hiring of CDOs; however, they were now called Community Services Officers, CSOs.

Thus, the local councils, which had been relegated in the early 1970s and had lost a number of their powers, were given a new power in the mid-1970s; they became one level in the administration of the state's community intervention. Although powers in the area of community intervention were not seen by many local councillors to compensate for the loss of powers in more crucial areas such as housing, the community was an area where a politics had emerged. The management of community politics and the involvement of local councils in that management was therefore not unimportant.

Intervening in the Community: the Second Phase

As far as the CDOs were concerned, the disestablishment of the CRC, and specifically of its CD programme, was a tragic mistake. The first stage of the programme had begun to show signs of success in the building-up of strong, confident community organisations. The second stage, namely, improved community relations, would never have a chance to emerge because of the state's actions in curtailing the programme. The CDOs thus saw the relationship between CD and sectarianism as a straightforward one of mutual exclusivity. They added a new element to the traditional economistic argument about NI. In the past the economistic argument had been that combined activity over employment and housing issues would lead to decreasing sectarianism. The CD addition to the argument was that sectarianism could also decline as a result of combined activity in the arena of community politics, over issues of redevelopment, roads, etc. This is why, it was believed, CD would lead to improved community relations and why the curtailment of the programme was seen as a tragedy.

In fact, as we shall see, the evidence that CD led to improved community relations is slight. It would seem, then, that sectarianism is not so easily overcome. If that is so, the lesson of the CRC is that there was a fallacy in the economistic strategy.

As far as the British state was concerned, there was another lesson to be learned from the experience of the first phase of community intervention. The CRC and the Ministry of Community Relations had represented a small, but nonetheless real, direct attack on sectarian attitudes. This, as we have pointed out, derived from the initial and naïve application of a racial model to NI. But in the four years since the British state's first major intervention into reforming NI, British administrators had overcome that naïveté and plumped for a more lasting and technocratic solution to the NI problem. They had geared up to govern, and part of that process of efficiency required the management of community politics. The state's intervention in the community became less and less concerned with confronting sectarian attitudes head-on, and more explicitly involved in reproducing capitalist social relations. In this sense, the strategy became less a specific community intervention strategy for NI than an extension to NI of the British state's new-found management of community politics in Britain.

Rose and Hanmer (1975) have analysed this process of the British state's management of community politics in terms of the application of Etzioni's (1968) 'cybernetic model.' This model sees corporate society operating as does a cybernetic system, that is, on the basis of the principle of subsidiarity. In short, no higher level of a system should be given tasks to perform which a lesser level can adequately perform. Subsystems thus have a great deal of autonomy. But such autonomy is only possible because of an intricate series of feedback mechanisms. So, the subsystem is autonomous only when it is performing the function required of it. If it oversteps its function, the presence of sensitive feedback mechanisms guarantees instantaneous moves by higher levels in the system and the loss of autonomy by the subsystem, at least temporarily. For Etzioni the future of efficient government is seen to lie in the application of the cybernetic model, thus combining maximum possible freedom with maximum possible control. Rose and Hanmer concluded that the technocratisation of government in Britain was bringing about such a system, and saw the proof of this in the whole area of community politics.

There is a danger in Rose and Hanmer's approach of too conspiratorial an assessment of the activities of the British state. But in as far as it is a valid approach, it says something, not just of the British state's community intervention at home, but also in NI. When Lord Donaldson finally announced the demise of the CRC in August 1974, he foresaw an 'essentially tripartite alliance of community groups, local government and local agencies (*Irish News* 31/8/74) — in short, a reproduction at the local level of the alliance that the British were attempting to forge through Sunningdale at the regional level. The overall need for NI was seen to be the establishment of a new alliance, no longer of Unionists only, but of 'modernising' politicians. The thrust of British policy was that the ruling alliance in the North was no longer to be the all-class one of Unionism, but the all-religion one of bourgeois power-sharing. This alliance was to be reproduced at local as well as regional level. In short, the British goal of sponsoring 'proper class politics' in NI extended not just to political parties, but also to the community, to the management of 'proper class politics' at the community level.

At the time of the CRC's demise, it is estimated (see Duffy, Perceval et al. 1975, appendix 6) that there were almost 800 community groups in NI, and although the vast bulk of them (450) was in Belfast, they were spread throughout NI. There is no doubt that the CRC's CD programme contributed in some part to the burgeoning of community groups, but probably to a smaller extent than the CDOs themselves would like to believe. But, from the British state's point of view, more important than the question of the origin of these groups is that of their management after the demise of the CRC. Gouldner (1970) has argued that, with the cut-back of the War on Poverty in the United States, the state could not afford to ignore the existence of the many community organisations which had been in part spawned by that state-sponsored programme. What emerged was 'reform at a distance.' Reform became technocratic and was carried out with 'thin-lipped, business-like rationality.' A similar process has occurred in Britain in the aftermath of the Community Development Project. In NI the process had begun already in the last days of the CRC, but it has taken off since the CRC's demise. Some indicators of the process are the increase in NIO finanical assistance to sport (£5 million in 1978 compared with less than £½ million eight years earlier; see *Belfast Telegraph* 20/11/78), in leisure facilities and in the provision of community workers. (According to Department of Education figures, there are at present 21 full-time and 10 part-time Community Services Officers employed by district councils.) The growth of expenditure on community and leisure services in Belfast is evident from Table 2.

Table 2: Revenue Expenditure, Belfast City Council, 1975-9

Year ending March 31	Community Services (£s)	Leisure Services (£s)	Total Council Expenditure (£s)
1975	4,487	45,689	5,290,156
1976	28,912	71,505	7,097,969
1977	91,548	189,668	8,836,326
1978	110,569	788,227	10,469,384
1979	213,359	1,361,408	11,876,945

SOURCE: Belfast City Council, *Summary of Accounts and Statistics*, 1975–79

Gouldner's incisive analysis could lay more emphasis than it does on one important mechanism in the increasing technocratisation of community intervention, that is, the growth of a 'community industry.' At first, the community groups which had emerged were discrete and atomised, each struggling for its own disparate and localised goal. But very soon there emerged umbrella organisations. The most significant of these was perhaps the Greater West Belfast Community Association, formed in February 1973 and claiming to represent approximately 70 community groups in Protestant and Catholic West Belfast. There were similar umbrella organisations in east and north Belfast, but the Greater West Belfast Community Association proved to be not only the most active but also the most radical. However, even it was not as revolutionary an innovation as many believed at first. In fact, the relationship of its central committee with many of the constituent groups was at most negligible, meaning that it was less of an integrated body, in the sectarian sense, than it appeared to be on paper. Furthermore, it suffered the consequences of an organisational malady, namely, that its officers became separate and aloof from the people in the constituent community groups. It was an organisation of organisations rather than of people. As such, its officers became 'community leaders,' and the stage was set for the later development of an indigenous community industry.

Yet, despite the relative unrepresentativeness of these umbrella organisations, there is no denying that pressure for a regional NI community umbrella did emerge from the grass roots. So, when Community Organisations of NI was established at a meeting in Derry in 1975, it did represent to some extent a popular striving for strength in numbers. Yet, in a very real sense, what was a gain on the part of the community groups was also a loss, for the building of a community hierarchy coincided neatly with the interest of the British state at that point in time. In fact the push from below which brought about the community hierarchy made it that much easier for the British state to establish what Donaldson had called the 'tripartite alliance.' The process did not have to be executed with each and every one of the 800 groups, because a community hierarchy already existed.

Griffiths, Hayes and the CDOs had asked for the expansion of the CRC's CD programme under their control. After the demise of the CRC that expansion occurred, but very definitely under the control of government. The NIO, and in particular one of its chief ministers, Lord Melchett, became increasingly involved in community intervention. Melchett's BAN (Belfast Areas of Need) Project channelled money from the Department of Education into areas of social malaise in Belfast (see Project Team 1976). The NIO has also given financial assistance to many other programmes, including the much-publicised collaboration between Melchett and the Save the Shankill group in drawing up a £1 million plan for the provision of community facilities in a working class area of Belfast experiencing the devastation of redevelopment (see *Belfast Telegraph* 22/11/78).

The overall result of increased state intervention and funding in the community has been the formation of something beginning to approximate the cybernetic model proposed by Etzioni and criticised by Rose and Hanmer. There is a much greater deal of collaboration between government and the community hierarchy than there has been before. This is not to say that the government has complete control of the community hierarchy. On the contrary, there is no monolith involved here, but rather two separate interests which sometimes coincide. Real divisions are revealed in the occurrence of severe clashes between government and the community hierarchy (as in the Bone area of north Belfast, where one local group relentlessly pressurised Melchett for the establishment of a community education centre; see Rowlands, Gaffikin, Griffiths and Ray 1979).

The cybernetic model requires efficient feedback systems, and these also began to emerge through such institutions as the BAN area teams, Community Education Forum and all the other schemes to which government money is given. It is in the context of these feedback institutions that the term 'community leader' becomes important, for it is to these people that the autonomy is given (as well as the finances) and it is also these people who sit on the committees which distribute the finances and provide feedback to government. All of this is not merely the co-option of individuals, but the creation of a community industry in NI. That creation was, paradoxically, made all the easier by the pre-existence of the community hierarchy which had been instituted precisely to give the community groups greater strength.

And what of those community groups? They struggle on day by day, often becoming as separated from the community industry as they are from government institutions. There are both positive and negative aspects of their increasing alienation from the community industry. On the positive side is the possibility that, despite the growth of the hierarchy, real hardship will give rise to spontaneous outbursts of organisation outside the hierarchy. Such is the case of the Turf Lodge women who successfully agitated for the demolition of their flats and the Divis Demolition Committee pursuing a similar aim. Both groups operated largely outside the community hierarchy, statutory bodies and established political groups.

However, the examples of successful independent actions on the part of community groups are as yet quite few. For the most part the experience of community groups at the receiving end of the increased community intervention has been that of atomisation rather than success. Atomisation occurs mainly through the medium of money. In point of fact, despite the phenomenal growth of the community industry and its finances, remarkably little money is spent on the support of community groups and the provision of community services by local councils, as Table 3 shows. Moreover, the vast bulk of recurrent expenditure is on salaries to professional community workers and the running of resource and community centres. On average only 16% of community services expenditure goes directly through local councils to community groups. Yet, that average hides a wide range of responses to community groups, Belfast's expenditure being proportionately greater than Larne's, for example. There are a number of factors which could explain these differentials, but one in particular needs to be emphasised.

Local councillors, to varying degrees, are at least suspicious, if not downright antagonistic, towards community groups. Gerry Fitt, for example, expressed his antagonism openly.

> '... we, the elected representatives, know the problems which beset our constituencies... I do not think any of us would claim to be theorists or academics, and if we applied our knowledge, if we spoke of the problems that we know exist in our constituencies, it may be of far more importance than some university graduate going into an area and asking questions.' (HC Deb. V.77 c. 1366)

Community groups are seen to be outside the democratic process, and their existence is seen in fact to subvert that process. This assessment is especially prevalent in NI where many community groups contain paramilitary group members wearing another hat. Local councillors have frequently opposed the state's encouragement of community groups. Ivan Cooper, himself a councillor and an SDLP Assembly member, echoed the words of his party leader, Gerry Fitt, when announcing the demise of the CRC.

> 'The present arrangements... did not provide for the proper involvement... of the elected representative... this is a trend... which strikes at the root of our democratic system... the CRC has acted as a buffer between the government and community groups,

whereas what I believe is necessary is more direct contact'
(Assembly Deb. V.3 c. 72).

In these sentiments Cooper prefigured the growth of the post-
CRC technocratic community industry.

He also revealed a shared interest with civil servants who in
the pursuit of rationality and efficiency prefer a hierarchical
chain down which government money can pass automatically
without them having to decide on the respectability of each
group. The civil servants in the Ministry of Community Relations

*Table 3: Breakdown of Expenditure on Community Service in
District Councils, 1979* (Councils ranked in descending order by
size of population.)

Council	CSOs (%)	Resource and Community Centres (%)	Voluntary Groups (%)	Total (£'000s)
Belfast	24.0	44.8	31.2	338
Derry	9.7	78.6	11.6	76
Newry/Mourne	15.6	78.8	5.6	40
Lisburn	34.8	55.7	9.5	23
Craigavon	21.0	74.4	4.6	104
Newtownabbey	11.9	79.9	8.3	46
Castlereagh	35.5	64.5	0	47
North Down	32.0	67.4	0.5	19
Fermanagh	44.5	28.0	27.5	14
Ballymena	26.2	72.9	0.9	26
Ards	38.6	60.2	1.2	15
Down	24.1	68.0	7.8	14
Armagh	10.4	76.8	12.8	12
Coleraine	9.9	74.2	15.9	12
Dungannon	0	91.7	8.2	6
Omagh	45.5	51.4	3.1	13
Strabane	14.9	78.7	6.4	36.0
Antrim	25.2	73.8	1.0	22
Magherafelt	51.0	0	49.0	2
Larne	35.9	63.9	0.2	15
Banbridge	0	0	0	0
Carrickfergus	17.9	51.0	31.1	30
Cookstown	37.8	55.8	6.4	4
Limavady	33.9	63.6	2.5	4
Ballymoney	100.0	0	0	1
Moyle	91.0	9.0	0	2

SOURCE: Compiled from figures supplied by Department of Education

were careful to work through official channels, even in funding community groups. As one of them, Pat Carvill (1973) noted:

> 'Where local authorities are unable or unwilling to provide facilities, we would be quite happy to grant aid a voluntary group.'

The antagonism of civil servants towards community groups is expressed even more clearly by John Oliver (1978:242), a senior civil servant at Stormont.

> 'A well-meaning but dangerously vague concept of community action is offered as a replacement [to party politics]. Potentially more dangerous still is the astonishing new growth of community associations, some with dubious connections, but nevertheless intent on imposing their will on housing, roads, redevelopment, community halls, libraries and so on to the virtual exclusion of elected politicians and of rational argument, financial considerations, ordered priorities and other realities of public administration. The alternative to elected representative government can only be anarchy or tyranny in the long run.'

In this sense, civil servants and local councillors share a common interest. Both have had difficulty accepting the rhetoric and largesse of Lord Melchett and his open encouragement of community groups, and are happiest dealing through channels which keep the community groups 'in their place' and bolster the position of local councillors. It should not be surprising, then, that many local councillors show an extreme caution about where community services funds go. Salaries and plant are seen as a safer bet than community groups who may threaten their power and influence.

Even in those councils most committed to backing community groups directly the amount of money which reaches the groups is miniscule. On the other hand, the amount of red tape to be cut through to acquire that money is great. The minutes of Belfast City Council's Community Services Committee, to take the council with the largest expenditure on community services, are filled with the consideration of requests by community groups for grants. The requests are mainly for very small amounts of money for the most mundane purposes, as Table 4 shows. For the most part, these requests are quickly passed over and the bulk of the Committee's time is spent considering weightier matters involving much larger sums. For example, the Committee on 20/6/78 agreed to spend £38,000 on a Community Arts project, but 100% of that amount came from the Departments of Education and

Environment, and was merely administered by the council. The only expenditure of the council in this scheme was £480 on a minibus.

The end result of all this is that Belfast's community groups are controlled at a very low cost. Each group is reduced to approaching the council as an individual group, and often arguing with the Community Services Committee for months over slight amounts of money.

Table 4: Grants to Community Groups, Belfast City Council, May 1978

Organisation	Expenditure £s	Rate of Grant Aid %
Lower Falls Residents' Association	90	50
Lower Falls Redevelopment Association	850	50
Roden Street Residents' Association	200	75
Hamill Street Residents' Association	200	75
Clonard Community Council	622	75
Middle Falls Environmental and Community Development Association	200	75
Crescent Community Association	200	75
	3,200	50
Woodvale Community House	200	50
	691	75
Silverstream Community Association	1,245	75
Community Shop Association	1,000	50
	1,280	75
Steadfast Community Association	95	75
Springhill Housing Action Committee	200	75
Oakley Community Association	200	75
Whitewell Community Association	150	75
Torr Heath Community Centre	630	75
	380	50

SOURCE: Minutes Presented to Belfast City Council, May 1978

It is not only with the council that the individual community groups argue. Such friction occurs among groups in the same area, and between groups in different areas. The irony is that, in the case of intra-area struggles, the only gain for the victor group, apart from a measure of local hegemony, is the rather dubious perk of being in some way integrated into the community hierarchy, thus attaining the eligibility to wrangle with the local council for the small amount of finances available. When such time-consuming, often demoralising struggle occurs between areas, given the sectarian geography of NI, sectarianism can enter in as a major element in community politics.

Sectarianism and Community Politics

Despite the reforms of the last decade, sectarian attitudes and utterances are still very much alive. Often they are of the old blood-curdling variety. Note this manifesto of Charles Poots, DUP councillor in North Down.

> 'If I was in control of this country it would not be in the same state as it is now. I would cut off all supplies including water and electricity to Catholic areas. And I would stop Catholics from getting social security. It is the only way to deal with enemies of the state and to stamp out the present troubles' (cited in *Sunday News* 2/3/75).

The last few years have seen the partial blunting not so much of sectarianism but of the language of sectarianism. This is exemplified in the following statement of Councillor William Wilson of Ballymena. His espousal of Protestant domination is not couched in the strident 1930s sectarian tones of Brookeborough, but in the 'realistic' and 'objective' sectarian tones of the 1970s. Wilson had discovered that one travelling family from the South of Ireland had recently been housed in Ballymena and that two others were camping on waste ground. He urged the setting-up of special 'tinkers' camps' in Catholic areas.

> 'You must of necessity put them in a Catholic area or at least where they are convenient to their church and the schools. Ballymena is a predominantly Protestant district' (cited in *Sunday News* 17/11/76).

But as a result of the reforms many of the direct mechanisms of sectarian patronage are no longer immediately available to sectarian councillors. Poots is not 'in control of this country' in the same sense as his predecessors were, so the only way he can 'cut off all supplies, including water and electricity, to Catholic areas' is outside official structures such as local councils. This is in fact what did occur during the UWC strike of 1974, and was the tactic of the DUP and others during the abortive Paisley/Baird 'lock-out' of 1977. Nevertheless, sectarian councillors have a forum to give practical expression to their sectarian consciousness.

Where councils are dominated by loyalists, the policies that emerge after often informed by fundamentalist Protestant morality. Thus, Cookstown, Limavady and Larne councils have at various times prevented the opening of their new swimming pools on Sundays in moves reminiscent of the closing of play parks in the 1950s. Such actions are often justified in the grandest manner.

> 'I'm convinced the pool will never prosper because this council allowed the Lord's Day to be desecrated. And if we violate God's Law, His curse will be upon it. I guarantee the pool will never pay while it remains open on the Lord's Day.' (Councillor Jack McAuley, Larne council, cited in *Sunday News* 23/11/75).

In fact, the opposite is true. Critics of Craigavon's ban on Sunday opening pointed out that the closure of the Recreation Centre was probably costing the council £2,000 a week (see *Sunday News* 11/1/76). But such economic rationality is lost on sabbatarian councillors who have successfully closed not only swimming pools, but recreation centres, a youth club in Banbridge, a leisure centre on the Shankill Road in Belfast, and so on. All these closures emerged from the operations of formal democracy in a sectarian setting.

Such sectarian utterances and attitudes can emerge in matters over which the local councils no longer have control, as Poot's statement shows. Similarly, councils no longer control education, but that does not prevent sectarian agitation over education issues. Ballymena council, for example, has attempted unsuccessfully on a number of occasions to have all references to Darwin's 'ape theory' removed from schools in its area, schools it no longer controls.

These incidents show that even in the reformed district councils the old loyalist world-view is alive and well, a world-view that combines an opposition to Catholics with opposition to the welfare state. Rev. T.A.B. Sawyers, Deputy Grand Chaplain of the Orange Lodge of Ireland, summed it up when he said at the July 12th celebration in Tobermore:

> 'Is it not an appalling fact that a few of those Ulster babies, pronounced a few years ago the healthiest in the UK, filled as they were in the formative years with gallons of free orange juice, should be responsible for acts of savagery and butchery unsurpassed in history ancient or modern?' (cited in *Sunday News* 13/7/75).

The crucial question is how one is to explain the persistence of such utterances and attitudes. One answer frequently given is that they are residual. They are seen as a hangover from the past; they will disappear as the influence of reformism grows. But it is apparent that demands are frequently made by loyalist councillors that appear in themselves progressive, but which are made in order to belittle or negate Catholic gains in the same area, whether real or imagined. For example, should socialists and feminists delight in the demand of an Official Unionist councillor from Lisburn for state nursery facilities in his council area? Or should they reject it when they read on to discover that he is enraged that Poleglass, the proposed Catholic housing estate in the council area, is to have nursery facilities? Stances can be taken that appear progressive, but are in fact not. The reason for this is not least that those taking the stances are doing so for sectarian reasons. Social democratic reformism and sectarianism can co-exist.

Such co-existence is apparent in one area over which local councils have a measure of control, namely, community intervention. From the beginning of the state's community intervention it was apparent that some elements in local government would seek to administer that intervention in a sectarian manner. By 1975 Armagh council had refused to take over a new £49,000 community centre in the Callan Bridge estate, and Magherafelt council was baulking at the suggestion of a community centre in Draperstown (see *Sunday News* 2/9/75). Often such actions were justified in terms of lack of funds to run the facilities, as was the reason given by Craigavon council, for example, when it refused to take charge of a community hall from the Housing Executive (see *Sunday News* 12/9/76). However, the old-style sectarianism beneath the surface is only thinly veiled. Armagh and Magherafelt are loyalist-controlled councils; Callan Bridge and Draperstown are Catholic areas.

More recently, Belfast council agreed to postpone the building of a leisure centre in the Catholic Oldpark area on the grounds that it would probably be used only by Catholics. That it should be so, given not only the sectarian geography of north Belfast but also the high level of inter-sectarian violence in the area, should surprise no one. In fact, most leisure centres and community centres are used by Catholics only or Protestants only for similar reasons. So, the objections of Councillor Frank Millar, who proposed the postponement, are in fact dubious. He argued that if the council decided to go ahead with the project 'it would be clearly seen they were prepared to provide facilities for one section of the community only and would be doing so in a sectarian manner' (cited in *Belfast Telegraph* 11/11/79). At the very least, Millar demands a 'fairness' that is unrealistic where sectarian class relations exist. He is also less than consistent, for he did not oppose the building of another leisure centre which, although adjacent to the 'Catholic' one, was in Protestant territory and would therefore be used by Protestants only.

In the same vein Larne Councillor Jack McKee, DUP, accused the NIO of bending over backwards to provide recreational facilities in communities of murderers and gangsters, while law-abiding areas were neglected. To anyone attuned to the language of sectarianism, it is immediately clear that he was referring to Catholic and Protestant areas respectively. Protestant Larne, he pointed out, had 18,000 people, but only one community centre. (He did not mention that at the time Larne had three community centres at the planning stage.) And he concluded: 'It seems people have to be killers and rioters in this country before they get any attention' (cited in *Sunday News* 9/10/77). McKee is following DUP party policy in this regard. The *Protestant Telegraph*, mouthpiece of the DUP and of Free Presbyterianism, has complained that,

> 'while the government is more than willing to pour millions into leisure projects and various work efforts, invariably in republican areas, it is noticeable that no comparable efforts are being taken to eradicate terrorism' (15/4/78).

Of the six leisure centres already in existence in Belfast, for example, three are in Protestant areas and are likely to be used almost exclusively by people from the areas; two are in Catholic areas, and the clientele of the sixth is mixed. A similar division will occur in the nine further leisure centres proposed by Belfast City Council (from information provided by Department of Leisure Services, Belfast City Council).

Criticism of Belfast council, at least, cannot be on the basis of the 'fairness' of allocation. What can be criticised is the notion of 'fairness' itself. More than 'fairness' is required to correct imbalance.

The ability of Councillor McKee and the DUP to ignore the equitable distribution of leisure centres neatly demonstrates that community politics can be as much a matter of sectarian politicking as jobs and houses traditionally were. Such sectarian politicking can be found not just on the part of local councillors who have some role in the provision of community facilities, but even, paradoxically, in the community industry itself. One result of the growth of the industry has been that community workers and 'community leaders' have of necessity tended to work more closely together as the industry has grown. As these community workers and 'leaders' are both Catholic and Protestant, there would seem to be some slight validity to the claim that community work leads to improved community relations. But, if such improved relations exist, it is only within the industry and not between the communities in which the workers work and the 'leaders' lead. Furthermore, working together with someone from across the 'sectarian divide' in the community industry does not of necessity diminish sectarian attitudes and utterances outside the narrow range of issues on which the industry is active. Nowhere is this more apparent that in the person of one of the joint secretaries of the Greater West Belfast Community Association. This man was tireless in putting forward the position of the Association and its constituent groups, and was able and willing to oppose government at any turn on behalf of the Association. At the same time, he was capable of the crassest sectarianism, as is shown by an interview he gave to a student paper, *Gown* (see Delargy 1976:6), while wearing another hat, that of UDA spokesperson.

'Gown: How long will a civil war last?

UDA: We would like it to be over in a week.

Gown: What about those Catholics who have no arms?

UDA: How do we know they've no arms? We will assume that Catholics are fully armed and on that assumption we will take action against them.

Gown: Can anybody surrender?

UDA: We cannot take prisoners. They are a liability.

Gown: Will you win?

UDA: While there are Protestants here, there will be a NI as a part of Britain.

Gown: What will be the conditions under which Catholics will stay?

UDA: There will be no room for RCs in a new state.'

The case is an extreme one, but perhaps serves to illustrate the fact that CD, rather than inevitably limiting sectarianism, was equally capable of being limited by it.

It is patently obvious that sectarianism and community politics can co-exist. This is because 'community politics' is not an abstraction, but is politics in and between communities divided along sectarian lines. Because of such division, even actions which have no direct or immediate connections with sectarianism can have sectarian consequences. The CRC was about the combatting of sectarianism, while the provision of leisure centres and community centres is not — it is about the formalisation, centralisation and technocratisation of community intervention and it results in benefits for only sections of the communities in which such centres are built. But the sectarian division of those communities in NI leads to the sectarian allocation of the centres. This sectarianism need not derive from sectarian intention on the part of those making the decision. In fact, there can be a scrupulous pursuit of 'balance' on the part of the reformist state when it comes to providing facilities. But such 'balance', even if attained, is itself sectarian, requiring, for example, one leisure centre in a Protestant area for every one in a Catholic area. Similarly the Housing Executive designates a Protestant housing action area for every Catholic one designated, again pursuing 'balance', even when it is obvious from the Executive's own surveys that it is in Catholic areas that the worst housing conditions are to be found. The same limitation is apparent as regards the Fair Employment Agency, a reformist body that comes in for a lot of opposition from loyalists because it has some teeth. But it can be argued that a policy of equality in employment would require not just 'fairness' or 'balance' but positive discrimination in order to counter the present imbalance whereby Protestants are more likely to be in skilled employment and Catholics in unskilled.

To equate the absence of sectarian intentions with the absence of sectarianism is a mistake. Sectarian geography may determine the nature of an action much more surely than the intentions of the actors. To build a leisure centre in a working class area is to build a 'sectarian' leisure centre. Similarly, the sectarian division of labour can determine the consequences of an action; to seek to set up a factory needing skilled workers in a society where those workers are predominantly Protestant is of necessity to locate in a Protestant area, thus perpetuating the sectarian division of labour.

It is for this reason that local councils, even those not noted for their sectarian attitudes and utterances, accept both the sectarian division of labour and sectarian geography in the hiring of employees, having 'green' plumbers, for example, to work in Catholic areas, and 'orange' plumbers for Protestant areas. In those work situations where there is no need for 'green' labourers,

then there are none. For example, Catholics in Belfast are buried
in cemeteries owned by the Catholic Church. As only Protestants
are buried in council cemeteries, the council tends to hire only
Protestant gravediggers. The 'devout' Protestant or Catholic can
thus have the consolation of dying knowing that the last sod
shovelled over his/her coffin will be dug by someone using the
same foot as him/herself.[3] In short, even actions carried out with
non-sectarian intentions can give rise to sectarian consequences
because sectarianism is not merely a matter of intentions. This is
true not least in the area of the state's intervention into the
community.

Two final examples should demonstrate that sectarianism is
not merely a matter of 'intentions'. Wiener (1975:127) recounts
how the Hammer Redevelopment Association managed, after a
lot of effort, to 'persuade' the Mobile Rodent Control Unit to do
something about the rats in their area. However, as there was
only one such unit for the whole city, this meant that the rats in
other redevelopment areas were able to run wild while the Unit
was in the Hammer. Wiener (1975: 127)concludes:

> 'localised action simply meant community groups competing
> against each other with the one protesting loudest gaining a
> temporary advantage as resources (contractors, rodent control
> units, etc.) were rushed in to dampen the community agitation.'

Examples of such sectionalism facilitated by the capitalist state's
intervention in the community are not unique to NI. But, when
the areas concerned are respectively Protestant and Catholic, the
sectionalism encouraged can be sectarian.

The sectarian distribution of facilities operates in both
Catholic and Protestant areas, even though the mechanisms of
distribution are different in each. In Protestant areas the
importance of local councillors should not be under-estimated;
hence the focus here on their actions and utterances. In Catholic
areas the power of the Catholic Church is still crucial, even
though it is in some ways declining, not least because of 'the
troubles'. And although not immediately involved in the decision-
making process as councillors are, the Catholic clergy can
influence policies. Dearlove (1973:213) has examined the willingness of policy-makers to accept the recommendations of interest
groups. He argues convincingly that such willingness is based on
three criteria: the group concerned, the actual recommendation
and the style of the group attempting to influence policy. As far as
the Catholic Church is concerned, especially since its rapproche-

ment with Unionism from the mid-1960s, the state is likely to lend an ear to the clergy's policy recommendations. Where the state deals with interest groups on the basis of 'respectability,' the Catholic Church has a headstart on community groups; it does not have to prove its 'respectability' to the state.

Moreover, the actual physical control of areas by the clergy often makes it difficult for the state to ignore the church, even if it wanted to. The example of one Catholic area in Belfast is noteworthy. Ardoyne is a solidly Catholic area surrounded by Protestant areas and very strongly policed by the Catholic clergy. The church's influence extends not just to the local schools and parish halls, but to youth clubs and pre-school playgroups; priests even sit on the management committees of the two largest drinking clubs in the area. Consequently, when the NIO distributed money to Ardoyne under the BAN project, it was inevitable that most of it would end up in schemes controlled by the church. Local community workers estimate that £½ million of BAN money went to the church in Ardoyne. In short, the normal operation of state intervention in the community had sectarian consequences. But, even more than that, when coupled with the church's deliberate attempts to maintain its position, the control became complete.

Conclusion

In a time of capitalist crisis the capitalist state takes drastic action to restabilise the economy. In Britain at present this entails a commitment to a monetarist policy which is having profound effects throughout the whole society, not least in cutting back community intervention. Because of direct rule the British state pursues a similar policy in NI.

The 'community' is an asset to capitalism; hence the capitalist state's management of class relations in the community. But the 'community' is also, and at the same time, a liability to capitalism. Given that many of the institutions and programmes of community intervention are either recent or experimental, and given that community intervention is regarded as superfluous by hard-headed monetarists, a strong lobby is now urging a drastic cutback of community intervention. Because it is an asset, it cannot be done away with altogether; but because it is a liability, cutbacks have already begun. For example, in Belfast, as we have already seen, the amount of money available to community groups is slight, but even that is being cut back. Belfast City

Council has cushioned the blow somewhat by allowing its Community Services Department to continue to grant-aid community groups even though it is now over-spending on its 1979/80 estimates; the extra money is coming from the rates (see *Belfast Telegraph* 3/1/80). But the cushioning is only a temporary stay of execution; community services are as eligible a target for cuts as any other. Similarly, the NIO has decided not to renew the three-year Community Worker Research Project when it expires in 1981, thus putting fourteen community workers out of jobs (see *Belfast Telegraph* 17/1/80). It will be a trimmed community industry that will continue into the 1980s.

Accompanying this trimming is an increase in administrative arrogance. Frequently there is no longer even lip-service to participation. Thus, when Minister of State Philip Goodhart (sic) was asked why he had raised rents without consulting the NIHE, he replied:

> 'Of course they would like more consultation; everyone would like more consultation. But one has to remember that the vast amount of money for housing in NI comes not from rent, but from the taxpayer' (interview on BBC Radio Ulster, 12/3/80).

The logic is that, as guardians of the taxpayers' money, government ministers must make all the decisions. The rhetoric of the halcyon days of Lord Melchett is gone.

What consequences cutbacks in community intervention will have for community politics is open to question. But what is predictable on the basis of past experience is the future relationship between community politics and sectarianism. Cross-sectarian links will sometimes emerge on issues such as common opposition to the building of Belfast's inner city motorway. But to believe that such links will ultimately sound the death knell of sectarianism is to work on the basis of a false logic. Sectarianism and reformist community politics are not timeless, abstract opposites. The state's intervention in the community is directed to the management of class relations in the community. In the specific historical circumstances of NI these class relations are sectarian. Consequently, community politics and sectarianism can co-exist. Furthermore, even community interventions not inspired by sectarian intentions on the part of the interveners can have sectarian effects.

Ultimately the position that community politics can kill sectarianism rests on the belief that sectarianism is merely a set of attitudes. As such, it is open to demise through education, legislation and the presence of a different set of attitudes. This was the position of the British state in its first phase of intervention in the community in NI. But the priority shifted, and the British state moved into its second phase of managing class relations in the community, sectarianism and all. It does not seek to encourage sectarian attitudes and utterances in the way that Stormont at its worst did. And it keeps a watch on the most blatant aspects of such official encouragement of discrimination through a few mechanisms such as the Ombudsman and the Fair Employment Agency. For the rest, the British state is content to work within sectarian class relations, accepting sectarian geography, the sectarian division of labour and capital.

Community politics is about much less than reversing NI's history. It is about struggle with the state over the provision of communal facilities. The removal of sectarian class relations is a political feat which community politics alone is incapable of accomplishing.

NOTES

1. The East Belfast CD team noted an encounter with one councillor who accused them of causing trouble 'by dividing the people . . . He had done work in the electoral area and he resented anyone else being involved . . . He went on to say that anyone who came into his area to do any work would not come out again.' (Sam Bailie, CDO, memo to CRC 30/8/72)
2. There were 24 CDOs in all during the CRC's life-time, although never more than 16 at any one time. 13 of the total were Catholics and 11 Protestants.
3. In colloquial speech, someone who digs with the same foot as oneself is of the same religion as oneself.

7

Reforming Repression

Social Democratic Ideology and Repression

Repression is one of the more widely discussed areas of state practice in the North, but one of the least analysed. This chapter examines the ideologies surrounding repression, which have played an important part in the attempt by the British state to contain the NI crisis in the last ten years. During a decade of military and civil rule which latterly has imposed a semblance of stability, British governments have been increasingly able to represent their management of the crisis — internationally, domestically and to some extent in Ireland itself — as legitimate and even 'progressive'.

Their approach is rooted in the social democratic ideology of Britain which presumes that the state embodies a consensus on the rule of law and on the parliamentary means by which law may be reformed. Social democracy makes the distinction between 'violence' which is the illegitmate praxis of the citizenry, and 'force' which is the necessary and legitimate business of the state carried on in the name of the people such that they may live with 'peace' and 'order'. As Young (1979:19) puts it,

> 'direct coercion is a minor part of social democratic forms of government, and is applied only against criminals and terrorists, marginal social categories against which coercive reaction is not a subject of dispute.'

NI presents a major contradiction to the British state for, while it is constitutionally within the UK, it cannot be held up as a regional exhibit of social democratic consensus. Since its inception, the Unionist state has used repressive legislation specifically designed to suppress and contain the Nationalist aspirations of Catholics and, more specifically, Republicanism. The *Civil Authorities (Special Powers) Act* empowered the

Minister of Home Affairs to make any regulation which he thought necessary for the 'maintenance of order' (without the formality of consulting Stormont) and to authorise such specified procedures as arrest without charge or warrant, internment without trial, flogging, execution, destruction of buildings, requisitioning of land or property and the prohibition of meetings, organisations and publications. The Minister had direct control over policing, which was carried out through two paramilitary agencies, the RUC and the Ulster Special Constabulary. The sectarian composition of the RUC until the present crisis was approximately 90% Protestant, 10% Catholic. From 1945 to 1969 the force was slowly increased from 2,700 to 3,000. In contrast, the part-time force of 'B Specials' was exclusively Protestant and could be expanded swiftly to meet IRA campaigns, as was demonstrated in the 1950s. In the latter half of the decade, 3,500 men were hurriedly recruited within three years, bringing the force up to 13,700 by 1958. As institutionalised forms, the police and the legal system constituted the most powerful expression of Unionist authority.

Since 1969, repression has been developed considerably. The military and paramilitary agencies of the state have rapidly grown in size and become much more sophisticated (see Ackroyd *et al* 1977). The RUC alone has been increased by 268% and is supported by 8,000 troops in the Ulster Defence Regiment (UDR) and approximately 14,000 in the British Army. (In the mid-1970s there were 25,000 British troops in the North.) If ancillary security agencies and personnel are included, this means that someone is employed in policing 'the troubles' for every 38 persons in NI. Law and the legal system have been adapted to process those engaged in political violence, for example through changes in the rules of evidence and the suspension of jury trials. The average daily prison population numbered 2,947 in 1978 compared to 617 in 1969 — almost a five-fold increase in ten years (May Report 1979:41). The penal regime has been altered on several occasions to re-categorise prisoners.

Ultimately the British state reduces the 'NI problem' to one of containing 'terrorism'. On this basis, the state has presided over the reconstitution of repression within the North and, to a lesser extent, within Britain itself. But that reconstitution has faced a continuing ideological struggle over the contradiction between the formal integration of NI within the UK, and the policy of isolating political violence and the broader politics which it expresses. The struggle falls into three identifiable periods. Firstly, at the onset of the crisis, the concern was to persuade the Unionist leadership to adopt 'British standards' of policing and to create the conditions of stability in which such standards might emerge. Secondly, there was a period of transition, the early part of which saw the use of internment, Bloody Sunday, the fall of Stormont and the military assault on the 'no-go' areas. The period is punctuated by negotiations with all parties, including the Provisionals and the Southern government, the peak of which was the Sunningdale conference. The Ulster Workers Council strike (1974) brought this period to an abrupt end. In the third period the British state resigned itself to direct rule, in the absence of any alternative form of government, and vigorously continued its attempt to redefine legality according to social democratic criteria.

Direct rule has aggravated the problem of distancing NI from Britain. Although the British state's ideological management of repression is complicated by the capacity of the mass media to relay events in the North throughout the world, the state is primarily concerned with the reaction of UK audiences. It is therefore important to understand how the media have treated NI.

The 'Reality' of Northern Ireland

Before 1968 there was minimal UK coverage of NI. British audiences were singularly unprepared to comprehend the rioting and police reaction as rooted in the political history of Ireland or, more immediately, in the context of an Orange state resting on distinctly 'un-British' standards and practices. Having no picture of the *lack of consensus* on which affairs in the North had been run, audiences interpreted violence on the streets within the framework of British 'consensus politics'. Fundamentally, 'the troubles' came to be seen as an *irrational breakdown* in social and political relations and not as a manifestation of a basic fissure in class and sectarian relations firmly embedded at every level within the state apparatuses.

The BBC was bound into the Unionist establishment and successive NI Controllers pledged themselves 'to keep an iron grip on all local news and allow nothing to go out which suggested that anything in NI could or would ever change' (Schlesinger 1978: 208). The local BBC assumed the position of principal producer and censor of all BBC output on Irish matters, a position which has been formally consolidated in a code of written rules since 1972. Within a relatively short period (1968–1970), the ambiguous response of the British press to Civil Rights campaigning changed to one which integrated the 'Irish insurrection' into 'a cocktail of dangerous illegitimacy' threatening the British state from all sides (Chibnall 1977:141). From this moment onwards, the theme which emerged with increasing force was that 'responsible debate had to be restricted to the discussion of the most effective means of eradicating the [insurrectionary] behaviour' (*ibid*:19).

The change appeared as a shift in emphasis rather than a dramatic switch in support for the various parties to the conflict. It was, however, orchestrated in several respects by major initiatives from British politicians and from within various branches of the Unionist state. While a considerable number of programmes on the Irish issue have been withdrawn from the schedules, often at the last minute, (see Campaign for Free Speech on Ireland 1979), this has not appeared as censorship in the strict sense of the word. As Schlesinger (1978:23) has observed, 'ministerial intervention has been elusive, and there was nothing in the BBC's approach to editorial control which approximated to popular imagery of classic totalitarian censorship, with its directives and specially planted supervisory personnel'. But the point Schlesinger makes is that *formal* censorship is *unnecessary*, since the BBC polices itself within a context of increasingly well-organised and explicitly propagandist state news sources, a context shared by other media. Given that the professional imperatives of media workers tend to make violent incidents the major rationale for reporting NI, it is to be expected that the Army, the Police and the NI Office are the most prominent sources of news. The Army in particular has continuously strengthened and revised its public relations efforts, applying both 'sticks and carrots' methods, to ensure their version of events reaches the media first, to influence individual journalists and above all to convey its own role as non-partisan — difficult and dangerous, yes, but one carried out with judicious sensitivity. Through interviews with 'the soldier on the street' and carefully constructed statements from HQ, British audiences learn to discriminate between the necessary force of the Army and the senseless violence of the IRA, the principal enemy.

More recently, the content of news from NI has developed a dual theme. Alongside the de-contextualised violence, stories have been placed providing equally uninformative (and presumably 'abnormal') glimpses of 'the other side of life in NI'. Following the abortive attempts to construct a framework for consensus politics between 1972 and 1975, the media within NI clearly responded to Roy Mason's theme of a 'return to normal life' and the 'downward trend in violence'. Normal life stories, like their 'violence' counterparts, are necessarily devoid of political questions; they convey a sense of the 'remarkable' pursuit of everyday life amidst violence and destruction. Considered as 'consensus mobilisation', such images widen the scope of the principal enemy target from the law and order field to the arena of local politics. A key agency in this development was the NI Office Information Service, which now produces daily broadsheets on the activities of Ministers and their wives, policy changes and reviews, and full texts of speeches. The broadsheets are written in such a manner that their contents can be directly consumed by the media with the minimum of editing; context is supplied and key phrases headlined. It is by no means unusual either to read in the local daily papers, or hear on local radio, statements which, although they appear interpretive, are nonetheless direct copies of the material emanating from the Information Service.

The long-standing official commitment to a developed politics for the North appears to rest on the assumption that the British state can, over a period of time, significantly alter the nature of local politics and political ideologies. A major element of the necessary groundwork, as conceived by the last Labour administration, was to suspend and deem irrelevant all discussion of repression and to prevent politics in other areas from falling into the 'traditional' grooves of sectarianism and constitutionalism. Ideologically, a distinction was fostered between the 'outmoded' politics of the past and a 'way-forward' politics whereby political practice would be confined to a number of discrete areas of social disorganisation. A new consensus was seen to lie in getting 'both sides' to agree on the urgency and severity of NI's social problems — in particular, bad housing and unemployment. For example Mason (2/1/79) once stated,

> 'there is an area of life here which depresses me more than anything else and that is the sterility of political debate. I am not blaming particular individuals for this, but I fear that the basic language of party politics is still the political rhetoric of ten, fifty or one hundred years ago.... The future lies not in demonstrations or destruction but in effort, employment and enjoyment of life. We must progress to the achievement of a normal society, piece by piece to the establishment of peace, and step by step to the status of a normal and healthy society.'

In such a way, Mason (18/10/78) could pose as neutral in the local squabble, and also appeal directly to those businessmen, civil servants, trade unionists, welfare professionals and other state workers who shared his privatised notion that 'the vast majority of people here are, like ordinary people anywhere, concerned with their families, their homes, their jobs and the future'.

Reforming the Men in Green

An important strand in British ideologies of repression involves demonstrating domestically and internationally that direct intervention in NI from 1968 onwards has accomplished a number of major reforms in the organisation and practices of the local state. One such reform concerns the police, whose activities attracted widespread criticism in Britain and elsewhere from the mid-1960s onwards. The Unionist response to Civil Rights marchers was largely repressive; it was inability to contain the ensuing reaction which forced the Orange state to seek technical and military assistance from Britain.

Callaghan, who as Home Secretary was in close contact with the Unionist government, agreed that the immediate and primary problem was the 'maintenance' or re-establishment of law and order. Callaghan (1973:77) also seemed to recognise, however, that the RUC was seen by the Catholic minority as a sectarian force wielded in the direct political interests of Unionism:

> 'it was always in my mind that, by British standards, the NI cabinet and Parliament was little more than an enlarged county council . . . with an unhealthy political control over the police'.

In these terms, normalising the police force was thought to involve three things — disarmament, reorganisation and de-sectarianisation. One of Callaghan's ideas was to reinforce the RUC by importing British policemen, with their experience of Grosvenor Square. This would not only forestall and perhaps prevent the deployment of troops but also allow British methods and ideologies of policing to permeate the ranks of the RUC on the basis of first-hand experience. The plan was strongly resisted by senior British officers and by the Police Federation, who did not wish to commit themselves either to an unfamiliar situation or to an alien political authority. Troops were sent in instead, but the British state still pursued the basic policy of fashioning a 'neutral' police force ('as in Britain').

Much of what was contained in the Hunt Report (1969) on the reform of the police was inspired by (Sir) Robert Mark's earlier observational tours of policing in NI. By British standards, Mark saw the RUC as a demoralised, unprofessional force, working in atrocious and siege-like conditions, lacking an adequate leadership and intelligence network. As he described the effects of the rioting,

> 'the men are bewildered and angry at the reaction of the press and the public. They have all been on duty for long periods but there has been no real organisation by the top-level command for proper reliefs or even for such ordinary domestic details as hot meals at night. All this should have been done and would have been done in any equivalent demonstration in Britain.' (cited in Callaghan 1973:56)

When the RUC was approached by the English Special Branch (sent over to 'sort out' the RUC) for files relating to terrorist activity, the RUC could produce only out-of-date material on the IRA (McGuffin 1973:84). The RUC denied that similar files existed on extreme Loyalists despite the fact that O'Neill had proscribed the UVF immediately after the shooting of four Catholic hotel workers in June 1966. Ironically, O'Neill had spent the weekend of the shootings in France observing the fiftieth anniversary of the wiping out of the original UVF in the battle of the Somme.

This serves to illustrate the superficiality of the British assessment of what was wrong with the RUC. 'Unhealthy political control' of the police was less a problem *per se* than a symbol of the nature of policing in a sectarian state. To give a more dramatic example, the Cameron and Scarman Reports (1969 and 1972) interpreted police brutality as a minor and 'unfortunate' breakdown in discipline — 'a number of policemen were guilty of misconduct which involved assault and battery, malicious damage to property . . . and the use of provocative sectarian and political slogans'. (Cameron 1969:73)

The repressive branch of the state would in no fundamental sense be transformed by the implementation of Hunt's proposals. Nevertheless, the British attempt to de-politicise the force succeeded in inflaming Right-wing Unionists and Loyalists as they perceived the control of repression slipping from Stormont to Westminster. The Inspector General of the RUC resigned and was replaced by Sir Arthur Young (seconded from his post as London Metropolitan Commissioner); a Police Authority was established and an Office of Director of Public Prosecutions created to replace political control over prosecutions. Recruitment was stepped up and investment in new buildings and equipment increased. Especially offensive to the Protestant Right was Hunt's suggestion of changing the colour of the RUC uniform from green to blue (the British model). The new uniforms were manufactured but never used.

The major institutional reform was the decision to disband the B Specials, the direct descendant of the UVF whose principal *raison d'être* was to fight to hold the line of partition in the 1920s (see Farrell 1976). 'Disband' is not the right word, as Unionist Ministers argued when vetting the Hunt Report prior to publication. Hunt had used 'disband' in the text but the Unionists changed this to 'replace'. The difference in emphasis could not be said to have affected what transpired subsequently, but it does describe developments more acccurately. In place of the B Specials, a new RUC Reserve force and the UDR were established, the latter formally constituted as a regiment of the British Army. The Labour Party *intended* to create a non-sectarian UDR. As the UDR grew, however, Catholic participation fell as Table 1 shows.

Table 1: Catholic Participation in the UDR

Date	UDR Membership	Percentage of Catholics
April 1970	1,800	20
November 1970	3,869	16
November 1971	5,500	8
November 1972	9,102	4
1979	c.8000	2

SOURCES: Deutsch and Magowan (1973;1974); SDLP Submission to Secretary of State's Conference 1980

Catholics were beginning to resign from the UDR early in 1971 — a trend denied by the Army. But it was the introduction of internment (Aug 1971) which was the primary stimulus. Assassinations of UDR members began the day after the first internment swoop; by the end of the year, four of the regiment had been shot dead. Certainly no rigorous attempt was made to prevent the Specials from joining either the UDR or the expanding police force. On the contrary, the Minister of Home Affairs (John Taylor, now one of NI's Euro-MPs) is said to have ensured the hurried recruitment of 300 Specials to the RUC and moreover licensed a number of gun clubs of ex-Specials (Central Citizens' Defence Committee 1973). The UDR was quickly infiltrated by

Loyalist paramilitaries (Farrell 1976:362). The Commanding Officer of the UDR said in a television interview that if a member of the regiment belonged to the Protestant paramilitary UDA he would probably take no action (26/10/72). A few months earlier Whitelaw (22/7/72) seems to have advocated such infiltration by saying 'the IRA must be condemned by the people and while people ought not to take the law into their own hands they might help by joining the UDR or RUC Reserve'. Similarly, the new Police Authority reflected an extension of Unionist control in both its composition and its failure 'to assert itself in such a way as to alter the public conception of the police force as an agent of the Unionist Government'. (Boyle, Hadden and Hillyard 1975:22)

The Hunt reforms, while momentarily providing symbolic challenges to Unionist control, provided an injection of resources and manpower into the Unionist police force. The intention of disarmament folded under political pressure which stimulated re-equipment. Effective checks on the exercise of police power were not developed; rather, the forms of mediation between the RUC and the public became more sophisticated. The force was encouraged to develop community relations work, to appoint community policemen, and to humanise its approach to youth (e.g. through the famous Blue Light Disco). The latter formed part of a wider youth policy of introducing Intermediate Treatment, Community Service Orders, investment in recreational facilities, co-ordination of youth club provision etc. But it is the area of complaints procedures which has gradually become the most politically prominent form of mediation in fragmenting and individualising collective hostility towards the RUC.

The criminalisation policy, discussed in the next section, and the rigid determination of the Labour Party to continue Direct Rule as the 'least-of-all-evils' form of government for the North, provide the historical context of the surfacing of the political storm surrounding RUC interrogations from 1976 onwards. In addition, consideration must be given to the specific role of Mason and the Chief Constable (Newman until 1979) and their apparent obsession with terrorist conviction rates. As Holland (1979:17) has written,

> 'there have been times since Mr Mason first arrived in Belfast in 1976 when it has seemed that the whole of British government policy in NI has been directed to that one bright moment each month when the Secretary of State can announce [to the British Parliament] how many people he has put in jail in the previous 28 days'.

The impact of the non-jury Diplock courts introduced under the *Northern Ireland (Emergency Provisions) Act* 1973 (EPA) is clearly seen in Table 2 which shows the dramatic increase in the numbers convicted of offences against the person observable from 1974 onwards.

Table 2: Persons found guilty of offences against the person

	Total	Murder	Wounding
1972	282	9	106
1973	355	18	122
1974	516	26	444
1975	688	73	493
1976	578	52	457
1977	639	75	491

SOURCE: Ulster Year Book 1978/9

Convictions in the Diplock courts are obtained in 90-95% of all cases heard; in the vast majority of these, conviction is secured on the basis of a confession by the accused. The Bennett Report (1979) on interrogation procedures corroborated the high conviction rates (at 94%) and suggested that confessions had played an increasing role since 1976. By 1977 the legal profession knew that confessions could be rejected as evidence only if it could be proved that they were obtained by 'torture or inhuman or degrading treatment' — a very high standard of proof. Indeed, Bennett (1979:52) revealed that less than 15 statements of the 2,293 persons appearing before the special courts between 1976 and 1978 had been ruled inadmissable on grounds of ill-treatment. The hurdle which this standard presents can be further illustrated by examining the outcome of complaints against the RUC in which assault is alleged (since a conviction against the interrogators would undoubtedly mean a confession being ruled inadmissable).

Table 3: Complaints against RUC alleging assault

	Total	Those arrested under emergency legislation
1975	180	n.a.
1976	384	220
1977	671	443
1978	327	266

SOURCE:Bennett Report 1979, Appendix 2

Between 1972 and 1978, 10 police officers were prosecuted for alleged offences in the course of interrogation, but none was finally convicted. Nor have disciplinary proceedings been brought since 1974 in respect of the interrogation of persons in custody (Bennett 1979:113). As Amnesty International (AI) found, it is virtually impossible to convict an individual policeman of criminal misconduct because of the problem of identifying the accused, although a court may have established that an offence was committed (see Table 3 for the number of cases involved). AI's report (1978:67) stated, 'complaints of criminal misconduct which do not result in prosecution are classified as "unsubstantiated", even though the maltreatment alleged may be found by the authorities investigating the complaint to have taken place'. The creation of the Police Complaints Board in 1977 has done little to alter the situation. The Board deals only with internal disciplinary matters and its powers must be deferred in those cases where there is a possibility of criminal proceedings. A 'double jeopardy' law exists whereby an officer 'cannot be accused of the disciplinary offence of using unnecessary violence towards a prisoner if a court has already acquitted him of the criminal offence of assault on the basis of the same set of circumstances'. (Bennett 1979:100)

The Secretary of State, the DPP, and the Chief Constable effectively control and protect a system of interrogation which enabled them to ignore widespread concern over maltreatment of suspects voiced amongst others by police doctors, the UDA, the Police Authority, NI Civil Rights Association, and the SDLP. For several years the Chief Constable maintained that allegations of maltreatment were simply part of a propaganda campaign to discredit the RUC and that such injuries as existed were self-inflicted. The Police Federation not only subscribes to this view but uses it to demand extensions of the Emergency Provisions and Prevention of Terrorism Acts. As the chairman stated recently,

> 'the concentrated attack on the interrogation procedures which culminated in the Bennett Report will do nothing but hamper the defeat of terrorism . . . if the hands of the police are tied still further then undoubtedly more gunmen and bombers will go free to indulge as they please in this cruel prolonged and useless campaign'. (*Police Beat* July 1979:14)

He went on to say that 'the activities of the "Godfathers" could be combatted 'without departing too far from the present rule of law' by making silence of suspects an offence and by arguing that 'it should be sufficient to establish a prima facie case of belonging to a proscribed organisation if an officer not below the rank of superintendent states . . . that the accused is a member of such an organisation'.[1]

Since the abolition of Stormont, the defence of 'police impartiality' has increasingly rested on apologies for maltreatment and the demonstration of the willingness of the overwhelmingly Protestant RUC to act against Protestant paramilitaries. This context of 'even-handedness' informed the publicity surrounding the prosecution of Loyalists for 'terrorist-type offences' (e.g. the 'Shankill butchers'), and helps to explain Mason's repeated emphasis on the 'courageous response' of the RUC to the Paisley/UDA strike of 1977. One month after the publication of the Bennett Report, Mason (4/4/79) addressed the annual passing out parade of the RUC in these terms:

> 'the people of the Province can rest assured that the policing of the Province is in excellent hands. The RUC have come through with great courage and great integrity'.

His successor has similarly congratulated the force for the strides it has made in recent years in developing professionalism and in demonstrating impartiality to the citizens of NI: 'The more professional you are, the more impartial you are seen to be, the more people will rely on you and treat you as friends'. (Atkins 5/6/79)

Law and Order and Legal Relations

The reform of the RUC paved the way for the re-assertion of the police as the 'legitimate' protector of a 'legitimate' state. It is the basis on which the British, from the abolition of Stormont onwards, began to construct the NI crisis in terms of a law and order problem to be dealt with by the normal indigenous police force, and started to mobilise the law and legal process in the fight against 'terrorism'. The role of the military was increasingly played down, while the primacy of the police and the rule of law was promoted. Initially, with world attention focused on the RUC and the Specials, the British Army was portrayed as an intervention both unavoidable and neutral. To a limited extent it was welcomed by Catholics in that the Army was seen as more likely than the RUC or Specials to prevent Loyalist incursions into Catholic ghettos. It also heralded the collapse of Stormont. But as the Joint Security Committee moved towards a policy of 'demonstrations of force' in the summer of 1970 — drenching the ghettos with CS Gas and at one stage imposing a curfew in the

Lower Falls — the Catholic and Protestant working class increasingly sought the protection of their respective paramilitary organisations. The policy provided the impetus for the Provisionals' move from a defensive to an offensive strategy. While the media continued to portray the Army's role as keeping the mobs apart, the Army was gradually coming to see the Catholic ghettos in general, and the Provisionals in particular, as their central problem. Relations deteriorated rapidly with the introduction of internment, the murders of Bloody Sunday and the Army's use of systematic torture (for which Britain was later condemned in the European Court of Human Rights).

Images of British soldiers in Second World War tin hats drinking cups of tea with women in the Bogside were therefore tarnished soon after the troops arrived and shattered altogether by the final flourish of the Unionist government — internment. The consensus in 'terrorist management' circles is that internment was a *tactical* error. An exception here is the political scientist Paul Wilkinson (1977:156) who has argued that,

> 'I cannot accept that the abandonment of internment was other than an act of incredible folly, a self-inflicted wound on the part of the civil authorities. It is an affront that men and women known by the police, the Army, and the community at large to be terrorist leaders and assassins are allowed to walk the streets of NI in broad daylight'.

But in resisting the introduction of internment the Army felt that it lacked precise intelligence on whom to intern. As in the treatment of cancer, the malignant should be accurately burnt out from the normal, neither leaving malignancy to spread, nor damaging the healthy cells. Mistakes could exacerbate the overall military problem. Van Straubenzee, one of Whitelaw's team from 1972–3, claims that he began to phase out internment because the criminal law is a more effective and politically less embarrassing means of control than dawn raids by soldiers. In this way, the British state constructed the strategy of criminalisation — the denial of political recognition of any group or person 'outside the law'. And from this emerges the false dichotomy of military versus 'normal legal' means in the 'defeat of terrorism' within and outside of NI — a popular debate in political and military circles. It is false because in reality both apparatuses are used and because the dichotomy disguises the political nature of legal relations. In essence the dichotomy is an argument over more or less repression. Van Straubenzee (1979:157) has this to say on the international political value of maximising the use of law:

> 'I am certain that in our regular dealings with the United States it was necessary to try and knock some kind of sense into the woolly-headed people who were sending money over in large quantities and, indeed, into politicians like the Kennedys who depended on Irish votes and who put their politics first, that to be able to say we were doing it (repression) within the law was of inestimable value'.

The idea which is enshrined in the criminalisation strategy is that the 'rule of law' commands greater respect than the 'rule of the military'. The law is not an alternative to troops, but a framework of 'higher authority' within which the military can be said to be acting.[2] Internment, technically not 'outside the law', nevertheless belonged to the sphere of discredited 'Unionist law' which the Tories had condoned and had come to defend. On the other hand, 'British law', administered in an 'even-handed' manner, so the thinking goes, might increase the legitimacy of the British state and its repressive apparatuses. There are two major contradictions here. One is that the repressive apparatuses are themselves sectarian and the second is that 'exceptional law' is required to deal with the threat of those who regard the state as illegitimate. Thus, although the Unionists' *Special Powers Act* was repealed (as demanded by the Civil Rights movement), it was replaced by the more comprehensive EPA. Major-General Clutterbuck (1979:69) captures the mood of ruling class thinking on this second issue:

> 'I think the biggest danger lies in over-reaction .... That is what we have to avoid in the use of police or soldiers. I suggest that it is vital that the police and Army should act within their own country's laws, and that if they are not adequate they should get Parliament to create new ones'.

'Exceptional law' on its own proved to be unworkable since the crisis in legal relations had worked its way into the heart of the legal process — the criminal trial. The Diplock Report, which recommended the introduction of non-jury courts and modifications of the rules of evidence for 'scheduled offences', established a crucial link in the chain of repression. Significantly, it passed over 'the inherent contradiction in seeking to encourage the use of courts and public confidence in them while at the same time maintaining a system of extra-judicial detention which struck at the very root of public conceptions of justice according to the law'. (Boyle, Hadden and Hillyard 1975:95)[3]

Bloody Sunday (13/1/72) marked a watershed in all this because it destroyed the remnants of the Army's neutral image locally and damaged it internationally. Boulton (1973:151) writes,

> 'Catholics talked of "Bloody Sunday" but John McKeague went on television to say that Loyalists called it "Good Sunday" and were only sorry that more IRA scum had not got what they clearly deserved . . . Bloody Sunday, following as it did the shock report of Sir Edmund Compton revealing extensive and systematic "ill-treatment" of internees, emphasized the consequences of committing British security forces to the support of Stormont.'

The need to reconstitute the very foundations of the state in terms of the 'British rule of law', and to justify every policy and action in terms of that law, began to gel in the consciousness of the Tory cabinet, as it had done some years earlier in the minds of some Labour ministers. Very quickly, Direct Rule became inevitable: to execute the policy, the British would need unfettered control, not just of the Army, but of every branch of the state. This moment also signalled the start of an intensified Army campaign to give fuller rein to 'low-intensity operations'. Bloody Sunday had created 'the illusion of battle', to use Kitson's (1969) phrase; the task now was to gain (forcibly) the 'allegiance of the population'. The Army unleashed its offensive to enter into the 'war of propaganda', to adopt saturation intelligence techniques, to use cameras, computers and lasers, to bring in the SAS to pinpoint and eliminate 'key activists' and so on.

These changes in emphasis from military to legal forms of control were not accomplished without struggle and contradiction. A few examples are enough to illustrate the point. Intelligence-gathering means searching Catholic homes in the middle of the night and widespread 'P checks' on the streets during the day. SAS 'cracksquads' and regular patrols assassinate in error. Soldiers have shot soldiers. Internment and interrogation involved institutionalised brutality and, in the case of internment, systematic torture and sensory deprivation. Official reports into the latter were not merely 'cover-ups', in the sense of failing to penetrate the silences of the perpetrators and their command structures; they went to great lengths to explore whether any action had been *illegal*, thus appealing to the law as the final authority. Beneath this canopy they engaged in exhaustive discussions of the meaning of words — cruelty, torture, permanent (damage), ill-treatment, brutality and so on (see McGuffin 1974). Thus as Hall (1974:287) has commented, 'the *meaning* of the physical forms of interrogation was symbolically legitimated by a purely semantic device'. Of the sixty known cases of soldiers *fatally* shooting innocent persons, only seven have been brought to trial: none was convicted (Fisk 1978). Sectarianism permeates the whole legal process — in the selection of charges, the granting of bail, the incidence of conviction and acquittal and the level of sentencing (Boyle et al 1975). The decision to end internment was followed by the withdrawal of special category status for scheduled offences committed after 1976. From 1 April 1980 no political offenders qualify for special status. These decisions have led to the 'dirty protest' in the H Blocks by Republican prisoners who refuse to accept the designation 'criminal'. Thus prisoners who have committed similar offences, but at different times, serve their sentences under different conditions.[4] Terrorist offences, defined in law as those involving violence for political ends, are considered as 'political' in the courtroom but 'criminal' for the purposes of punishment. One final example: while the enemy, 'terrorism', had been identified and denied all political legitimacy by all major political parties throughout the British Isles, 'men condemned as "thugs" and "murderers" were invited to talk to senior British ministers in Cheyne Row'. (Fisk 1978:85) Such talks were prevalent during the phase of attempts to establish a constitutional settlement, and especially at the end of that period (January 1975) during the latter stages of the bombing campaign in Britain (*Sunday Times* 18/6/78).

Nevertheless, the 'law and order' ideology continues to weld together repressive practices as necessary and legitimate. Again, Mason's contribution is noteworthy. As a propagandist of the 'NI problem', Mason is unsurpassed.[5] His distinctive contribution (that of the last Labour government as a whole) lay in giving substance to the repression theorists' emphasis on deploying both reform and repression in the management of political unrest. An instructive account of the situation has been given by the military strategist ex-Colonel Evelegh, currently enjoying a measure of popularity as a 'NI expert' with the BBC. Evelegh (1978:54) bemoans the Catholic ghettos' lack of social and environmental services and civil servants because it creates a 'competition to govern' between illegitimate organisations. Thus, as he puts it, the Army became 'the only credible representative of civil government in the Catholic areas'; or, more accurately, the state had no credibility whatsoever. Although the no-go area barricades had long since been removed (1972) at the time to which he is referring (1975), large areas of Belfast were in effect governed by 'Nationalist and Loyalist paramilitaries' (ibid:50). Evelegh therefore argues for reforms in the administration of state services and for increases in social services, but he does so in the following terms:

> 'a campaign against terrorist-backed insurrection... is not a military campaign alone: it is possible for the military to repress an area into a sort of calm, but the trouble will burst out again as soon as their pressure is reduced. Such a campaign is not only political... (or) only an economic one ... Nor is such a campaign a question of social services, welfare or housing. In a counter-terrorist campaign, the battle runs across every level and every activity of society. Thus the conflict must be seen by Government in terms of co-ordinating the whole social system'. (ibid:52)

In Mason's eyes the two principal enemies of NI were 'terrorism and unemployment', and he declared his intention to attack both with vigour. On several occasions, unlike his predecessors, he stated that he would *never* 'parley with terrorists'. His definitive statement is contained in a document entitled *Protecting Human Rights in NI*, published in February 1979. It begins,

> 'over the past ten years much has been done to ensure that human rights in NI should be as well protected as elsewhere in the UK — indeed there are those who have said that there are more measures to maintain fair treatment and give *legal protection* to human rights in NI than in most other parts of Europe' (my emphasis).

The document continues by listing a number of reforms — universal franchise, proportional representation, the outlawing of discrimination, the creation of a centralised housing authority and the setting up of the Police Authority. Under the heading 'special steps to Protect the Citizen', the Diplock Courts are paraded as models of justice:

> 'All NI courts and the NI judiciary are completely independent of Government control... and they are an integral part of the legal system in the UK. The courts play a fundamental role in the protection of human rights in NI... No-one is imprisoned for his political beliefs, and there are no political prisoners in NI'.

This ideology of the humanity and universality of the rule of law is constantly reiterated by representatives of the British state. For instance, Lord Hailsham (5/9/79) said the following in a speech which later gained notoriety when Thatcher quoted some of the key phrases in representing her Irish policy to the Conservative Party annual conference of 1979:

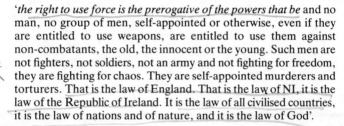

> '*the right to use force is the prerogative of the powers that be* and no man, no group of men, self-appointed or otherwise, even if they are entitled to use weapons, are entitled to use them against non-combatants, the old, the innocent or the young. Such men are not fighters, not soldiers, not an army and not fighting for freedom, they are fighting for chaos. They are self-appointed murderers and torturers. That is the law of England. That is the law of NI, it is the law of the Republic of Ireland. It is the law of all civilised countries, it is the law of nations and of nature, and it is the law of God'.

During his visit to Belfast, Hailsham was asked if the Diplock courts could be described as 'less just' than jury courts. His reply rejected the implication of degrees of justice under the law: through the Diplock courts, 'justice is done'.

Ulsterisation

With such full-blown ideologies of normalisation and the righteousness of the legal system, it would be contradictory to have the police confined to barracks or limited in the areas they can handle. A 'normal' situation can more adequately be represented if the indigenous forces (the RUC and UDR) and not the 'exceptional forces' (the Army) are playing the leading 'law and order role'. The impact of the Ulsterisation policy between 1974 and 1979 is shown in Maps 1 and 2. The success of the policy is represented more commonly in the publication of 'league tables' of violence and security forces operations. For instance, it is pointed out that shooting incidents, explosions, civilian and security forces' deaths are all declining — as is the necessity to search houses (74,556 in 1973; 15,462 in 1978). (For full figures see *Hansard* 15/6/79.) Such empirical evidence is used to prove that, step by step, the 'NI problem' is being solved. It is taken as more than an indicator of declining conflict, for the statistics are understood as a measure of change in social relations — the separation of the fish from the water, to use the popular idiom (Kitson 1969), and the willingness of 'all the people' to search for peace and political reconciliation within the UK. As suggested earlier, Ulsterisation has presented the indigenous forces with a number of legitimacy tests. In 1974 the Army and RUC in effect fraternised with the UWC strike. When Paisley and the UDA called the 'show-of-loyalty' strike on the general

CALL TO ACTION

> If all those slaughtered since the I.R.A. offensive commenced could march past a given point with a ten second interval between them, that long, grim procession of the dead would take 5 HOURS.

> If all those injured and maimed since the I.R.A. offensive commenced could march past a given point with a ten second interval between them, that longer, grimmer procession would take 2½ DAYS.

WHENEVER ANOTHER CIVILIAN, POLICEMAN OR SOLDIER IS KILLED, ALL RIGHT THINKING PEOPLE CRY OUT WITH ANGUISHED HEARTS

WHY CAN'T SOMETHING BE DONE? WHERE ARE OUR LEADERS?

Mr. Roy Mason has stated arrogantly that nothing more will be done than what has been done. He claims that his security policy will not be altered. That it is winning the war.

Ulster people ask —

IF THIS IS VICTORY WHAT WOULD DEFEAT BE LIKE?

MR. ROY MASON AND THE BRITISH GOVERNMENT SAY: "WE WILL DO NOTHING"

<u>OUR DEMANDS</u> — Our demands are most reasonable by any civilised and democratic standards.

1. TO BEGIN A POWERFUL AND EFFECTIVE OFFENSIVE AGAINST THE IRA.
2. TO ANNOUNCE STEPS TO BRING BACK STORMONT BY IMPLEMENTING THE CONSTITUTIONAL SETTLEMENT AGREED BY THE CONVENTION.

WE CALL ON ALL LOYALISTS AT 12 MIDNIGHT ON MONDAY, 2nd MAY, 1977 TO JOIN US IN A COMPLETE STOPPAGE AND WITHDRAWAL OF LABOUR AND A TOTAL WITHHOLDING OF CONSENT OR SUPPORT TO DIRECT RULE

THE GOVERNMENT HAS FAILED IN ITS RESPONSIBILITY — WE NO LONGER CAN KEEP OUR PART OF THE CONTRACT BETWEEN THE RULED AND THE RULERS

MASON CRIES "BACK ME" — WE SAY "BACK ULSTER"

GOD SAVE ULSTER — GOD SAVE THE QUEEN

The blood our fathers spilt.
Our love, our toils, our pains,
Are counted us for guilt,
And only bind our chains.
Before old England's eyes.
The traitor claims his price.
What need of further lies?
We are the sacrifice.

Believe, we dare not boast,
Believe, we do not fear.
We stand to pay the cost.
In all that men hold dear.
What answer from the North?
One Law, one Land, one Throne.
If England drive us forth.
We shall not fall alone!

RESTORE DEMOCRACY

forward by action
UNITED UNIONIST ACTION COUNCIL
to victory

SAVE ULSTER

Belfast *Newsletter* 29 April 1977

question of government security policy in 1977, it was essential for the state to demonstrate the RUC's capability to break up road blocks and prevent intimidation. The importance of the confrontation was not that it expressed the death throes of Loyalism, but that it provided an opportunity for bolstering the credibility of the RUC for withstanding this 'major threat to law and order', as well as for further refinements of the security apparatuses.

Ulsterisation is sometimes seen simply as the British state's reconstitution of a Protestant army (or armies), but the policy faces a number of contradictions. At the political level, Unionists and Loyalists often complain of the force used against Protestants (e.g. the UDA strikers or Protestant football fans) and contrast this with the security forces' failure to destroy terrorism once and for all, and to move against Catholic rioters. A number of District Councils have passed an ominous package of 'security proposals' which include demands for systematic mass raids on 'Republican ghettos' and another 'Falls Road curfew', the closing and sealing of the border, the death penalty and the abolition of remission. Unionist MPs protested to the Secretary of State that the Army did not shoot dead those involved in the display of guns during the August 1979 anniversary demonstrations (marking the introduction of internment and the arrival of troops), and actually permitted the BBC to film the event. Within the police there is the opinion that 'normalisation' has proceeded too rapidly (leaving the RUC exposed) and that Ulsterisation is held back by too rigid an Army control over the UDR. The RUC call for military support is therefore a call for greater deployment of the UDR. The tensions between the Army, its indigenous regiment and the RUC are usually presented as technocratic problems of co-ordination and communications, but they are clearly under-pinned by professional rivalries and, more importantly, *political* differences over tactics (see *Hibernia* 18/11/79). Within the Army itself, the current debate revolves around the question of 'untying the hands of the security forces' — the push for the final military solution. While the secret Army security review, which the IRA acquired and leaked in March 1979, argued that total military suppression was impossible, the General Officer Commanding NI (Creasey) publicly made the case that the Army can win. The RUC argue that they are better equipped than the Army to sift the massive flow of low-grade intelligence for the sort of evidence required for court convictions. The appointment of former MI6 head Sir Maurice Oldfield as 'security co-ordinator' stems directly

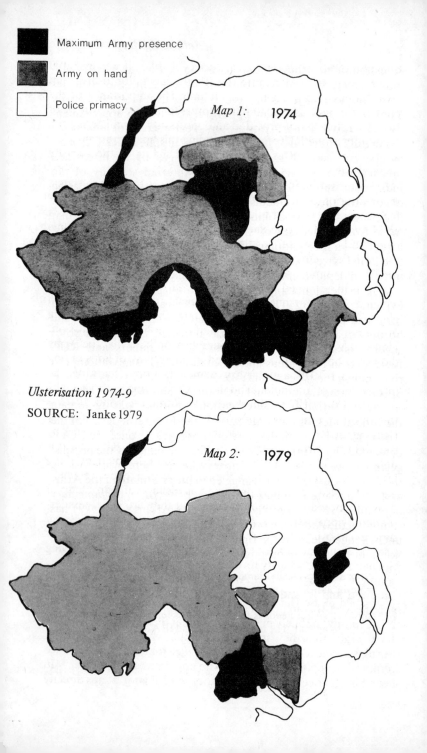

Maximum Army presence

Army on hand

Police primacy

Map 1: 1974

Ulsterisation 1974-9
SOURCE: Janke 1979

Map 2: 1979

from the political differences sketched above — the 'heads-on-a-plate' demands of the Protestant ultra-Right, the struggles between the indigenous forces and the British Army, and finally Thatcher's radical-Right populism. Oldfield's appointment inevitably gives senior Army officers greater scope for influencing the overall direction of security policies, in spite of RUC denials to the contrary. Already there are signs of an intensified intelligence approach, involving an internal scrutiny of the indigenous forces for possible leaks of strategic information concerning the movements of individuals and the existence of installations of various kinds. Similarly, the Army argues that there is a distinct lack of 'high-grade information' on terrorist activity — a recognition of the inadequacies of the confidential telephone system and surveillance techniques. This suggests an increased deployment of the SAS and other specialist units.

A further limitation of the Ulsterisation policy is immediately evident from Map 2. The character of the war with the IRA has a rural and urban form. Indeed Janke (1979) has referred to the border areas as being virtually a 'liberated zone'. This poses severe risks of assassination to UDR members and RUC Reservists in rural areas and inevitably restricts any attempt to re-establish the type of control exercised for fifty years by the B Specials based on individual intimate local knowledge.

Ulsterisation and the 'extension of normal policing' remain the official ideology and the basis of the long-term desire of the British to withdraw their own troops to barracks once the IRA is defeated. Thatcher symbolically ratified the policy by the populist gesture of wearing a UDR combat jacket and beret while visiting the Army's outpost in Crossmaglen in the aftermath of the Army and Mountbatten killings of August 1979 (*Ulster Commentary* September 1979; *Observer* 2/10/79). As Atkins (26/10/79) has reminded the American press, the constitutional position of NI is unchallengeable, as is the right of the British to use troops there 'for national defence purposes':

> 'those who cynically clamour for an end to its [the Army's] active role in aid of the police in NI know perfectly well that nothing would please Her Majesty's Government and the people of NI more . . . All it needs is for the fruitless terrorist campaign . . . to come to an end. The ball is firmly in the IRA's court — not ours'.

WILL JOINING THE UDR AFFECT YOUR SOCIAL LIFE?

Of course it will.

For a start, we'll ask you to give us a couple of your nights each week. And maybe the odd weekend. Anything from 12 to 20 hours a week in all.

You'll find it tiring, and often dangerous.

But there is a brighter side. As well as helping to bring the Troubles to an end, you'll enjoy new social surroundings.

Every UDR Company Headquarters has its own social centre, where you can get together with your family and friends. You'd be hard pushed to find a better place in the Province to relax in your off-duty hours.

And you won't have to look over your shoulder every time the door opens.

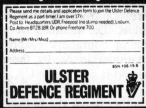

Please send me details and application form to join the Ulster Defence Regiment as a part-timer. I am over 17½.
Post to: Headquarters UDR, Freepost (no stamp needed), Lisburn, Co. Antrim BT28 1BR. Or phone Freefone 700.

Name (Mr/Mrs/Miss) _____

Address _____

BSN-106-15-6

ULSTER DEFENCE REGIMENT

Conclusion

We have argued that repressive practices and their ideological representations have developed a dual character in the British state's attempt to stabilise NI. By 1972, the 'NI problem' had become 'dangerously' internationalised and the British policy of propping up the Stormont regime, through open military repression on the streets and through internment, was thoroughly discredited. At this moment, and without the obstacle of a NI government, the British accelerated the drive for reforms and the reconstitution of the rule of law, while at the same time drawing upon the latest repertoire of counter-insurgency thinking and practices derived from colonial experiences elsewhere. In so doing, it became increasingly possible to divert international concern by representing the conflict as a discrete problem of criminality and by pointing to the considerable efforts being made to modernise the state's approach to 'social problems' and 'democratic politics'. 'Extra-legal' internment was relaced by the 'legal' conveyor-belt system of interrogation, remand (up to two years in many cases) and Diplock courts' sentencing. Open street warfare dwindled in regularity from a daily occurrence to an anniversary event. Political offences were re-categorised as ordinary crime. The Irish-American connection was scrutinised for links with terrorism and finally Southern politicians were encouraged to declare their support for, and take an active role in, defeating 'the men of violence'.

The duality of British policy referred to above is echoed by the two main British currents opposing it. On the one hand, the practice of civil libertarians is to police the inhumanities of the state and the erosion of citizenship rights which the law formally protects. They condemn political violence, thereby abstracting repression from the struggle over the legitimacy of NI as part of the UK. The weakness of this strategy is its assumption that the form of bourgeois legality in NI *could be* similar to that in Britain. Undoubtedly, there is some credibility in arguing that since NI is part of the UK, universality of law should apply, but recent history demonstrates the limitations of the argument. On the other hand, the radical Left speaks less of 'abuses' than of systematic state repression of the Nationalist population in its liberation struggle against the British state. The Left is more ambiguous on the question of political violence, but its practice is organised around the demands of 'troops out' and 'self-determination for the Irish people'. Its appeal lies in the simplicity of the connection it makes between Britain's historical domination of Ireland and repression in the Northern segment today; it is less concerned with *reforming* the repressive apparatuses than with *exposing* their true form. Thus the central focus of the Left is on instances of repression and the Provisionals' campaign. Yet there is still a sense in which the radical Left in Britain monitors repression in the North as if the political context were no different from the 'revolutionary moment' of 1972. If the Irish question is to be successfully re-inserted into British politics by breaking the Labour Party's adherence to 'bipartisanship' (Bell 1979), then the Left must struggle to present the crisis of NI in new ways. Part of that struggle involves recognising the British state's reform of repression and the impact of the changing emphasis from military to legal forms of stabilisation.

Notes:

1. The Irish Republic's *Offences Against the State Act* 1972 allows for conviction on a charge of membership of an illegal organisation on the word of a Chief Superintendent.
2. In fact the Army had no legal authority to arrest people until the *NI (Emergency Provisions) Act* 1973.
3. When they talk of 'public conceptions of justice according to the law', these authors are clearly presuming a social democratic consensus on the rule of law which (as we have argued) may have some basis in Britain but none in NI.
4. Special Category prisoners who are put in compounds, rather than individual cell blocks, may wear ordinary clothes and need not do prison work.
5. His appeal to Unionists was confirmed recently by the suggestion that he be offered a Unionist seat at Westminster should he not be re-selected as the Barnsley Labour candidate.

8

Conclusions

The 'reform' of the NI statelet in the post-war period has involved replacing the trappings of formal representative democracy with the trappings of formal social democracy. The transition was accelerated between 1968 and 1974 by the abolition of Stormont, the removal of Unionist Party control over repression, and the bureaucratisation of local government through centralising housing provision and creating new administrative units to manage health and social services, education and planning. For almost 50 years the Partition settlement had stabilised the North of Ireland by insulating it from Great Britain and the rest of Ireland. Within its confines, 'formal democracy' appeared to prevail, based on an impregnable two-to-one Protestant majority. Control over the coercion of the dissident Catholic minority and over local patronage was left to the Unionist Party while the UK state maintained overall control over the economy and the public finances of the NI administration. After 1945 new forms of capital accumulation and the emergence of a reformist social democratic state in Britain began, imperceptibly at first, to undermine the political structures of the Unionist state and its relationship to the rest of the UK.

NI was affected by the expansion of the British state apparatus required for its growing intervention in restructuring capital and in developing welfare state services. Stormont came to function more directly as an agent of the British state by implementing welfare reforms and directly encouraging the restructuring of the local economy. The consequences for the Unionist Party were two fold. Firstly, the highly decentralised local authority system — based on Orange clientelism and on the systematic local policing of Catholic 'apartheid' — was gradually undermined by the centralising forces of British social democracy operating through Stormont. Secondly, the Unionist Party was ill-equipped to oversee an increasingly complex and interventionist state apparatus, much less to reproduce in NI a political consensus similar to that shared by the main parties in Britain in the 1950s and 1960s. Its oligarchical leadership was internally divided on a whole range of questions such as state intervention in the economy, welfarism, relationships to the British (and Irish) governments, concessions to Catholics and the management of Protestant working class disaffection over unemployment. While the Unionists' working class supporters favoured state interventionism in many areas, they did not necessarily want to see the resultant benefits extended to the Catholic minority. Nevertheless the relationship of the Catholic class alliance to the state was changing — the Catholic working class benefitted from the welfare reforms, if not from the restructuring of the economy. Meanwhile the Catholic middle class was coming into increasing contact with the now more complex state apparatus. Yet it faced here all the disabilities crystallised in the local operation of Protestant democracy — notably the nature of state repression and the clientelism operated by the Unionists at local level. It was these disabilities which initially provoked the Civil Rights movement.

Given its structure and internal divisions, the Unionist Party as such was unable to come to terms with the challenges presented by state interventionism in the new political and economic circumstances of the 1960s. The Stormont bureaucracy, as an agent of the UK state (in alliance with elements in the Unionist cabinet), was increasingly coming to supplant the Unionist Party as the political 'organiser' of the tension-ridden Protestant class alliance. This was especially the case in its mediation between the traditional Protestant bourgeoisie and the Protestant working class. The former opposed the allegedly preferential treatment given by the state to incoming multi-national enterprises, while the latter supported the provision of new jobs which traditional industry had failed to deliver. However, the Unionist Party still constituted the Protestant alliance in one key area — control of the local repressive apparatuses, which had remained immune from post-war reform. It was the collapse of local 'law and order' which finally undermined the political insulation of NI from Westminster politics and forced the central state to assert its ultimate constitutional responsibility for repression.

The thrust of Westminster policy between 1968 and 1974 was to install a local political arrangement which would reproduce in NI the ideological consensus which seemed to underpin British politics. Initially the British government sought to shore up the Unionist Party while encouraging the 'moderate' elements within it. When this attempt collapsed, the SDLP and Alliance Party were brought into a 'power-sharing' Executive in order to legitimate the new 'social democratic' structures. The 'extremists' on both sides were excluded from the political compromise, if not from informal contacts with the Army and some civil servants. The agreement failed to involve many of the Unionist politicians who had formed an uneasy alliance with the Protestant para-militaries since the abolition of Stormont. It failed also to obtain IRA acquiescence.

Bipartisanship prevailed in Britain on these initiatives based on the perceived necessity to restore stability and thereby re-insulate the NI problem from Westminster politics. Differences in emphasis between Tory and Labour Party policy did exist, however. The former placed more emphasis on constitutionalism, as in the 'power-sharing' settlement, and on consultation with 'elected representatives', while pursuing a more dictatorial line vis-à-vis extra-parliamentary groupings. Labour, on the other hand, favoured a form of technocratic centralism as evidenced in its concession (on Army advice) to the UWC strike, which ended the 'power-sharing' agreement. This policy also informed the subsequent highly centralised and co-ordinated civil and military management of NI — especially the strategy of both *more* 'reform' and *more* repression under Mason. Little effort was devoted in this period to bolstering the legitimacy of 'squabbling' politicians and there was rather more consultation and co-operation with non-Parliamentary groupings such as trade unions, community groups and various reform lobbies.

The analysis in the foregoing case studies suggests that it is not sufficient to accept uncritically as 'reforms' the changes in the political, administrative and legal structures in NI resulting from British 'intervention'. Instead these must be evaluated in terms of the way they express the underlying social relationships in which they are embedded. Our detailed analysis of different areas of state intervention has attempted to examine the way in which these social relationships are being 'reconstituted' within the UK state apparatus in NI. In a capitalist state these relationships must have a class form; in the specific historical circumstances of NI, however, class relations are simultaneously sectarian.

The most obvious contradictions of 'reform' clearly lie in the restructuring of the specifically repressive state agencies. The local security forces have been re-armed and massively expanded. In the case of the RUC this has been accompanied by encouraging within the force a new professional ideology of 'impartial' policing along British lines. The full-time and part-time UDR are now increasingly recognised by Westminster politicians as 'British Army professionals'. The practical results of these policies in NI, regardless of the ideology, is the official arming of one side of the sectarian divide — the Protestants. The IRA campaign has followed 'Ulsterisation' in that, from the imposition of internment in 1972, it has been increasingly directed at assassinating members of the police, the prison service and the UDR. Given that the vast majority of these are Protestants, the IRA strategy inevitably became 'sectarian'. Similarly, despite police attempts to demonstrate impartiality, their role, and especially the role of the UDR, is largely directed at suppressing Catholic dissent. Potential Loyalist opposition to Direct Rule has been defused by incorporation into the security forces — a strategy which has many historical precedents. This incorporation even suggests an increment of economic (if not physical) security for Protestants, as the Tories cut public expenditure in all areas except defence and the internal security industry. Repression policy also facilitates an internal politics within Unionism in the competition between the DUP and the Official Unionist Party to establish which has the hardest line on 'security'.

Sectarian class relations have been reproduced through other 'reforms' also. While local government has been reformed, its lack of significant powers considerably reduces the gain to those disadvantaged by the old system, but local councils still remain as arenas where the veneer of formal democracy serves to reproduce sectarian class relations. Trade unions have become more 'respectable', with representatives on many state bodies. In this role they help to manage rather than to confront sectarian class relations. Community politics increasingly present opportunities for state technocratic management of scarce resources on a divisive Protestant/Catholic basis. They no longer serve to expose sectarian class structure in the sense that they did, for example, during the establishment of 'no-go' areas in working class districts. Reform of housing provision has proved to be somewhat more contradictory. Here, right in the heart of a UK state apparatus committed to the formal technocratic management of local politics, the realities of housing management force the recognition of differential 'Catholic' and 'Protestant' housing need. This explicit recognition contrasts to the practice elsewhere within the state. For example, security forces are not officially labelled 'Protestant', nor are industrialists, judges, or civil servants, whatever the practical reality might be beneath the rhetoric of political management. Thus there are contradictions within a state ideology committed to 'serving the public interest'. While it seeks on the one hand to assert the 'end of the sectarian state' by pointing to reforms of 'sectarian discrimination' and its commitment to 'impartial management', its ultimate reliance on sectarian class relations challenges that assertion at all levels in the everyday operation of the state.

Historically the state in NI has depended for its separate existence on sectarian class divisions. Forms of political management have been altered as these divisions and the state itself have been reshaped in response to new forms of capital accumulation and the emergence of new political structures in Britain. As the 'public sector' has expanded to directly employ over 40% of the labour force and to indirectly support the jobs of many in the so-called private sector, sectarian class division has been incorporated into the heart of the state apparatus itself, as our case studies demonstrate. This reality threatens the illusion of separation between reform and repression on the British 'mainland' model. The state's ideological response to this threat has been to reduce the problem to a military one — the forces of 'law and order' versus the 'terrorists' — or to a problem of anachronistic sectarianism abstracted from class relations.

The much-discussed crisis of the British welfare state, however, is also evident in NI. Even as the state apparatus expanded in NI, foreign investment and manufacturing employment declined. Unemployment has reached new post-war dimensions. Direct Rule has presided over a reduction in housing provision and steeply rising rents and domestic energy costs, sharpening divisions in the process. Current Tory Party policy of finding a new devolution settlement for NI coincides with its more general policy of diffusing class conflict and responsibility for public expenditure cuts, to local authorities and different sectors of the state apparatus. This delegation of responsibility, while consistent with a populist attack on big government, threatens to reconstitute a local Unionist state in NI, albeit in a more internationally 'acceptable' guise. The Labour Party has already laid the groundwork by reconstituting sectarian class divisions within the administrative and military apparatuses. Labourist politics within NI, whether practised by trade unions or political groupings, would appear unable to challenge such a reconstitution as they tend to abstract sectarianism from class division. The political task for the Left, then, lies not in ignoring sectarian division but in directly opposing its multi-faceted reconstitution by the UK state in NI. The question of the reformability or irreformability of the NI state must not be posed at a general or abstract level remote from an analysis of the state's relationship to sectarian class division.

In the short run there is a pressing necessity to highlight politically the 'emerging solution' to the NI problem which lies behind the allegedly 'temporary expedient' of Direct Rule. This means challenging the consensus of the Tories and Labour alike on remaining 'politically silent' on NI while they search for an 'internal compromise'. This consensus is shared also by political parties in the Irish Republic to a considerable extent (for reasons that need to be analysed elsewhere). Failure to challenge the current ideological insulation of the NI crisis may have far-reaching consequences in helping to strengthen repressive and reactionary forces, not only in NI, but throughout the British Isles as a whole.

The UK state is not 'above' the NI problem, it is an integral part of that problem.

Bibliography

Ackroyd, C., Margolis, K., Rosenhead, J. and Shallice, T., *The Technology of Political Control*, Penguin, Harmondsworth, 1977.

Akenson, D.H., *Education and Enmity*, David and Charles, Newton Abbot, 1973.

Amnesty International, *Report of an Amnesty International Mission to Northern Ireland (November-December 1977)*, London, 1978.

Aunger, E.A., *Social Fragmentation and Political Stability: a Comparative Study of New Brunswick and Northern Ireland*, unpublished Ph.D. dissertation, University of California, Irvine, 1978.

Barratt Brown, M., *From Labourism to Socialism*, Spokesman Books, Nottingham, 1972.

Barritt, D.P. and Carter, C.F., *The Northern Ireland Problem: a Study in Community Relations*, Oxford University Press, London, 1962.

Belfast and District Trades Council, *Annual Report*, Belfast, 1978.

Belfast Bulletin 7, 'Trade Unions in Northern Ireland', Workers' Research Unit, Belfast, 1979.

Bell, G., *The Protestants of Ulster*, Pluto Press, London, 1976.

—— *British Labour and Ireland: 1969-79*, The Other Press, London, 1979.

Bennington, J., *Local Government Becomes Big Business*, CDP, London, 1976.

Bew, P., Gibbon, P. and Patterson, H., *The State in Northern Ireland*, Manchester University Press, 1979.

—— 'Some Aspects of Nationalism and Socialism in Ireland: 1968-1978', in Morgan, A. and Purdie, B., (eds.) 1980.

Birrell, D., Murie, A., Hillyard, P. and Roche, D., *Housing in Northern Ireland*, Centre for Environmental Studies, London, 1971.

Black, W., 'Industrial Development and Regional Policy', in Gibson, N.J. and Spencer, J.E. (eds.), 1977.

Bleakley, D., 'The Northern Ireland Trade Union Movement', *Journal of the Statistical and Social Inquiry Society of Ireland* 20, 1953:156-69.

—— *Trade Union Beginnings in Belfast and District*, unpublished M.A. dissertation, Queen's University, Belfast, 1955.

Boal, F., Murray, R. and Poole, M., 'Belfast: the Urban Encapsulation of a National Conflict', in Clarke, S.E. and Obler, J.L. (eds.), *Urban Ethnic Conflict: a Comparative Perspective*, Institute for Research in Social Science, University of North Carolina, 1976.

Boserup, A., *Who is the Principal Enemy? Contradictions and Struggles in Northern Ireland*, Independent Labour Party, London, 1972.

Boyle, K., Hadden, T. and Hillyard, P., *Law and State: the Case of Northern Ireland*, Martin Robertson, London, 1975.

British and Irish Communist Organisation. *The Irish Communist*, monthly.

Boulton, D., *The UVF 1966-1973: an Anatomy of Loyalist Rebellion*, Torc Books, Dublin, 1973.

Buckland, P., *The Factory of Grievances: Devolved Government in Northern Ireland, 1921-39*, Gill and Macmillan, Dublin, 1979.

Budge, I. and O'Leary, C., *Belfast: Approach to Crisis*, Macmillan, London, 1973.

Burton, F., *The Politics of Legitimacy: Struggles in a Belfast Community*, Routledge and Kegan Paul, London, 1978.

Busteed, M.A., 'Small-Scale Economic Development in Northern Ireland', *Scottish Geographical Magazine* 92 (3), 1976.

Byrne, D., 'The De-Industrialisation of Northern Ireland', Department of Sociology and Social Policy, Ulster Polytechnic, Northern Ireland (mimeo), 1979.

—— 'Housing in Belfast: the Politics of Reproduction in a Different Place', Durham University (mimeo), 1979.

Callaghan, J., *A House Divided*, Collins, London, 1973.

Campaign for Free Speech on Ireland, *The British Media and Ireland*, London, 1979.

Campaign for Labour Representation in Northern Ireland, *Ulster: What the Labour Party Needs to Do*, Belfast, 1980.

Carlin, T., 'Interview with Eugene McEldowney', *Irish Times*, 17 November 1979.

Carr, A., *The Belfast Labour Movement: Part 1 — 1885-93*, Athol Books, Belfast, 1974.

Central Citizens' Defence Committee, *The Black Paper: the Story of the Police in Northern Ireland*, Belfast, 1973.

Chibnall, S., *Law-and-Order News: an Analysis of Crime Reporting in the British Press*, Tavistock, London, 1977.

Clutterbuck, R., 'Terrorism: a Soldier's View', in *Ten Years of Terrorism*, Royal United Services Institute for Defence Studies, London, 1979.

Cockburn, C., *The Local State*, Pluto Press, London, 1977.

Compton, P., *Northern Ireland: A Census Atlas*, Gill and Macmillan, Dublin, 1978.

Connolly, J., *Ireland Upon the Dissecting Table*, Cork Workers' Club, Historical Reprint 11, 1975.

Cooper and Lybrand (NI) Associates Ltd., *The Current Economic Situation and Prospects for 1980*, Cooper and Lybrand, Belfast, 1980.

CSE State Group, *Struggle Over the State: Cuts and Restructuring in Contemporary Britain*, CSE Books, London, 1979.

Counter-Information Services (CIS) Anti-Report 10, *Courtaulds Inside-Out*, CIS, London, n.d.

Darby, J., *Conflict in Northern Ireland*, Gill and Macmillan, Dublin, 1976.

—— and Morris, G., *Intimidation in Housing*, Northern Ireland Community Relations Commission, Belfast, 1974.

—— and Williamson, A. (eds.), *Violence and the Social Services in Northern Ireland*, Heinemann, London, 1978.

Dearlove, J., *The Politics of Policy in Local Government*, Cambridge University Press, 1973.

Delargy, J., 'Interview with UDA Spokesman', *Gown* 22 (7), 6 February 1976.

De Paor, L., *Divided Ulster*, Penguin, Harmondsworth, 1970.

Deutsch, R. and Magowan, V., *Northern Ireland: a Chronology of Events*, volumes 1 and 2, Blackstaff Press, Belfast, 1973/4.

Devlin, B., *The Price of My Soul*, Pan Books, London, 1969.

Dickey, A., 'Anti-Incitement Legislation in Britain and Northern Ireland', *New Community* 1 (2), 1972:133-8.

Direct Labour Collective, *Building with Direct Labour: Local Authority Building and the Crisis in the Construction Industry*, CSE Books, London, 1978.

Dohrs, F.E., *The Linen Industry of Northern Ireland*, unpublished Ph.D. dissertation, Northwestern University, Chicago, 1950.

Duffy, F., Perceval, R. *et al, Community Action and Community Perceptions of Social Services in Northern Ireland*, New University of Ulster, Coleraine, 1975.

Elliott, S., *Northern Ireland Parliamentary Elections Results, 1921-1972*, Political Reference Publications, Chichester, 1973.

—— and Smith, F.J., *Northern Ireland Local Government Elections of 1977*, Queen's University, Belfast, 1977.

Etzioni, A., *The Active Society*, Collier-Macmillan, London, 1968.

Evelegh, R., *Peace-Keeping in a Democratic Society: the Lessons of Northern Ireland*, Hurst and Company, London, 1978.

Farrell, M., *Northern Ireland: the Orange State*, Pluto Press, London, 1976.

Fisk, R., *The Point of No Return*, Andre Deutsch, London, 1975.

—— 'The Effect of Social and Political Crime on the Police and British Army in Northern Ireland', in Livingston, M. (ed.), *International Terrorism in the Contemporary World*, Greenwood Press, London, 1978.

Gallagher, F., *The Indivisible Island*, Gollancz, London, 1957.

Garnsey, R., 'The Experience of Courtaulds Ltd. in Northern Ireland', in Wilson, T. (ed.), 1965.

Gibbon, P., *The Origins of Ulster Unionism*, Manchester University Press, 1975.

—— 'The Northern Ireland State 1921-1941', Paper presented to the British Sociological Association Annual Conference (mimeo), 1977.

Gibson, N.J., 'Some Economic Implications of the Various "Solutions" to the Northern Ireland Problem', in Vaizey, J. (ed.), 1975.

—— and Spencer, J.E. (eds.), *Economic Activity in Ireland: a Study of Two Open Economies*, Gill and Macmillan, Dublin, 1977.

Ginsburg, N., *Class, Capital and Social Policy*, Macmillan, London, 1979.

Gough, I., 'State Expenditure in Advanced Capitalism', *New Left Review* 92, 1975.

—— *The Political Economy of the Welfare State*, Macmillan, London, 1979.

Gouldner, A., 'The Sociologist as Partisan: Sociology and the Welfare State', in Reynolds, L. and J. (eds.), *The Sociology of Sociology*, McKay, New York, 1970.

Green, A.J., *Devolution and Public Finance: Stormont from 1921 to 1972*, Studies in Public Policy No. 48, Centre for the Study of Public Policy, University of Strathclyde, Glasgow, 1979.

Griffiths, H., *Proposals on Structure and Training for an Enlarged Field Programme*, Community Relations Commission, Belfast (mimeo), November 1971.

—— *Community Development in Northern Ireland: a Case Study in Agency Conflict*, New University of Ulster, Coleraine, 1974.

Hackett, General Sir J., 'Containing the Explosive Mixture', *Hibernia*, 9 August 1979.

Hall, R., 'Capitalist Development in the Periphery: the Case of Dungannon', Department of Sociology and Social Policy, Ulster Polytechnic (mimeo), 1979.

Hall, S., 'Deviance, Politics and the Media', in McIntosh, M. and Rock, P. (eds.), *Deviance and Social Control*, Tavistock, London, 1974.

Harbinson, J., *The Ulster Unionist Party 1882-1973*, Blackstaff Press, Belfast, 1973.

Harrison, J., *Marxist Economics for Socialists: a Critique of Reformism*, Pluto Press, London, 1978.

Harvey, D., 'The Urban Process Under Capitalism', *International Journal of Urban and Regional Research* 2, 1978:101-31.

Hayes, M., 'Some Aspects of Local Government in Northern Ireland', in *Public Administration in Northern Ireland*, Magee University College, Derry, 1967.

Hechter, M., *Internal Colonialism*, Routledge and Kegan Paul, London, 1975.

Hemel Hempstead Constituency Labour Party, *Ireland: an Alternative*, Hemel Hempstead, 1979.

Hepworth, N.P., *The Finance of Local Government*, Allen and Unwin, London, 1978.

Hibernia, 'Special Reports: Secret Security', 18 November 1979.

Holland, M., 'Roy Mason's Guilt', *Magill* 2 (7), 1979.

Hyman, R., *Marxism and the Sociology of Trade Unionism*, Pluto Press, London, 1973.

Inside Politics, 'An Interview with Patrick Macrory', BBC Radio Ulster, November 1978.

Irish Congress of Trade Unions (ICTU), *Report of Annual Conference of the Irish Congress of Trade Unions*, Dublin, 1977.

Irish Transport and General Workers' Union (ITGWU), *Fifty Years of Liberty Hall*, Dublin, 1959.

Isles, K.S. and Cuthbert, N., 'Economic Policy', in Wilson, T. (ed.), 1955.

Janke, P., 'Ulster, a Decade of Violence', *Conflict Studies* 108, Institute for the Study of Conflict, London, 1979.

Kennedy, S. and Birrell, D., 'Housing', in Darby, J. and Williamson, A. (eds.), 1978.

Kitson. F., *Low Intensity Operations*, Weidenfeld and Nicolson, London, 1969.

Labour and Trade Union Co-ordinating Group, *Workers Break the Stoppage*, Belfast, 1977.

Labour Research, 'Northern Ireland: Economic Dependency', *Labour Research* 66 (2), 1977: 36-7.

Larkin, E., 'The Devotional Revolution in Ireland', *American Historical Review* 77 (3), 1972:852-84.

Lawrence, R., *The Government of Northern Ireland*, Clarendon Press, Oxford, 1965.

Lyons, F.S.L., *Ireland Since the Famine*, Fontana, London, 1973.

McAllister, I., *The Northern Ireland Social Democratic and Labour Party*, Macmillan, London, 1977.

McCann, E., *War and an Irish Town*, Penguin, Harmondsworth, 1974.

McCarthy, C., *The Decade of Upheaval: Irish Trade Unions in the 1960s*, Institute of Public Administration, Dublin, 1973.

—— *Trade Unions in Ireland, 1884-1960*, Institute of Public Administration, Dublin, 1977.

—— and Blease, W.J., 'Cross-Border Industrial Co-operation: Limits and Possibilities', *Administration* 26 (3), 1978:352-72.

McGuffiin, J., *Internment*, Anvil Books, Tralee, 1973.

—— *The Guineapigs*, Penguin, Harmondsworth, 1974.

McInerney, M., *Trade Unions Bid for Peace in the North*, Irish Times Publications, Dublin, 1970.

Masters, M. and Murphy, D., 'British Imperialism and the Irish Crisis', *Revolutionary Communist Papers* 2, May 1978.

Merrett, S., *State Housing in Britain*, Routledge and Kegan Paul, London, 1979.

Micklewright, M.A., *The Geography of Development in Northern Ireland*, unpublished Ph.D. dissertation, University of Washington, 1970.

Miller, D.W., Queen's Rebels: Ulster Loyalism in Historical Perspective, Gill and Macmillan, Dublin, 1978.

Moore, B., Rhodes, J. and Tarling, R., 'Industrial Policy and Economic Development: the Experience of Northern Ireland and the Republic of Ireland', *Cambridge Journal of Economics* 2, 1978:99-114.

Moore, R., 'Race Relations in the Six Counties', *Race* 15, 1973.

Morgan, A. and Purdie, B. (eds.), *Ireland: Divided Nation, Divided Class*, Ink Links, London, 1980.

Morrissey, M. and S., 'Northern Ireland: Why the Trade Unions are Central', *Marxism Today*, November 1979:17-23.

Murie, A., 'Spatial Aspects of Unemployment and Economic Stress in Northern Ireland', *Irish Geography* 7, 1970:53-67

National Labour Movement Delegation, *Report of Visit to Ireland*, London, 1976.

Nealon, T., *Ireland: a Parliamentary Directory*, Institute of Public Administration, Dublin, 1974.

Northern Ireland Civil Rights Association (NICRA), *We Shall Overcome*, NICRA, Belfast, 1979.

Northern Ireland Committee (NIC) of the Irish Congress of Trade Unions, *Memorandum on the Protection of Human Rights in Northern Ireland and the Involvement of the NIC of the Irish Congress of Trade Unions*, NIC, Belfast, 1978.

—— *Jobs: an Action Programme*, NIC, Belfast, 1979.

Northern Ireland Community Relations Commission (CRC), *Housing in Northern Ireland*, Proceedings of Conference, February 1972.

Nugent, R.T., 'Encouragement for New Industries', *The Banker*, September 1946:165-7.

O'Connor, J., *The Fiscal Crisis of the State*, St. Martin's Press, New York, 1973.

O'Dowd, L., Tomlinson, M., 'Urban Politics in Belfast: Two Case Studies', *International Journal of Urban and Regional Research* 4 (1), 1980:72-95.

Official Unionist Research Department, *Putting People First in Housing*, Belfast, 1973.

Oliver, J., *Working at Stormont*, Institute of Public Administration, Dublin, 1978.

O'Loghlen, B.A., 'The Patterns of Public Expenditure in Northern Ireland and the Republic: 1954-1965', *Administration* 17 (2), 1969.

Parkin, F., *Marxism and Class Theory: a Bourgeois Critique*, Tavistock, London, 1979.

Parson, D., *Regional Planning, Housing Policy and Community Action in Northern Ireland*, unpublished M.A. dissertation, University of California at Los Angeles, 1979.

Perrons, D., *The Role of Ireland in the New International Division of Labour: a Proposed Framework for Regional Analysis*, Working Paper No. 15, Urban and Regional Studies, University of Sussex, 1979.

Police Beat, Chairman's Address to Annual Conference 3, July 1979.

Probert, B., *Beyond Orange and Green: the Political Economy of the Northern Ireland Crisis*, Zed Press, London, 1978.

Provisional United Trade Union Organisation (PUTUO), *Second Report*, Dublin, 1957.

—— *Draft Constitution for a Trade Union Centre for Ireland*, Dublin, 1957.

Purdie, B., 'Belfast Labourism 1905-1925', *Ireland Socialist Review* 7, 1980:8-15.

Revolutionary Communist Group, *Hands Off Ireland*, quarterly.

Rolston, B., 'Whatever Happened to the Likely Lads?', *Fortnight*, 9 May 1975.

—— 'Community Work: Control or Liberation? Towards an Alternative Theory', in *Proceedings of Sociological Association of Ireland Third Annual Conference*, Queen's University, Belfast, 1977:28-33.

Rose, H. and Hanmer, J., 'Community Participation and Social Change', in Jones, D. and Mayo, M. (eds.), *Community Work Two*, Routledge and Kegan Paul, London, 1975.

Rose, R., *Northern Ireland: a Time of Choice*, Macmillan, London, 1976.

Rowlands, D., Gaffikin, F., Griffiths, S. and Ray, D., *The Community Education Project: Final Report*, Department of Further Professional Studies in Education, Queen's University, Belfast, 1979.

Ryan, W.P., *The Irish Labour Movement*, Talbot Press, Dublin, 1919.

Saunders, P., *Urban Politics: a Sociological Interpretation*, Penguin, Harmondsworth, 1980.

Schlesinger, P., *Putting 'Reality' Together: BBC News*, Constable, London, 1978.

Simpson, J., 'Local Government in a Developing Economy', *Administration* 14 (2), 1966.

Sinn Fein, the Workers' Party, *The Irish Industrial Revolution*, Repsol Publications, Dublin, 1977.

Smiles, W., 'Ulster's Order-Books Now', *The Banker*, September 1946:162-4.

Social Democratic and Labour Party, Submissions to Secretary of State's Conference, 1980.

Steed, G.P.F., 'The Northern Ireland Linen Complex: 1950-70', *Annals of the Association of American Geographers* 64, 1974:397-408.

—— and Thomas, M.D., 'Regional Industrial Change: Northern Ireland', *Annals of the Association of American Geographers* 61, 1971:344-60.

Sunday Times, 'What did we Promise the Provos?', 18 June 1978.

Tomlinson, M., 'The Electricity Industry in Northern Ireland', *Scope* 33, May 1980.

Vaizey, J. (ed.) *Economic Sovereignty and Regional Policy*, Gill and Macmillan, Dublin, 1975.

Van Straubenzee, W., 'International Law and International Terrorism', in *Ten Years of Terrorism*, Royal United Services Institute for Defence Studies, London, 1979.

Walsh, F., 'The Changing Industrial Structures of Northern and Southern Ireland', *The Maynooth Review* 5 (2), 1979:3-14

Whyte, J.H., *Church and State in Modern Ireland 1923-1970*, Gill and Macmillan, Dublin, 1971.

Wiener, R., *The Rape and Plunder of the Shankill*, Notaems Press, Belfast, 1975.

Wilkinson, P., *Terrorism and the Liberal State*, Macmillan, London, 1977.

Wilson, T. (ed.), *Ulster Under Home Rule*, Oxford University Press, London, 1955.

—— (ed.), *Papers on Regional Development*, Basil Blackwell, Oxford, 1965.

Workers' Association, *What's Wrong with Ulster Trade Unionism?*, Belfast, 1974.

Workers' Research Unit Bulletin 4, 'Derry Ten Years After', Workers' Research Unit, Belfast, 1978.

Young, J., 'Left Idealism, Reformism and Beyond: From New Criminology to Marxism', in *Capitalism and the Rule of Law*, National Deviancy Conference/Conference of Socialist Economists, Hutchinson, London, 1979.

Government Publications

Benson Report, *Northern Ireland Railways*, Cmd. 458, Belfast, 1963.

Bennett Report, *Report of the Committee of Inquiry into Police Interrogation Procedures in Northern Ireland*, Cmnd. 7497, London, 1979.

Cameron Report, *Disturbances in Northern Ireland*, Cmd. 532, Belfast, 1969.

Carter, R., *Housing Finance: the Facts*, Department of the Environment, Belfast, 1977.

Carvill, P., 'The Administration of the Social Needs (Grants) Act' Ministry of Community Relations, Belfast (mimeo), 1973.

Collins Report, *City of Belfast: Inquiry into Administration*, Belfast, 1928.

Department of Commerce, *Industrial Development in Northern Ireland: Facts and Figures*, Belfast, 1976.

Department of the Environment, *Housing Return for Northern Ireland 1944-1979*, Belfast.

—— *Report of the Working Party on Tenant Participation and New Forms of Tenure*, Belfast, 1976.

—— *Housing Proposals in West Belfast*, Belfast, 1978.

—— *Northern Ireland Housing Statistics*, Belfast, 1979.

Department of Manpower Services, *Northern Ireland Labour Market: a Guide in Graphs and Charts*, Belfast, 1979.

Diplock Report, *Report of the Commission to Consider Legal Procedures to Deal with Terrorist Activities in Northern Ireland*, Cmnd. 5185, London, 1972.

Dunlop Report, *Inquiry into the Finances and Administration of Whiteabbey Sanatorium*, Belfast, 1941.

Educational Development in Northern Ireland, Cmd. 470, Belfast, 1964.

Fair Employment Agency (FEA), *An Industrial and Occupational profile of the Two Sections of the Population in Northern Ireland*, Belfast, 1978.

—— *Second Report of the Fair Employment Agency for Northern Ireland: 1 April 1977 — 31 March 1978*, Belfast, 1979.

—— *Third Report of the Fair Employment Agency for Northern Ireland: April 1978 — March 1979*, Belfast, 1980.

Hall Report, *Economy of Northern Ireland: Report of the Joint Working Party*, Cmd. 446, Belfast, 1962.

Hunt Report, *Report of the Advisory Committee on Police in Northern Ireland*, Cmd. 535, Belfast, 1969.

Interim Report of the Planning Advisory Board, *Housing in Northern Ireland*, Cmd. 224, Belfast, 1944.

Isles, K. and Cuthbert, N., *Economic Survey of Northern Ireland*, Belfast, 1957.

Lockwood Report, *Higher Education in Northern Ireland*, Cmd. 475, Belfast, 1965.

Lowry Report, *Belfast Corporation Inquiry*, Belfast, 1962.

McCall Report, *Belfast Corportation Housing Allocations Inquiry*, Belfast, 1954.

Macrory Report, *Report of the Review Body on Local Government in Northern Ireland*, Cmd. 546, Belfast, 1970.

Matthew Report, *Belfast Regional Survey and Plan*, Cmd. 451, Belfast, 1963.

May Report, *Committee of Inquiry into the Prison Service*, Cmnd. 7673, London, 1979.

Megaw Report, *Inquiry into the Housing Schemes of Belfast Corporation*, Cd. 30, Belfast, 1926.

Ministry of Health and Social Services, *Administrative Structure of the Health and Personal Social Services*, Belfast, 1969.

Northern Ireland Development Programme, 1970-75, Belfast, 1970.

Northern Ireland Economic Council, *Londonderry as a Location for New Industry*, Belfast, 1966.

—— *The Clothing Industry in Northern Ireland*, Belfast, 1979.

Northern Ireland Economic Reports for 1968 and 1973, Belfast, 1969 and 1974.

Northern Ireland Housing Executive, *Annual Reports*, Belfast, 1971-79.

—— *Housing Condition Survey 1974*, Belfast, 1974.

—— *Northern Ireland Household Survey*, Belfast, 1975.

—— *Belfast Household Survey 1978: Preliminary Report*, Belfast, 1979.

Northern Ireland Housing Trust, *Annual Reports*, Belfast, 1947-71.

Northern Ireland Information Service, 'Trade Unions', in *Information Briefs on Northern Ireland*, Belfast, 1979.

Northern Ireland Office, *Protecting Human Rights in Northern Ireland*, Belfast, 1979.

Nugent Report, *Report of the Committee on the Finances of Local Authorities*, Cmd. 369, Belfast, 1957.

Porter Report, *Committee on Rent Restriction Law of Northern Ireland*, Belfast, 1975.

Project Team, *Belfast Areas of Special Social Need Report*, Belfast, 1976.

Quigley Report, *Economic and Industrial Strategy for Northern Ireland: Report of a Review Team*, Belfast, 1976.

Report on Proposals for Dealing with Unfit Houses, Cmd. 398, Belfast, 1959.

Reshaping of Local Government: Further Proposals, Cmd. 530, Belfast, 1969.

Reshaping of Local Government: Statement of Aims, Cmd. 517, Belfast, 1967.

Scarman Report, *Violence and Civil Disturbances in Northern Ireland in 1969*, Cmd. 566, Belfast, 1972.

Ulster Commmentary, 'Prime Minister Among the People', September 1979.

Wilson Report, *Economic Development in Northern Ireland*, Cmd. 479, Belfast, 1965.

INDEX

(Numbers in italics denote graphics.)

CSE Books

CSE Books was founded by members of the Conference of Socialist Economists to promote the practical criticism of capitalism which the CSE as a whole is committed to and to facilitate wider participation in the debate and analysis going on in the CSE. Rather than forming ourselves into an academic editorial committee which sits in judgement of authors and in ignorance of readers, we want to engage politically in current debates and struggles. By coordinating with CSE activities in general, by publishing *Head & Hand: A Socialist Review of Books*, and by organising dayschools on issues thrown up by our own publications, we hope to narrow the gap which exists in bourgeois society between the producers and consumers of books.

For further information on CSE Books titles and the CSE Bookclub, write to 55 Mount Pleasant, London WC1X 0AE.

New Titles

Living Thinkwork: Where Do Labour Processes Come From? Mike Hales.
Mike Hales describes his experience doing operations research at ICI, where even mental workers learn that ultimately 'You're not paid to think'. Through an account of 'scientific' work in a capitalist firm, his book shows the place of knowledge-production in the politics of management. A concrete intervention in Marxist theory of the labour process, this book is also a document in the history of the 'class of '68', exploring the contradictory social relations between theory and personal experience, theory and practice, and academic and industrial work. 192 pages illust.
Hb 0 906336 14 7 £10/Pb 0 906336 15 5 £3.50.

Science, Technology and the Labour Process: Marxist Studies, volume I. Ed. Les Levidow & Bob Young.
This series of collections will analyse scientific and technological practices in terms of the capitalist labour process, especially the current restructuring of capital. The articles in the first volume take up the following areas: mental labour, microelectronics, Marx on technology, genetic engineering, Grunwick's fixed capital and scientific conceptualisation.
Hb 0 906336 20 1/Pb 0 906336 21 X.

Value: The Representation of Labour in Capitalism, ed. Diane Elson.
Marx's theory of value has been a controversial and constant matter of debate since the time it was first published. This collection of essays focuses on some of the more difficult and neglected concepts at the very beginning of *Capital*: abstract labour as the substance of value; the relative and equivalent forms of value; exchange value as a necessary mode of expression of value; the commodity as a symbol. The book also contains a useful annotated bibliography of all Marx's references to value. 192 pages.
Hb 0 906336 07 4 £12.00 / Pb 0 906336 08 2 £4.95

Also available from CSE Books

Technology and Toil in Nineteenth Century Britain, ed. Maxine Berg. A collection of documents designed to illustrate the neglected early history of deskilling, technological unemployment and assembly line alienation. The fifty-one selections reveal differing practices in a wide range of industries and provide a context in which the better known analyses of work and technology left by Babbage, Ure, Owen and Marx may be analysed. 250 pages illust.
Hb 0 906336 02 3 £10.00 / Pb 0 906336 03 1 £3.50.

Economy and Class Structure of German Fascism, Alfred Sohn-Rethel. A classic Marxist study of the founding of the Nazi state in the early 1930s. Sohn-Rethel managed to infiltrate the office of the Mittel-europaeischer Wirtschaftstag, a business institute whose members included representatives of every significant section of German finance capital, and the book is based on his experiences as an editorial assistant on the MWT's newsletter. 160 pages.
Hb 0 906336 00 7 £5.95 / Pb 0 906336 01 5 £2.50.

Struggle Over the State, CSE State Group
Building on the current upsurge of Marxist interest in the state, this collectively produced work combines recent theoretical progress with informed and up-to-date description of the restructuring of the UK state in the crisis of the 1970s. 144 pages illust.
Hb 0 906336 13 9 £5.95 / Pb 0 906336 12 0 £2.50.

The Conference of Socialist Economists

The Conference of Socialist Economists was formed in 1970. Since that time there have been many changes. CSE is committed to the development of a materialist critique of capitalism in the Marxist tradition. The membership of CSE now covers a broad spectrum of political and research activities which generates a wide-ranging debate, for CSE is as far as possible, unconstrained by the traditional academic divisions of intellectual labour into, say, 'economics', 'politics', 'sociology', or 'history'.

Instead the groupings are around the CSE working groups. Currently, groups actively working on material are the Ideology Group, Housing, Capital and the State, State Economic Policy, Capitalist Labour Process, Political Economy of Women, European Integration, Health and Social Policy. There is a Labour Process Historians' Group and there may at different times be other groups in operation. Groups are in various parts of the country.

For further information on membership, write to CSE, 55 Mount ant, London WC1X 0AE.